T. E. Schmauk

Bible History

T. E. Schmauk

Bible History

ISBN/EAN: 9783337171865

Printed in Europe, USA, Canada, Australia, Japan

Cover: Foto ©Lupo / pixelio.de

More available books at **www.hansebooks.com**

The Work You Did Last Year.

BIBLE STORY.
Single Stories.

Jesus Born in Bethlehem.

The Child Jesus Brought to the Temple.

The Wise Men From the East.

The Flight Into Egypt.

The Boy Jesus in the Temple.

Jesus Baptized.

Christ Tempted by the Devil.

The Marriage-feast at Cana.

Peter's Draught of Fishes.

The Centurion's Servant Healed.

Christ Stills the Storm.

The Daughter of Jairus.

The Widow's Son at Nain.

Feeding of the Five Thousand.

Transfiguration of Christ.

The Good Samaritan.

The Prodigal Son.

The Rich Man and Lazarus.

Jesus Blesses Little Children.

Lazarus Raised From the Dead.

Christ Enters Into Jerusalem.

Christ's Suffering in Gethsemane, Betrayal and Arrest.

Jesus Before Caiaphas, Herod and Pilate.

Christ Crucified.

Risen and Ascended to Heaven.

The Pouring Out of the Holy Ghost.

God Makes the Heavens and the Earth.

The Forbidden Fruit, and the Fall.

Cain and Abel, the First Two Brothers.

The Flood.

Building the Tower of Babel.

God Calls Abraham.

The Burning of Sodom.

Abraham Offering Up Isaac.

Isaac Blessing Jacob and Esau.

Jacob Dreams of the Ladder.

Joseph Dreams of His Brethren.

Joseph Sold, in Prison, and Before Pharaoh.

Joseph Makes Himself Known.

Moses Born.

The Ten Plagues.

The Passover and the Crossing of the Red Sea.

At Mount Sinai.

Joshua and the Fall of Jericho.

Samson Breaks the Pillars.

Little Samuel.

David Kills Goliath.

Absalom Caught in the Oak Tree.

King Solomon.

Elijah Calls Down Fire From Heaven.

Elisha Restores the Woman's Son.

Daniel in the Lion's Den.

BIBLE HISTORY.

SECOND GRADE TEXT-BOOK

IN

LUTHERAN LESSON SERIES FOR INTERMEDIATE
SUNDAY-SCHOOLS.

NEW AND OLD TESTAMENT HISTORY.

...BY AUTHORITY OF THE...
General Council of the Evangelical Lutheran Church
in North America.

PHILADELPHIA:
GENERAL COUNCIL PUBLICATION BOARD.
1899.

PREFACE.

This is the second text-book of the Graded Series. It is a decided advance over Bible Story in method and in bulk of matter. The difference in the two grade books is that between an advanced primer and a reader; between a story-book and a school history.

Bible History is essentially a reading book. Scholars are expected to become readers of a series of events in their connection, and to reproduce them in recitation. The teacher's questions are few and comprehensive, and the scholar in replying is to be the narrator of a whole scene. The spiritual application of the lesson is to be drawn from the page of memory passages prefixed to each chapter.

In last year's work, the scholars have absorbed the matter of fifty-two Bible Stories and have had a year's practice in detailed analysis. They have been taught to note and examine. Here they are to be taught to remember in bulk and combine. There is much more for them to do, and to think. They must carry a whole train of events in mind, and narrate them, in response to a single question. It is a process in which even younger children delight, though ability in this line is often lacking. The method cultivates a gift of continuous narration and a habit of looking out for and retaining connections.

PREFACE

The result will be an insight into the life of Christ and into Bible History, in their relations, and a connected hold on the train of events, which is not to be expected of scholars brought up on the lesson-leaf system.

The fifty-two Bible Stories already at the scholar's command, are not repeated, but only alluded to, in Bible History. Incidentally the book will enlarge the story knowledge of the scholar by supplying additional matter, including particularly conversations, parables, situations and historical (as distinguished from personal) events. Matters of date and chronology, of custom, locality and government are relegated to next year's book, Bible Geography. Much purely personal matter has been saved for Bible Biography; and all consideration of text and writers and authorship is reserved for Bible Literature. Thus the History in this book is unincumbered, and the thread of incident should lead the reader on rapidly and with increasing interest.

The language used throughout is largely that of Scripture itself, except where the limits rendered it necessary to pass swiftly over a whole scene, or a series of scenes, in a single sentence; or where introduction and connection are made. Even here Scriptural clauses are preferred. No references to Scripture are given, however, because it is counter to the intention of the book to divert the scholar's mind to text and verse and source and form.* That comes later. The book hurries along syn-

---

* The chapters from which the history is taken are given roughly and as a whole in every lesson.

PREFACE

thetically. Spelling and pronunciation of words are excluded on a similar principle, (although a Pronouncing Index of proper names is being prepared for insertion at the close of the volume). This is not the place for giving such knowledge, however important it may be. Even those inner details of a scene that come strictly within the scope of the book are often pushed out, so that the main purpose of the book may be subserved in the space of the fifty-two Sundays' recitations, to which the book is confined. This main purpose is to fit the scenes into their connection and the events into their bearing, so that the succession and connection will be impressed on the mind, as a guide and frame for the scholar's future study.

Special mention is due to the Rev. H. H. Bruning, Ph.D., Prof. M. H. Richards, and the Rev. W. A. Snyder for valuable aid in the correction of proofs, to the Rev. E. P. H. Pfatteicher for the selection of the memory page of Scripture and catechism passages, and to the Rev. Wm. J. Finck, for the preparation of the Pronouncing Index of Proper Names.

THEODORE E. SCHMAUK,

Editor for the General Council Sunday-School Committee.

November 10, 1898,

THE METHOD OF READING.

The only thing that the scholar has to commit to memory, is his page of Scripture and Catechism passages. But these he is to study well, so that by the end of the year he will have in his mind an unfading treasure of the most glorious portions of God's Word. Let the teacher insist on the thorough mastery of at least *a part* of this page by every scholar.

The rest of the scholar's work is simply reading and thinking. He should read over the chapter and the stories at home before the lesson is taught in class, and should give especial attention to the connection of events, at the close of each lesson. He should see whether he can string all the stories, like a row of pearls, each in their proper succession, from the beginning of the book.

Each of the chapters is rather long and contains an abundance of matter. For the object this year is to give the scholar bulk of material. It will not do therefore for the teacher to dwell too long upon details. After hearing the scholars recite their Scripture, the teacher will read over the Summary of Events of the preceding Sunday's Lesson to the Scholars, and will then at once proceed to have the scholars read their chapter for the day. This may be done in two ways. The one is the method of silent reading. It is a very good way. Each scholar in the class is to read the paragraph silently (together with such of the Stories as refer to that paragraph), and then the teacher asks the questions on that paragraph and asks the questions at once. This method has the great advantage of keeping the whole class occupied simultaneously.

The other method is to have the class read through the whole chapter, the main paragraphs first, and then the Stories, in rotation, each scholar taking a sentence. After this has been done, the teacher will ask all the questions in rotation.

The teacher should draw the scholar's attention to the fact that when he asks a question, the scholar is to use both what he has read in the main paragraphs and in the Stories, in making answer. There are no questions on the Stories alone, but they are covered by the questions on the main text.

The lessons are so rich that the teacher will be tempted to spend too much time on them. He should always leave some minutes at the close to have the scholars repeat the Summary of Events, as best they can; and to make a spiritual application. This latter can be done very well by saying a few words on one of the memory passages which the class has recited for the day.

THE SCRIPTURE TO BE LEARNED.

This page has been given greater prominence than any other part of the book. It is now or never that the boys and girls will make of their memories a treasure store-house of God's Word. The ability to memorize with ease will soon begin to pass away. In after years, may every mother be able to say to her child, and every teacher to his scholars, what Paul said to Timothy: "Continue thou in the things which thou hast learned, and hast been assured of. From a child thou hast known the holy scriptures, which are able to make thee wise unto salvation through faith which is in Christ Jesus. All scripture is given by inspiration of God, and is profitable for doctrine, for reproof, for correction, for instruction in righteousness, that the man of God may be perfect, thoroughly furnished unto all good works."

No especial emphasis is to be laid upon finding or knowing the various books of the Bible, or upon the external locations of chapter and verse this year. Instruction along this line will come later on. Here it is the inner power of the Word that is to be held fast. The Scripture to be Learned is to sink into character, soul and life, as a force by itself. It is to be the Word of God quick and powerful, and sharper than any two-edged sword, piercing even to the dividing asunder of soul and spirit.

The importance of this Memory Page has been pointed out to the scholars.

LUTHER'S CATECHISM.

Every scholar who does his duty, will have committed the whole catechism to memory by the time he has finished Bible History. He will not know it in its order and connection, but he will know it in a better way, namely in its heart and substance and in its hold on life and soul and character. The ordering and connection of the parts will be all the more impressive to him when he comes to the subsequent catechetical stage. To have gained such a living knowledge of the catechism in connection with Scripture narrative, is one of the greatest of the advantages of the present Bible History course.

HOW TO TEACH WITH THIS BOOK.

THE BOOKS.—The Scholar's Book, this year, is like your own, except that it is without questions. It is to be used by him as a reader or history. It is important that your scholars should be rather fluent in reading.

THE SUNDAY BEFORE YOU BEGIN.—Assign your class the first memory lesson, tell the scholars to read the first chapter over carefully at home, and that you will ask questions about it in class next Sunday. Explain briefly the difference between the questions and answers to be used now, and those to which they have been accustomed in Bible Story. Tell them that they are to *remember things together,* and to tell them to you in that way.

DURING THE WEEK.—You should read the whole lesson over thoughtfully; and particularly see where the answers come in, so that you will be ready to correct the scholar at once when he is wrong.

ON SUNDAY you have the following things to do:

1. *Recitation.*—Have every scholar repeat the page of memory passages.

2. *Review.*—Go over the last lesson's Summary of Events with the class.

3. *Reading Lesson.*—Get the class to read the lesson either by the silent method, or by the paragraph method explained above.

The main point is to have every scholar think, understand, and remember what he reads.

4. *Questioning.*—After reading each paragraph and its Stories by the silent method, or after reading the whole chapter and its Stories by the rotation method, ask the questions in the margin.

The questions you ask this year are very different from those you employed in Bible Story. There the scholars' answers were to be short and to the point. Here the scholar is to put many facts together, indeed to tell a whole story in answer to your question. He is to narrate what he recollects in a scene or paragraph. Do not allow him, therefore, to dispose of your question by a word or two in reply. If he cannot answer at length, ask him to open his book and read the paragraph over, and then close the book and tell you what he has read.

You will notice that some of the questions are marked with a star (*); this is to indicate that the fuller answer to them is to be found in one of the Stories. The questions take the stories into the chapter in regular order and when you ask them the scholars will see how and where these Stories fit into the history.

The entire lesson should be gone over in the recitation, and it will keep you busy to do it. Possibly your scholars thought Bible Story was a little easy for them. If so, they will have plenty of work in getting over the ground this year. Lift them out of last year's easy rut, and make them stretch their minds. The great contrast in method has been adopted intentionally, and the change ought wake up the scholars.

HOW TO TEACH

5. *Review.*—Let the class give a Summary of Events out of their memory, and then compare it with the Summary in the book.

6. *Application.*—Teach some spiritual lesson from one of the passages on the memory page; and illustrate it, if you can, by something in the history, or in the Stories.

7. *Assigning of Lesson.*—Read the memory page of the following lesson with your scholars, and tell them to commit it. Do not allow them to neglect committing these passages to memory. Be patient and persistent with each one. Where a scholar's ability is defective, shorten his lesson but make him recite something every Sunday.

Tell your scholars to read next Sunday's Chapter and Stories several times during the week.

8. *Time for Recitation.*—You ought to have at least 31 minutes every Sunday for the lesson, viz., for recitation of memory page, 5 minutes; for review of last Sunday's Summary, 1 minute; for reading of lesson, 8 minutes; for questioning on lesson, 10 minutes; for review on today's Summary, 3 minutes; for personal and spiritual application, 3 minutes; for assigning of next lesson, 2 minutes. Where only 20 minutes, or more, are allowed for the lesson, you may be able to hear the Scripture page recitation and to review last Sunday's Summary before the school opens; and you must condense your reading into 6 minutes and your questions into the same period of time.

CONTENTS.

Preface.. i.

Chapter 1. The Saviour Comes. History of His First Thirty Years............ 2
Chapter 2. The Saviour Begins Work. The Wilderness and Galilee............ 7
Chapter 3. The Saviour Goes to Jerusalem and Returns. In the Temple and In Samaria 12
Chapter 4. The Saviour Labours About the Sea of Galilee. At Capernaum and at Nazareth 17
Chapter 5. The Saviour Performs Miracles and Selects Disciples. Capernaum and by the Pool of Bethesda....................................... 22
Chapter 6. The Saviour's Great Sermon on The Mount of Beatitudes.......... 27
Chapter 7. The Saviour Meets with Opposition. Proud Capernaum and Other Cities 32
Chapter 8. The Saviour Teaches in Parables by the Sea of Galilee............ 37
Chapter 9. The Saviour King on Land and Sea. In the Desert, and the Borders of Sidon.. 42
Chapter 10. The Saviour Transfigured and Training the Disciples. On the Mountain and in the Plain.. 47
Chapter 11. The Saviour the Light of the World. Twice Again to Jerusalem.. 52
Chapter 12. The Saviour Eats Bread with a Chief Pharisee Near Jerusalem.... 57
Chapter 13. The Approach of the Crisis. To Bethany and to Jerusalem........ 62
Chapter 14. The Saviour Enters Jerusalem in Triumph and Teaches in the Temple. The Last Sunday, the Last Monday, the Last Tuesday. (Beginning of Passion Week)..................................... 67
Chapter 15. The Saviour Institutes the Lord's Supper and Comforts His Disciples. The Last Thursday.. 72
Chapter 16. The Saviour Suffers in Gethsemane and Under Pontius Pilate. The Last Thursday and Good Friday..................................... 77
Chapter 17. The Saviour "Cricified, Dead and Buried." Good Friday........ 82
Chapter 18. The Saviour "Rose Again from the Dead." Easter Sunday........ 87
Chapter 19. The Saviour Sends out the Apostles and "Ascended into Heaven." Forty Days After Easter.. 92
Chapter 20. The Holy Spirit Descends and the Church is Founded. Fifty Days After Easter, at Jerusalem... 97
Chapter 21. The Church is Persecuted, and Extended to Samaria and Galilee.. 102

Chapter 22.	The Church is Opened to the Gentiles. Paul is Converted and Peter Sees a Vision...	107
Chapter 23.	The Church Grows in Asia. Antioch and Paul's First Missionary Journey	112
Chapter 24.	The Church is carried to Europe. Paul's Second Missionary Journey	117
Chapter 25.	The Apostle of the Gentiles is Brought to Rome. Third Missionary Journey. Peter and Paul. End of Paul's Life...................	122
Chapter 26.	The First Coming of the Saviour to His Church and the City of the Living God. The End of the World and in Heaven........	127
Chapter 27.	The History of the World. From the First Man to the Flood. From Adam to Noah..	132
Chapter 28.	The History of the Patriarchs. Abraham......................	137
Chapter 29.	The History of the Patriarchs, Jacob and Joseph.................	142
Chapter 30.	The Children of Israel Go Out of Egypt...........................	147
Chapter 31.	The Children of Israel Come to Sinai, and to the Borders of Canaan	152
Chapter 32.	The Children of Israel Wander Forty Years in the Wilderness....	157
Chapter 33.	The Children of Israel March to the East of Jordan................	162
Chapter 34.	The Children of Israel Enter the Promised Land. Joshua........	167
Chapter 35.	The Children of Israel Under the Judges........................	172
Chapter 36.	The Times of the Judges—Ruth, Jephthah, Eli and Samson......	177
Chapter 37.	The Children of Israel Under Samuel............................	182
Chapter 38.	The Children of Israel Under Saul..............................	187
Chapter 39.	The Troubles of Saul and David................................	192
Chapter 40.	The Children of Israel Under David............................	197
Chapter 41.	The Children of Israel Under Solomon..........................	202
Chapter 42.	The Kingdom of Solomon Divided.............................	207
Chapter 43.	The Early and Wicked Kings of Israel...........................	212
Chapter 44.	Ahab and Elijah...	217
Chapter 45.	The Destruction of Ahab......................................	222
Chapter 46.	The Prophet Elisha...	227
Chapter 47.	Jehu, Jezebel and Joash, Amaziah and Uzziah...................	232
Chapter 48.	Israel In Prosperity, Confusion, and Captivity. The Empires of the East	237
Chapter 49.	Judah Under King Hezekiah...................................	242
Chapter 50.	Josiah, Jeremiah, and The Fall of Judah.........................	247
Chapter 51.	Daniel in the Babylonian Captivity, The Return of the Captives and the Rebuilding of Jerusalem................................	251
Chapter 52.	The Old Testament. Looking to the Coming of a Saviour.	

First Sunday.

THE SCRIPTURE TO BE LEARNED.

HOW ISAIAH PREDICTED THE SAVIOUR'S COMING.

How did Isaiah predict the Saviour's coming?*

For unto us a child is born, unto us a son is given: and the government shall be upon his shoulder: and his name shall be called Wonderful, Counsellor, The mighty God, The everlasting Father, The Prince of Peace. 9:6.

HOW MICAH PREDICTED IT.

How did Micah predict it?

But thou, Beth-lehem Ephratah, though thou be little among the thousands of Judah, yet out of thee shall he come forth unto me that is to be ruler in Israel; whose goings forth have been from of old, from everlasting. 5:2.

WHAT JOHN, THE EVANGELIST, SAID.

What did John say?

And the Word was made flesh, and dwelt among us, (and we beheld his glory, the glory as of the only begotten of the Father), full of grace and truth. 1:14.

WHAT THE CATECHISM SAYS.

What does the Catechism say?

I believe in Jesus Christ, God's only Son, our Lord, who was conceived by the Holy Ghost, born of the Virgin Mary.

---

*Teacher asks these questions until the whole class have recited these parts.

CHAPTER I.

The Saviour Comes.

HISTORY OF HIS FIRST THIRTY YEARS.

Let us now read the History of the Saviour's coming to earth.

THE Bible as a History goes back to the beginning of the world and forward to the end of time. It is not a record of races or reigns or rulers, but it is God's way of writing and God's main way of making history.

The Bible as a History.

How is the Bible a History?

The chief person in Bible History is God's Son. He came in the days when Cæsar Augustus was Emperor at Rome, and Herod was King of Judea. It was nineteen centuries ago. There was peace in all the world, and the Jews and Gentile nations were looking for a mighty monarch who would bring back the golden age. This period was the fullness of time.

Who is the chief person in Bible History?

When did Christ come?

The Days of Cæsar Augustus.

God's Son was in the beginning with God. He was before all worlds. All things were made by Him, and without Him was not anything made that was made. He is the everlasting Son of the Father, and is God.

Who is God's Son?

The Eternal Son.

The Father sent Him down from Heaven for our salvation. He forsook the throne of glory and entered the world in the likeness of men. That He would come, and would be born of a virgin, had been said long before by the prophets of the Old Testa-

Why did He come from heaven?

The Coming of God's Son.

Who said He would come?

a   3

FIRST SUNDAY.

<small>Who was John the Baptist?
Tell the story of John's parents.*</small>

ment. The birth of John the Baptist, the last of the prophets, the Messenger to prepare the way for the world's Saviour, was announced to Zacharias in the temple at Jerusalem. Six months af- <small>John, the Forerunner.</small> ter John's birth the infant Jesus was laid in the manger at

<small>Tell the story of the birth of Jesus.</small>

Bethlehem. The night He was born the <small>Jesus Born.</small> angel of the Lord came upon some shepherds keeping watch over their flock and brought them the good tidings of great joy. The shepherds has-

<small>Tell the story of Jesus' ancestors.*</small>

tened unto Bethlehem and found Mary and Joseph, and the Babe lying in a manger. After eight days the Babe was circumcised and named Jesus.

<small>Tell what occurred when Jesus was six weeks old.</small>

When Jesus was six weeks old, He was brought to the temple at Jerusalem, and presented to the Lord. Simeon and Anna saw Him there. Not long after- <small>Presentation in Temple.</small> wards some Wise Men came from the East to Jerusalem to seek the new-born King. They were guided by a star to Bethlehem, where the young Child was.

<small>Tell of the Wise Men and King Herod.</small>

On the road home they did not stop at Jer- <small>Wise Men.</small> usalem to see King Herod. For God had <small>Herod.</small> warned them in a dream not to go back to Herod, since he was only seeking the young child to destroy Him. God also warned Joseph to flee into Egypt <small>Flight into Egypt.</small> with the young Child and His mother. Joseph did so, and staid there until Herod died. He then came back, and settled with Jesus and Mary in his old home at Nazareth, where Jesus was subject to them. From Nazareth Joseph took Jesus up to

<small>Tell what took place after twelve years.</small>

the temple, when the boy was twelve years <small>Goes to the Feast.</small> old. We know nothing further of the youth of Jesus.

<small>*See Stories to be Read.</small>

THE STORIES TO BE READ.

The Story of the Parents of John the Baptist.

There was in the days of King Herod a certain priest named Zacharias, and his wife Elisabeth. They were both righteous before God. They had no child, and they both were now well stricken in years.

And it came to pass, that his lot was to burn incense when he went into the temple of the Lord. And the whole multitude of the people were praying without at the time of incense. And there appeared unto him an angel of the Lord standing on the right side of the altar of incense. And when Zacharias saw him he was troubled. But the angel said unto him, Fear not, Zacharias, for thy prayer is heard; and thy wife Elisabeth shall bear thee a son, and thou shalt call his name John. He shall be great in the sight of the Lord; and he shall go before Him in the spirit and power of Elias, to make ready a people prepared for the Lord.

And Zacharias said unto the angel, Whereby shall I know this? The angel answered, I am Gabriel, that stand in the presence of God; and am sent to show thee these glad tidings. And, behold, thou shalt be dumb, and not able to speak, until the day that these things shall be performed, because thou believest not my words.

And the people waited for Zacharias, and marvelled that he tarried so long in the temple. And when he came out, he could not speak unto them; and he beckoned unto them and remained speechless.

Now Elisabeth brought forth a son. And her neighbors and her cousins heard how the Lord had showed great mercy upon her; and they rejoiced with her.

And on the eighth day they came to circumcise the child; and they called him Zacharias, after the name of his father. And his mother answered and said, Not so; but he shall be called John. And they said unto her, There is none of thy kindred that is called by this name. And they made signs to his father, how he would have him called. And he asked for a writing table, and wrote, saying, His name is John.

FIRST SUNDAY.

And they all marvelled. And his mouth was opened immediately, and his tongue loosed, and he spake, and praised God. And all they that heard this, laid it up in their hearts, saying, What manner of child shall this be? And the hand of the Lord was with him.

The Story of the Ancestors of Jesus.

The table of Christ's ancestors goes back fully four thousand years. It is the only one of its kind. Matthew carries it back through David, and Ruth, to Abraham, to show how Jesus was connected with the father of the people of Israel, from whom He sprang according to the flesh. Luke carries it all the way back to Adam, to show Christ's connection with the whole human race.

SUMMARY OF EVENTS.

What Bible History is.

Ask each scholar to give, as best he can, "The Summary of Events."

The chief Person in Bible History.

The chief Time in Bible History. Fullness of Time.

The Son of God sent into the world. The earthly ancestors of Jesus.

His Forerunner, John. John's Parents.

The Birth of Jesus at Bethlehem. See *Bible Story*.

The Presentation at Jerusalem. See *Bible Story*.

The Wise Men and Herod. See *Bible Story*.

The Flight into Egypt and Return to Nazareth. See *Bible Story*.

The Boy Jesus. See *Bible Story*.

From what parts of the Bible is our narrative taken? John 1; Luke 1, 2; Matt. 2, and Mark 1.
What pictures did we have in "Bible Story" referring to this Chapter?
What shall we call this first Chapter? **The Saviour Comes.**
In conclusion, let the teacher again refer to the Scripture and Catechism answers that the scholar has learned.

Second Sunday.

THE SCRIPTURE TO BE LEARNED.

HOW PAUL SPOKE OF THE SAVIOUR WHO CAME TO SUFFER AND TO WORK.

Who, being in the form of God, thought it not robbery to be equal with God: but made himself of no reputation, and took upon him the form of a servant, and was made in the likeness of men: *What did Paul say of the Saviour Who came to suffer and to work?*

And being found in fashion as a man, he humbled himself, and became obedient unto death, even the death of the cross.

Wherefore God also hath highly exalted him, and given him a name which is above every name: that at the name of Jesus every knee should bow, and that every tongue should confess that Jesus Christ is Lord, to the glory of God the Father. Phil. 2:6-11.

HOW ISAIAH PROPHESIED OF THE SAVIOUR AS THE LAMB OF GOD.

The Lord hath laid on him the iniquity of us all. He was oppressed, and he was afflicted, yet he opened not his mouth: he is brought as a lamb to the slaughter, and as a sheep before her shearers is dumb, so he openeth not his mouth. 53:6-7. *How did Isaiah prophesy of the Lamb of God?*

WHAT DOES THE CATECHISM SAY AS TO HOW THE WORK OF THE SAVIOUR IS TO GO ON IN OUR HEARTS?

The old Adam in us is to be drowned and destroyed by daily sorrow and repentance, together with all sins and evil lusts.

---

*Teacher asks these questions until the whole class have recited these parts.

CHAPTER II.

The Saviour Begins Work.

THE WILDERNESS AND GALILEE.

When did John the Baptist begin to preach?
How was John clothed?*
What did he say to the Pharisees?*
To the multitudes?
To the publicans?*
To the soldiers?*

IT WAS in the fifteenth year of the reign of Tiberius Cæsar, when Jesus was about thirty years old, and Pontius Pilate was governor of Judæa, and Herod was tetrarch of Galilee, that the Word of God came unto John the Baptist in the wilderness. And he went into the region round about Jordan saying, Repent ye, for the kingdom of heaven is at hand. Great multitudes came out to hear John, and many were baptized by him. They wondered whether he were the Christ. But he said, I am not the Christ. I am not Elias. I am the voice of one crying in the wilderness. I baptize you with water; but one mightier than I, shall baptize you with the Holy Ghost and with fire.

What did he say of himself?
What did John say was the difference between Christ and himself?*
What would Christ do with the chaff?*

John in the Wilderness.

Jesus, who had left His home in Galilee, came to the river Jordan unto John to be baptized of him. John forbade Him, but finally suffered it. And when Jesus was baptized the heavens were opened, and He saw the Spirit of God descending like a dove and lighting upon Him; and lo, a voice out of the heavens saying, Thou art my beloved Son; in Thee I am well pleased. Being full of the Holy Spirit, Jesus was led up from the Jordan into the wilderness to be tempted of the devil. After forty days, and

Tell what you know of the baptism of Jesus?

Jesus Baptized.

Jesus Tempted.

8

SECOND SUNDAY.

the three temptations, the devil left Jesus, and behold angels came and ministered unto Him.

The next day John saw Jesus coming unto him and said, Behold the Lamb of God, that taketh away the sin of the world! Again the next day after, John was standing and two of his disciples; and he looked upon Jesus as He walked and said, Behold the Lamb of God! And the two disciples heard him speak, and they followed Jesus. **Andrew, Simon, Philip, Nathanael.** One of the two was Andrew. He found his brother Simon Peter. The next day Jesus found Philip. Philip found Nathanael and brought him to Jesus. On the third day there was a marriage in Cana of Galilee, and these disciples were there. The wine failed and Jesus told the servants to fill six water pots with water. When they bore the water **Marriage in Cana.** that had become wine unto the ruler of the feast, he said that the bridegroom had kept the good wine until last. This was the beginning of Jesus' miracles, and the first manifestation of His glory. After this He went down to the City of Capernaum, He, and His mother, and His brethren, and His disciples.

Side notes: What did John call Jesus? Who heard this? What did they say? Tell the story of Christ's finding His first disciples.* Whom did Andrew find? Whom did Philip bring? Tell the story of Nathanael.* What was the first miracle of Jesus? Where did He go after the marriage feast?

THE STORIES TO BE READ.

The Story of John's Preaching.

John himself had his raiment of camel's hair, and a leathern girdle about his loins; and his food was locusts and wild honey. All Jerusalem went out unto him. He said to the multitudes of the Pharisees and Sadducees that went out to be baptized of him, Ye offspring of vipers, who hath warned you to flee from the wrath to come. Now the axe lieth at the root of the trees; every tree therefore that bringeth not forth good fruit is hewn down, and cast into the fire.

SECOND SUNDAY.

And the multitudes asked him saying, What then must we do? And he answered and said unto them, He that hath two coats, let him impart to him that hath none; and he that hath food, let him do likewise. And there came also publicans to be baptized, and they said unto him, Master, what must we do? And he said unto them, Exact no more than that which is appointed you. And the soldiers likewise demanded of him, saying, And what shall we do? And he said unto them, Do violence to no man, neither accuse any one wrongfully; and be content with your wages. With many other exhortations therefore preached he good tidings unto the people.

The Shoe-Latchet and the Fan.

And all men mused in their hearts of John, whether he were the Christ or not.

John answered, saying unto them all, I indeed baptize you with water, but One mightier than I cometh, the latchet of whose shoes I am not worthy to unloose: he shall baptize you with the Holy Ghost and with fire; Whose fan is in his hand, and he will thoroughly purge his floor, and will gather the wheat into his garner; but the chaff he will burn with fire unquenchable.

The First Disciples—Andrew Finds Peter.

The two disciples followed Jesus. And Jesus turned and saw them following and said unto them, What seek ye? And they said unto him, Master, where dost thou live? He said unto them, Come and see. They came and saw where he dwelt and they staid with him that day, for it was only a few hours before night. One of the two that followed Him was Andrew, Simon Peter's brother. He first found his own brother Simon and said unto him, We have found the Christ. And he brought him to Jesus. And when Jesus saw him he said, Thou art Simon the son of Jonas: Thou shalt be called Cephas.

Philip Brings Nathanael.

Philip was of Bethsaida, the city of Andrew and Peter. Finding Nathanael, Philip said, We have found him of whom Moses

SECOND SUNDAY.

and the prophets did write, Jesus of Nazareth. Nathanael said, Can any good thing come out of Nazareth? Philip said, Come and see. Jesus saw Nathanael coming and said, Behold, an Israelite indeed, in whom there is no guile! Nathanael said, Whence knowest thou me? Jesus answered, Before Philip called thee, when thou wast under the fig-tree I saw thee. Nathanael answered him, Master, Thou art the Son of God; Thou art the king of Israel!

SUMMARY OF EVENTS.

The Word of God comes to John the Baptist. He is to prepare the Jews for the work of the Saviour.

Ask each scholar to give as best he can the "Summary of Events."

John preaches and baptizes in the wilderness. He warns the Pharisees and Sadducees. He tells the multitude what to do. He speaks of the shoe latchet and the fan.

Jesus, being about 30 years old, leaves His home and comes to John.

Jesus is baptized. See *Bible Story*.

Jesus is tempted by the devil. See *Bible Story*.

John points out Jesus as the Lamb of God.

Jesus returns to Galilee.

The first two disciples follow Jesus.

Andrew finds Peter.

Philip brings Nathanael.

Jesus performs His first Miracle and turns water into wine. See *Bible Story*.

Jesus goes down to Capernaum with His mother and brethren and disciples.

From what parts of the Bible is our narrative taken? Matt. 3, 4; Mark 1; Luke 3, 4; and John 1.

What pictures did we have in Bible Story referring to this chapter?

What shall we call this second chapter? **The Saviour Begins Work.**

In conclusion let the teacher again refer to the Scripture and Catechism answers that the scholar has learned.

THE SCRIPTURE TO BE LEARNED.

THE SANCTITY OF THE HOUSE OF GOD.

What should be our conduct in God's house?*

The Lord is in his holy temple: let all the earth keep silence before Him. Hab. 2:20.

GOD GAVE HIS ONLY BEGOTTEN SON.

Why did God give His Son?

For God so loved the world that he gave his only begotten Son, that whosoever believeth in him should not perish, but have everlasting life. John 3:16.

THE SON BROUGHT LIVING WATER.

What did He bring?

If thou knewest the gift of God, and who it is that saith to thee, Give me to drink; thou wouldest have asked of him and he would have given thee living water. John 4:10.

WHAT THE CATECHISM SAYS.

What does the Catechism say?

It (baptism) worketh forgiveness of sins, delivers from death and the devil, and gives everlasting salvation to those who believe; as the word and promise of God declare.

*Teacher asks these questions until the whole class have recited these parts

CHAPTER III.

Jesus Goes to Jerusalem and Returns.

IN THE TEMPLE AND IN SAMARIA.

NOW the Jews' passover was at hand, and Jesus went up to Jerusalem. He found in the temple those that sold oxen and sheep and doves, and the changers of money sitting. And He cast them all out.

At Jerusalem there was a man of the Pharisees, named Nicodemus, a ruler of the Jews. The same came to Jesus by night saying, Rabbi, Thou art a teacher sent from God. But Jesus told him that except a man be born of water and of the Spirit, he cannot enter the kingdom of God. Nicodemus did not understand. Jesus said there were things to tell still more difficult to believe. One of these was that as Moses lifted up the serpent in the wilderness even so must God's Son be lifted up on the cross. For God so loved the world that He gave His only begotten Son that whosoever believeth in Him should not perish, but have everlasting life.

After this Jesus and His disciples went into the Jordan Valley of Judea and preached. And all men came to Him. But the Pharisees heard that Jesus was making more disciples than John. When the Lord knew they had heard this, He left Judea to go again into Galilee.

The Night Interview of Nicodemus.

Born Again. Lifted on the Cross.

Jesus in the Jordan Valley.

Where did the Saviour go?
Tell what He did in the temple.
What did He say to those who sold doves?*
What did the Jews understand when He spoke of destroying and raising up the temple?*

With whom did Jesus have an interview?

What strange things did He tell Nicodemus?
Tell more fully of the surprise of Nicodemus.*

Where did Jesus go after Nicodemus left Him?
Why did He depart from the Jordan Valley for Galilee?

THIRD SUNDAY.

Where did He stop on His way?
Whom did He meet?
Describe the conversation between Jesus and this woman.
Why did the woman think Jesus could not give the living water?*
What did she ask Him about her father, Jacob?*
Why is this water better than any other?*
What did the woman do?
How did many come to believe?
What did they say He was?
What was the meat of Jesus?*

It was necessary to go through Samaria, and He came to a city of Samaria called Sychar. And Jacob's well was there. Being wearied with His journey, **Jesus at the Well.** Jesus sat by the well. About noon there came a woman of Samaria to draw water. Jesus asked her for a drink. She was surprised, for the Jews have no dealings with the Samaritans. Jesus told her that if she knew to whom she was speaking, she would ask for living water. She said, Sir, give me this water, that I thirst not. He said unto her that He was Christ. She left her waterpot, and went away into the city, and saith to the men, Come, see a man, who told me all the things that I ever did: can this be the Christ? They went out of the city and besought Him to abide with them: and He abode there two days. And many believed because of the word of the woman. Many more believed because of His word. Then they said to the woman, Now we believe, not because of thy speaking: for we have heard for ourselves, and know that this is indeed the Saviour of the world.

THE STORIES TO BE READ.

How Jesus Cast Out the Money Changers.

When he had made a scourge of small cords, he drove them all out of the temple, and the sheep and the oxen. And he poured out the changers' money, and overthrew their tables. To them that sold the doves he said, Take these things hence; make not my Father's house an house of merchandise. Then the Jews said unto him, What sign shewest thou unto us, seeing that thou doest these things? Jesus answered and said unto them, Destroy this temple, and in three days I will raise it up. The Jews said, Forty and six years was this temple in building,

THIRD SUNDAY.

and wilt thou raise it up in three days? But he spake of the temple of his body. When therefore he was raised from the dead, his disciples remembered that he spake this.

The Surprise of Nicodemus.

Nicodemus said, Master, we know that thou art a teacher come from God: for no man can do these signs that thou doest, except God be with him.

Jesus answered and said, Verily, verily, I say unto thee, Except a man be born anew, he cannot see the kingdom of God. Nicodemus saith unto him, How can a man be born when he is old? Jesus answered, Verily, verily, I say unto thee, Except a man be born of water and the Spirit, he cannot enter into the kingdom of God. That which is born of the flesh is flesh; and that which is born of the Spirit is spirit.

Nicodemus answered and said unto him, How can these things be? Jesus said to him, Art thou the teacher of Israel, and understandest not these things? Verily, verily, I say unto thee, We speak that we do know, and bear witness of that we have seen: and ye receive not our witness. If I told you earthly things, and ye believe not, how shall ye believe if I tell you heavenly things?

The Living Water.

Jesus said, If thou knewest the gift of God, and who it is that saith to thee, Give me to drink; thou wouldest have asked of him, and he would have given thee living water.

The woman saith unto him, Sir, thou hast nothing to draw with, and the well is deep: from whence then hast thou the living water? Art thou greater than our father Jacob, who gave us the well, and drank thereof himself?

Jesus said, Every one that drinketh of this water shall thirst again: but whosoever drinketh of the water that I shall give him shall never thirst; but the water that I shall give him shall become in him a well of water springing up unto eternal life.

THIRD SUNDAY.

The Meat of Jesus.

In the meanwhile the disciples prayed him, saying, Master. eat. But he said unto them, I have meat to eat that ye know not. The disciples said one to another, Hath any man brought him aught to eat? Jesus saith unto them, My meat is to do the will of him that sent me and to accomplish his work.

SUMMARY OF EVENTS.

The Saviour has been baptized and tempted and has begun His work.

The Saviour goes to Jerusalem to the Passover.

He drives out the money-changers and dove-sellers.

The Jews argue with Him about destroying the Temple.

He has a night-interview with Nicodemus.

He preaches in the Jordan Valley.

He departs for Galilee and stops at the well in Samaria.

The Samaritan woman.

From what parts of the Bible is our narrative taken? John 2, 3 and 4.
None of these scenes are in Bible Story.
What shall we call this third chapter? **The Saviour Goes Up to Jerusalem and Returns.**
In conclusion let the teacher again refer to the Scripture and Catechism answers that the scholar has learned.

Fourth Sunday.

THE SCRIPTURE TO BE LEARNED.

THE PHYSICIAN AND HIS PATIENTS.

They that are whole have no need of the physician, but they that are sick: I came not to call the righteous, but sinners to repentance. Mark 2:17.   <small>Who require a physician?*</small>

THE TEACHER AND HIS PUPILS.

I am the way, the truth, and the life: no man cometh unto the Father but by me. John 14:6.   <small>Who is the true teacher?</small>

THE PREACHER AND HIS CONGREGATION.

Seek ye first the kingdom of God, and his righteousness; and all these things shall be added unto you. Matt. 6:33.   <small>What does our great teacher and preacher say?</small>

WHAT THE CATECHISM SAYS.

I believe that Jesus Christ has redeemed me, a lost and condemned creature, secured and delivered me from all sins, from death, and from the power of the devil.   <small>What does the Catechism say?</small>

---

*Teacher asks these questions until the whole class have recited these parts.

CHAPTER IV.

The Saviour Labors About the Sea of Galilee.

CAPERNAUM AND NAZARETH.

Where did Jesus go after leaving Samaria?
Were the people in Galilee glad to see Him?
What did He do in Galilee?

TWO days after Jesus had met the woman at the well in Samaria, He returned to Galilee. The Galileans received Him with joy, for they had seen the things that He did at Jerusalem. His fame went through all their region. He taught in their synagogues and was glorified of all. When He came unto Cana, where He had made the water wine, a nobleman from Capernaum

What did He do at Cana?

met Him and besought Him to heal his son. **Heals Nobleman's Son.** Jesus told him to go home: his son would live. And it was so. And Jesus came to Nazareth, where He had been brought up. On the Sabbath He went into the synagogue and read from the book of the prophet Isaiah

What at Nazareth?
What was His text?
Tell the story and the result.*

and began to preach with wonderful words of grace. But when the people remembered who He was, **Preaches at Nazareth.** and when He spake the truth to them, they were filled with wrath, and rose up out of the synagogue and cast Him forth from the city and would have thrown Him headlong from the brow of a hill. But He passing through them, went His way.

Leaving Nazareth He came and dwelt in Capernaum, a city by the sea of Galilee. As the people pressed upon Him to hear the Word of God, He saw two boats standing; but the fishermen were gone out of them. He

FOURTH SUNDAY.

Teaches out of a Boat. entered one of them and had it pushed out a little from the land. Then He sat down and taught the multitude out of the boat. When He had finished speaking, He told the fishermen to go out into the deep and let down their nets. They enclosed a great multitude of fishes. As soon as the men came to shore they left their nets and followed Him. A little farther on, Jesus saw James and John in the boat mending the nets. He called them. When they had brought their boat to land, they left their father Zebedee in the boat with the hired servants and went after Him.

Tell the story of the fishermen and the nets.

On the Sabbath day Jesus entered into the synagogue and taught. A man with an unclean spirit interrupted Him. Jesus drove the unclean spirit out. Going to the house of Simon, He found the latter's wife's mother sick of a fever. He took her by the hand and raised her up. The fever left her, and she ministered unto them.

Drives out an Unclean Spirit.
Heals Peter's Wife's Mother.

Where did Jesus go on the Sabbath?
Whom did He heal?
Whom did He heal after service?

That evening at sunset, the whole city was gathered at the door. He laid His hands on every one of the sick and healed them. Early the next morning, He rose up and went out into a desert place and there prayed. The disciples came after Him and told Him that all the people were seeking Him. They would have that He should not go from them. But He said, I must preach the kingdom of God to other cities also; for therefore am I sent. And He went about in all Galilee teaching and preaching and healing. And great multitudes followed Him from Galilee and Decapolis and Jerusalem and Judea and from beyond Jordan.

Heals the sick in Capernaum.

What did He do at sunset?
What early the next morning?
Who followed Him?
What was the conversation?

Goes about all Galilee.

Where did He then go?
Who followed Him?

b

STORIES TO BE READ.

Jesus Heals a Nobleman's Son.

There was a certain nobleman, whose son was sick at Capernaum. When he heard that Jesus was come into Galilee, he went unto Jesus, and besought him that he would come down and heal his son; for he was at the point of death. Then said Jesus unto him, Except ye see signs and wonders, ye will not believe. The nobleman saith unto him, Sir, come down ere my child die. Jesus saith unto him, Go thy way; thy son liveth. And the man believed the word that Jesus had spoken unto him, and he went his way. And as he was now going down, his servants met him, and told him, saying, Thy son liveth. Then inquired he of them the hour when he began to amend. And they said unto him, Yesterday at the seventh hour the fever left him. So the father knew that it was at the same hour, in the which Jesus said unto him, Thy son liveth: and himself believed, and his whole house. This is the second miracle that Jesus did in Galilee.

Preaches at His Home.

He entered the synagogue and stood up to read. And there was delivered unto him the Book of Isaiah and he opened the book and found the place where it was written:

The Spirit of the Lord is upon me,
Because he hath anointed me to preach the Gospel to the poor;
He hath sent me to heal the broken-hearted,
To preach deliverance to the captives,
And recovering of sight to the blind,
To set at liberty them that are bruised,
To preach the acceptable year of the Lord.

And he closed the book, and gave it again to the minister, and sat down. And the eyes of all were fastened on him. And he said, This day is this Scripture fulfilled in your ears. And they wondered at his words of grace. But they said, Is not this Joseph's son? He said, No prophet is accepted in his own country. Many widows were in Israel in the days of the great famine, but unto none was Elias sent save unto the woman of Sa-

FOURTH SUNDAY. 21

repta; and many lepers were in Israel in the time of Elisha, and none of them was cleansed but Naaman the Syrian. And they were filled with wrath and rose up and cast him out of the city.

SUMMARY OF EVENTS.

Jesus returns from Jerusalem through Samaria.

He is received with honor in Galilee.

He preaches and teaches there.

He heals a Nobleman's son at Cana.

He is rejected at Nazareth.

He comes to the large city of Capernaum to live.

He teaches out of a boat and causes a miraculous draught of fishes. See *Bible Story*. "Peter's Draught of Fishes."

The next Sabbath He heals a man with an unclean spirit; and Peter's wife's mother.

At sunset He heals the sick of the city.

Early the next morning He goes out into a desert place.

He declines staying at Capernaum and goes about all Galilee.

From what parts of the Bible is our narrative taken? John 4, Luke 4, Matt. 4, Mark 1, Matt. 8.
What picture did we have in "Bible Story" referring to this chapter?
What shall we call this fourth chapter? **The Saviour Works About the Sea of Galilee.**
In conclusion let the teacher again refer to the Scripture and Catechism answers that the scholar has learned.

Fifth Sunday.

THE SCRIPTURE TO BE LEARNED.

THE RIGHTEOUSNESS OF THE PHARISEES REBUKED.

What did Jesus say of righteousness?*

For I say unto you that except your righteousness shall exceed the righteousness of the scribes and Pharisees, ye shall in no case enter into the kingdom of heaven. Matt. 5 : 20.

TRUE RIGHTEOUSNESS IN PRAYER.

How shalt thou pray?

But thou, when thou prayest, enter into thy closet, and when thou hast shut thy door, pray to thy Father which is in secret; and thy Father which seeth in secret shall reward thee openly. Matt. 6: 6.

THE COMMISSION TO THE DISCIPLES.

What did Jesus direct His disciples to do?

Go ye, therefore, and teach all nations, baptizing them in the name of the Father, and of the Son, and of the Holy Ghost. Matt. 28:19.

WHAT THE CATECHISM SAYS.

What does the Catechism say of baptism?

Baptism is not simply water, but it is the water comprehended in God's command, and connected with God's Word.

---

*Teacher asks these questions until the whole class have recited these parts.

CHAPTER V

The Saviour Performs Miracles and Selects Disciples.

CAPERNAUM AND BY THE POOL OF BETHESDA.

A Leper.

WHILE Jesus was in one of the cities, He healed a leper, who came to Him, full of leprosy. When after some days He entered again into Capernaum, and it was noised that He was in the house, so many at once gathered together that there was no room to receive them, not even about the door. As He was teaching, with Pharisees and doctors of the law out of every town sitting by, behold some came bringing a man sick of the palsy. He forgave the man's sins and told him to take up his bed and walk home. And the multitudes were all amazed and said, We never saw it on this fashion! Jesus went to the seaside and taught the people there. And as He passed by, He saw a publican named Matthew sitting at the receipt of custom. Jesus said to him, Follow Me; and Matthew left all, rose up, and followed Him.

A man with the Palsy.

At the Seaside.
Matthew.

After this there was a feast of the Jews, and Jesus went up to Jerusalem. While there He restored an infirm man at the pool of Bethesda. He told the Pharisees that He was the Son of God, and that He had a right to heal on the Sabbath. They were

The Man at the Pool of Bethesda.

Tell the story of the leper.*
What was the leper to do?*
What did he do?*

Tell the story of the palsied man.
What did Jesus say unto him?*
Who found fault?*
What did He then say?*
In what city was this?

How did Jesus call Matthew?

What do you know of the story of the impotent man at the Pool of Bethesda?

23

FIFTH SUNDAY.

<small>Tell about the plucking of corn.
What happened afterward?</small>

filled with madness because He defended His disciples for plucking corn when they were hungry on the Sabbath, and because He healed a man that had a withered hand on another Sabbath. **Angry Pharisees.** They went out of the synagogue, and communed one with an-

<small>How did Jesus answer the Pharisees?*</small>

other what they might do to Jesus. And they took counsel with the Herodians against Him, how they might destroy Him.

<small>When did Jesus choose the twelve apostles?
What are their names?*
Where did Jesus go?
Who were with Him?</small>

In those days He went out into a mountain to pray, and continued all night in prayer with God. **Praying in the Mountain. Choosing Twelve Apostles.** When it was day He called unto Him His disciples, and of them He chose and ordained twelve, whom also He named apostles. And He came down with them and stood in the plain. And a great multitude of people out of all Judea and Jerusalem and from the sea-coast of Tyre and Sidon came to hear Him.

THE STORIES TO BE READ.

The Story of the Leper.

There cometh a leper, kneeling down to him and saying. If thou wilt, thou canst make me clean. And being moved with compassion, he stretched forth his hand, and touched him, and saith unto him, I will; be thou clean. And as soon as he had spoken, the leprosy departed from him, and he was cleansed. And Jesus sent him out and said, Say nothing to any man: but show thyself to the priest, and offer the gift that Moses commanded. But he went out and began to publish it much, and to blaze abroad the matter, so that Jesus could no more openly enter into the city, but was without in desert places.

The Story of the Palsied Man.

Behold, they come unto Jesus bringing a man sick of the palsy, lying on a bed which was borne of four. And when they could not come near him because of the multitude, they went upon the housetop and uncovered the roof where he was. And when they had broken it up, they let down through the tiles the bed on which the sick of the palsy lay. And when Jesus saw their faith, he said unto the sick of the palsy, Son, be of good cheer, thy sins are forgiven thee. But there were certain scribes sitting there who began to reason within their hearts, saying, Why doth this man thus speak? He blasphemeth. Who can forgive sins but God alone? But Jesus said, Why reason ye these things? Wherefore think ye evil in your hearts? For which is easier, to say, Thy sins be forgiven thee, or to say, Arise, take up thy bed and walk? Then, that they might know that he had power to forgive sins, he turned to the sick of the palsy and said, Arise, and take up thy bed and go unto thy house. And immediately the man rose up before them, and took his bed, and departed to his own house, glorifying God.

The Story of the Impotent Man at the Pool of Bethesda.

There is in Jerusalem by the sheep gate a pool, which is called in Hebrew, Bethesda, having five porches. In these lay a great multitude of impotent folk, blind, halt, and withered, waiting for the moving of the water. And a certain man was there who had been sick for thirty-eight years. When Jesus saw him lying, he said, Wouldest thou be made whole? The sick man answered, Sir, I have no man, when the water is troubled, to put me into the pool: but while I am coming, another steppeth down before me. Jesus saith unto him, Arise, take up thy bed and walk. And immediately the man was made whole, and took up his bed and walked.

The Disciples Pluck Corn on the Sabbath.

Jesus went on the sabbath day through the cornfields: and his disciples were an hungered, and began as they went to pluck ears of corn, and to eat, rubbing them in their hands. But the Pharisees said, Thy disciples do that which is not lawful upon the sabbath. He said, Have ye never read what David did, how he went into the house of God in the days of Abiathar, and did eat the shewbread, which was not lawful? Or have ye not read

FIFTH SUNDAY.

in the law how that the priests in the temple profane the sabbath, and are guiltless? The sabbath was made for man, and not man for the sabbath: so that the Son of man is Lord even of the sabbath.

The Twelve Apostles.

Now the names of the twelve apostles are these: The first, Simon, whom he also named Peter. And Andrew his brother. James the son of Zebedee, and John the brother of James. And he surnamed these Boanerges, which is the sons of thunder. Philip and Bartholomew. Matthew the publican and Thomas. James the son of Alpheus, and Lebbæus whose surname was Thaddæus. Judas the brother of James, Simon the Canaanite called Zelotes, and Judas Iscariot, which also betrayed him.

SUMMARY OF EVENTS.

Jesus is on His way from the Passover at Jerusalem back to Capernaum.

He performs the Miracle of healing the leper. He enters Capernaum.

The Miracle of healing the man with the palsy. Calls Matthew.

The Miracle of healing the man at the Pool of Bethesda.

The Miracle of healing the man with the withered hand on the Sabbath.

The disciples pluck corn on the Sabbath.

The Pharisees' madness at these things.

The Choosing of the Twelve Apostles.

From what parts of the Bible is our narrative taken? Matt. 8-12, Mark 2-3, Luke 5-6.

None of these scenes are in "Bible Story."

What shall we call this fifth chapter? **The Saviour Performs Miracles and Selects Disciples.**

In conclusion let the teacher again refer to the Scripture and Catechism answers that the scholar has learned.

Sixth Sunday.

THE SCRIPTURE TO BE LEARNED.

THE POOR IN SPIRIT.

Blessed are the poor in spirit: for their's is the kingdom of heaven. Matt. 5:3. <small>Who shall inherit the Kingdom of Heaven?*</small>

THEY THAT MOURN.

Blessed are they that mourn: for they shall be comforted. v. 4. <small>Who shall be comforted?</small>

THE MEEK.

Blessed are the meek: for they shall inherit the earth. v. 5. <small>Who shall inherit the earth?</small>

THEY WHICH DO HUNGER AND THIRST AFTER RIGHTEOUSNESS.

Blessed are they which do hunger and thirst after righteousness: for they shall be filled. v. 6. <small>Who shall be filled?</small>

THE MERCIFUL.

Blessed are the merciful: for they shall obtain mercy. v. 7. <small>Who shall obtain mercy?</small>

THE PURE IN HEART.

Blessed are the pure in heart: for they shall see God. v. 8. <small>Who shall see God?</small>

THE PEACEMAKERS.

Blessed are the peacemakers: for they shall be called the children of God. v. 9. <small>Who shall be called the children of God?</small>

WHAT THE CATECHISM SAYS AS TO GOD'S CHILDREN AND GOD'S WORD.

When the word of God is taught in its truth and purity, and we, as the children of God lead holy lives in accordance with it; to this may our blessed Father in heaven help us! <small>When is the Name of God hallowed by us?</small>

---

*Teacher asks these questions until the whole class have recited these parts.

CHAPTER VI.

The Saviour's Great Sermon.

ON THE MOUNT OF BEATITUDES.

How did our Saviour begin His Sermon on the Mount?

How did He use the terms "Salt" and "Light?"

AND seeing the multitudes, He went up into the mountain; and when He had sat down, His disciples came unto Him and He taught them of those who are blessed in the kingdom of heaven. He compared them to salt that savors and to a light that shines. He told them not to **The Eight Blesseds. The Salt. The Light.** suppose that He came to destroy the law or the prophets.

What does He say of the Commandments?

He came to fulfil. If it was said to them of old time, Thou shalt not kill, He said, Every one who is angry with his brother shall be in danger **The Commandments.** of the judgment. If it was said to them of old time, Thou shalt not forswear thyself, He said, Swear not at all. If it was said, An eye for an eye, He said, Whoso-

Give the story of the Eye and the Tooth.*

ever smiteth thee on thy right cheek, turn to him the other also. If it was said, Thou shalt love thy neighbor, and hate thine enemy, He said, Love your enemies

Whom, did He say, we are to love?

and pray for them that persecute you. Be perfect as your Father in heaven is perfect.

He taught them, further, not to do their good deeds,

What did He say about good deeds and alms?

to be seen of men. Not to give alms with a **Sounding a Trumpet.** trumpet sounding before them, as the hypocrites do. Not to pray standing in the corners of the

SIXTH SUNDAY.

Praying on the Street Corners. streets or in the synagogues, to be seen of men, but to pray after the manner of the Lord's Prayer. Not to look sad when they fast, to be seen of men. Then their Father which seeth in secret, would reward them openly. *What about praying*

He taught them, further, not to lay up treasures upon **Moth and Rust.** the earth, but in heaven where neither moth **Mammon.** nor rust doth corrupt. Not to try to serve God and Mammon. Not to be anxious for what they should eat or what they should drink, or what they **What to Seek First.** should put on. But to seek first the kingdom of God, and all these things would be added unto them. *What about treasures? Give the story of the fowls of the air.**

He taught them not to judge, since with what measure they measured, it would be measured **Judge Not.** unto them again.

He told them to ask, to seek, and to knock; and that **Knock!** whatsoever they would have others do unto them, that they should do unto others.

He told them to enter in by the narrow gate. That **The Narrow Gate.** they should beware of false prophets. That a tree is known by its fruits. That the tree not bringing forth good fruit is cast into the fire. That **The Tree.** not every one who says Lord, Lord, shall **Lord! Lord!** enter into the kingdom of heaven, but he that doeth the will of His Father which is in heaven. That to some He will profess: I never knew you, depart from Me. *Tell the story of the strait gate.* What about false prophets? Tell the story of the tree.* What about those who say "Lord, Lord"?*

In conclusion He compared those who heard and **The House on the Rock; On the Sand.** acted on His words to a man building his house on a rock; and those who heard but did not act, to a foolish man building his *To what did He compare the persons who act on His words? Tell the story of the Wise Builder, of the Foolish Builder.**

SIXTH SUNDAY.

house upon the sand. And when He ended these sayings, the multitude were astonished at His teaching: for He taught them as one having authority, and not as their scribes.   **With Authority.**

THE STORIES TO BE READ.

The Story of the Eye and the Tooth.

Ye have heard that it hath been said, An eye for an eye, and a tooth for a tooth: but I say unto you, Resist not the evil: but whosoever smiteth thee on thy right cheek, turn to him the other also. And if any man would go to law with thee, and take away thy coat, let him have thy cloke also. And whosoever shall compel thee to go one mile, go with him twain. Give to him that asketh thee, and from him that would borrow of thee turn not thou away.

The Story of the Fowls of the Air.

Behold the birds of the heaven, that they sow not, neither do they reap, nor gather into barns; yet your heavenly Father feedeth them. Are ye not of much more value than they? Consider the lilies of the field, how they grow; they toil not, neither do they spin: and yet I say unto you, that even Solomon in all his glory was not arrayed like one of these. But if God doth so clothe the grass of the field, which to-day is, and to-morrow is cast into the oven, shall he not much more clothe you, O ye of little faith?

The Story of the Strait Gate.

Enter ye in at the strait gate: for wide is the gate, and broad is the way that leadeth to destruction, and many there be which go in thereat. For strait is the gate, and narrow is the way that leadeth unto life, and few there be that find it.

The Story of the Tree.

Every tree is known by its own fruit. For men do not gather grapes of thorns, or figs of thistles. Even so every good tree

SIXTH SUNDAY. 31

bringeth forth good fruit; but a corrupt tree bringeth forth evil fruit. Every tree that bringeth not forth good fruit is hewn down, and cast into the fire.

The Story of the Wise Builder.

Whosoever heareth these sayings of mine, and doeth them, I will liken him unto a wise man, which built his house upon a rock. And the rain descended, and the floods came, and the winds blew, and beat upon that house. And it fell not. For it was founded upon a rock.

The Story of the Foolish Builder.

Everyone that heareth these sayings of mine, and doeth them not, shall be likened unto a foolish man, which built his house upon the sand. And the rain descended, and the floods came, and the winds blew, and beat upon that house. And it fell. And great was the fall of it.

SUMMARY OF EVENTS.

After performing many miracles and selecting the twelve apostles, the Saviour preached the Sermon on the Mount:
The eight Beatitudes.
The figures of the Salt and the Light.
The commandments of old and Christ's commandments.
We are to love our enemies, and be perfect.
We are not to do good to be seen of men.
We are to lay up Treasures in heaven, and seek God's kingdom first. The Story of "The Fowls of the Air."
We are not to judge others, but to enter the strait gate ourselves. The Story of "The Strait Gate."
We, like the tree, shall be judged, not by our words, but by our fruits. The Story of "The Tree."
We are to hear and to do what we hear. The Stories of "The Wise Builder" and "The Foolish Builder."

None of the Sermon on the Mount is in "Bible Story."
What shall we call this sixth chapter? **The Saviour's Great Sermon.**
From what parts of the Bible is our narrative taken? Matt. 5, 6 and 7, Luke 6.
In conclusion let the teacher again refer to the Scripture and Catechism answers that the scholar has learned.

Seventh Sunday.

THE SCRIPTURE TO BE LEARNED.

EVEN JERUSALEM WOULD NOT.

Would Jerusalem obey? O Jerusalem, Jerusalem, thou that killest the prophets, and stonest them which are sent unto thee, how often would I have gathered thy children together, even as a hen gathereth her chickens under her wings, and ye would not! Matt. 23:37.

THE CONTROL OF OUR WORDS.

Must we watch our words? For by thy words thou shalt be justified, and by thy words thou shalt be condemned. Matt. 12:37.

OUR RELATIONSHIP TO CHRIST AND WHAT IT IMPLIES.

What are we to Christ? The Spirit itself beareth witness with our spirit, that we are the children of God: And if children, then heirs; heirs of God, and joint heirs with Christ; if so be that we suffer with him, that we may be also glorified together. Rom. 8:16, 17.

WHAT THE CATECHISM SAYS OF PUNISHMENT OF THE WICKED.

What does the Catechism say? I the Lord thy God am a jealous God, visiting the iniquity of the fathers upon the children unto the third and fourth generation of them that hate me: and showing mercy unto thousands of them that love me, and keep my commandments.

CHAPTER VII

The Saviour Meets with Opposition.

PROUD CAPERNAUM AND OTHER CITIES.

AFTER Jesus had ended His Sermon on the Mount, He went back to Capernaum. On the way He met some elders of the Jews who had come out to ask Him to heal the servant of a centurion in Capernaum. Soon after, the centurion himself appeared, and Jesus praised his faith and told him to go home for his servant was healed. The day after, He went unto a city called Nain. When He came near the gate of the city, a dead man, a widow's only son, was being carried out. Jesus told the mother not to weep and raised up the young man and gave him to his mother, and a great fear came on all the people. But He blamed that generation and found fault with the cities wherein most of His mighty works were done, because they repented not. On the other hand, He blessed the lowly.

And one of the Pharisees desired that He would eat with him. He went into the Pharisee's house, and sat down to meat. And a woman anointed His feet with an alabaster box of ointment. He said unto her, Thy sins are forgiven. Go in peace.

Soon afterward He went through every city and village, preaching the glad tidings of the kingdom of God.

The Centurion's Servant.

The Widow of Nain.

The Proud Cities.

The Alabaster Box of Ointment.

Where did Jesus go after preaching the Sermon on the Mount

What happened at Capernaum

Tell the story of the Widow's Son.

What does Jesus say to the weary and heavy laden?*

What does He say of the punishment of the cities?*

Tell the story of the woman anointing the Saviour's feet.*

What parable had He for Simon?*

How did He compare Simon and the woman?*

33

SEVENTH SUNDAY.

What did Jesus do in every city and village?
Who was brought to Him?
How did the Pharisees explain this miracle?
What did our Saviour reply?
What does He say of the Sin against the Holy Ghost?

What of every idle word?

What punishment did He predict for the Wicked City?
Who, did He say, would rise up in Judgment against them?

Whom does Jesus consider as His relatives?

The twelve disciples and many others were with Him. And He went into a house, and there was brought unto Him one possessed of a devil, both blind and dumb. He healed him, so that he both spake and saw. Then all the people said, Is not this the son of David? But when the Pharisees who came down from Jerusalem heard it, they said, This man casts out devils by the prince of devils. Jesus said, How can Satan cast out Satan? Whosoever shall speak a word against the Son of man, it shall be forgiven him; but whoso shall speak against the Holy Ghost, it shall not be forgiven him, neither in this world, nor in the world to come. And I say unto you, that every idle word that men shall speak, they shall give account thereof in the day of judgment. For by thy words thou shalt be justified, and by thy words thou shalt be condemned.

The Blind and Dumb.

The Sin Against the Holy Ghost.

Idle Words.

Then certain said, Master we would see a sign from thee. But He said, There shall no sign be given but the sign of the prophet Jonah. The men of Nineveh shall rise in judgment with this generation, and shall condemn it; because they repented at the preaching of Jonah, and behold a greater than Jonah is here! The queen of the south shall rise up in the judgment with the men of this generation, and shall condemn them; for she came from the uttermost parts of the earth to hear the wisdom of Solomon, and behold a greater than Solomon is here! While He yet talked, one said unto Him, Behold, Thy mother and Thy brethren stand without desiring to speak with Thee. He

The Men of Nineveh and the Queen of the South.

SEVENTH SUNDAY. 35

Mother and Brethren. said, My mother and My brethren are these which hear the word of God and do it. For whosoever shall do the will of My Father which is in Heaven, the same is My brother, and My sister, and mother.

The Punishment of the Cities.

Woe unto thee, Chorazin! woe unto thee, Bethsaida! For if the mighty works which have been done in you had been done in Tyre and Sidon, they would have repented long ago in sackcloth and ashes. But I say unto you, It shall be more tolerable for Tyre and Sidon in the day of judgment, than for you. And thou Capernaum, which art exalted unto heaven, shalt be brought down to hell. For if the mighty works which have been done in thee had been done in Sodom, it would have remained until this day. But I say unto you, That it shall be more tolerable for the land of Sodom in the day of judgment, than for thee.

"Come Unto Me."

Come unto me, all ye that labour, and are heavy laden, and I will give you rest. Take my yoke upon you, and learn of me: for I am meek and lowly in heart: and ye shall find rest unto your souls. For my yoke is easy, and my burden is light.

Story of the Woman Breaking the Alabaster Box of Ointment.

And behold a woman brought an alabaster box of ointment, and stood at his feet behind him weeping, and began to wash his feet with tears, and did wipe them with the hairs of her head, and kissed his feet, and anointed them with the ointment. Now when Simon the Pharisee, which had invited him, saw it, he said to himself, This man, if he were a prophet, would have known who this is that toucheth him. For she is a sinner.

A Parable for Simon.

And Jesus said, Simon, I have something to say unto thee.
He said, Master, say on.
Jesus said, There was a certain creditor, which had two debt-

c

SEVENTH SUNDAY.

ors: the one owed five hundred pence, and the other fifty. And when they had nothing to pay, he frankly forgave both. Tell me therefore, which of them will love him most.

Simon said, I suppose that he, to whom he forgave most.

Jesus said, Thou hast rightly judged.

She Loved Much.

And he turned to the woman, and said unto Simon, Seest thou this woman? I entered thine house; thou gavest me no water for my feet; but she hath washed my feet with tears, and wiped them with the hairs of her head. Thou gavest me no kiss: but this woman, since the time I came in, hath not ceased to kiss my feet. My head with oil thou didst not anoint: but this woman hath anointed my feet with ointment. Wherefore, I say unto thee, Her sins, which are many, are forgiven; for she loved much: but to whom little is forgiven, the same loveth little. And he said unto her, Thy sins are forgiven. Go in peace.

SUMMARY OF EVENTS.

After the Sermon on the Mount Jesus returns to Capernaum.
There He heals the centurion's servant. See *Bible Story*.
The day after He raises the son of the widow of Nain. See *Bible Story*.
He pronounces woes upon the seaside cities of Galilee.
He goes to Simon the Pharisee's house to meat.
He forgives the woman who showed her gratitude to Him by anointing with precious ointment. The Pharisees dislike it.
He heals a blind and dumb man.
The Pharisees say He heals through Satan.
He shows that He does not heal through Satan, and speaks of the sin against the Holy Ghost.
He tells that Nineveh and the Queen of Sheba will rise up to condemn the generation that rejects the Saviour.
He tells who are His brethren.

From what parts of the Bible is our narrative taken? Matt. 8, 11, 12, Mark 3 and Luke 7, 11.

What pictures of these scenes do you recall in "Bible Story?"

What shall we call this seventh chapter? **The Saviour Meets with Opposition.**

Eighth Sunday

THE SCRIPTURE TO BE LEARNED.

THE PARABLE OF THE SOWER.

A sower went out to sow his seed: and as he sowed, some fell by the wayside; and it was trodden down, and the fowls of the air devoured it.   *Give the Parable of the Sower.*

And some fell upon a rock, and as soon as it was sprung up, it withered away, because it lacked moisture.

And some fell among thorns; and the thorns sprang up with it, and choked it.

And other fell on good ground, and sprang up, and bare fruit an hundredfold.   Luke 8: 5-8.

THE POWER OF THE WORD.

The word of God is quick and powerful, and sharper than any two-edged sword, piercing even to the dividing asunder of soul and spirit, and of the joints and marrow, and is a discerner of the thoughts and intents of the heart.   Heb. 4:12.   *What is the power of God's Word*

WHAT THE CATECHISM SAYS.

We should so fear and love God, as not to despise His Word and the preaching of the Gospel, but deem it holy, and willingly hear and learn it.   *What does the Catechism say?*

CHAPTER VIII.

The Saviour Teaches in Parables.

BY THE SEA OF GALILEE.

How many parables did Jesus speak at this time? (Eight).

How many are given in our lesson? (Six).

What are they?

Relate the Parable of the Sower and the Seed.*

What were the four kinds of soil into which the seed fell?*

What four kinds of hearers of God's word are meant?*

Tell the parable of the Good Seed and the Tares.*

What is the field?

What, the good seed?

What, the tares?

When is the harvest?

Tell the parable of The Pearl.*

Give its meaning.

Of the Net.*

Give its meaning.

What did Jesus do in the storm?

What, when He came to the other side of the lake?

THE same day Jesus went out of the house, and sat by the seaside. When the multitude about Him pressed Him, He went into a boat and the multitude stood on the beach. He taught many things of the kingdom of heaven in parables. He spake of the Sower, of the Tares, of the Seed Growing Secretly, of the Mustard Seed, of the Leaven, of the Hid Treasure, of a Pearl, and of a Great Net. **In a Boat. Parables.**

When evening came, they took Him into the boat to cross over to the other side. A great storm arose, and He calmed it. On the other side there was a man out of his right mind, who could not be bound with chains or tamed, and who was in the mountains night and day cutting himself with stones. He saw Jesus from afar and ran and fell down before Him. Jesus cast the unclean spirit out of him, and sent it into a herd of swine, which ran down the steep mountain and were drowned in the sea. The man wished to be with Jesus, but Jesus told him to go home. He did so. **The Storm. The Man in the Mountains.**

When Jesus came back into His own country, He began to teach in the synagogue. But some sneered at

EIGHTH SUNDAY.

The Carpenter's Son. Him and said, Is not this the carpenter's son? As He saw the great multitudes, He was moved with compassion because they were as sheep without a shepherd; and He called His twelve disciples and sent them forth two and two. And Matthew made **At Meat with Matthew.** Him a great feast in his house. The Pharisees saw Him sitting at meat with many publicans, and they said, He eateth with publicans and sinners. Jesus said, They that are whole need not a physician, but they that are sick.

Jairus, a ruler of the synagogue, came to Him and begged Him to help his daughter, who was at the point of death. As He went on the way with Jairus, many followed and thronged Him. A **Jairus Comes.** sick woman in the crowd came behind and touched His garment. She was healed of her plague. Now people came telling the ruler, Thy daughter is dead. Jesus said, Only believe. He took the child by the hand and told her to arise. And she rose and walked.

From there as He passed by, He healed two blind men and charged them to tell no one. But they went forth and spread abroad His fame in all that land.

Margin notes: What did some say? How did He send out disciples? Who made Him a feast? What did Jesus say to the Pharisees? What did He do in the synagogue when He came back? Tell the story of Jairus' daughter and of the sick woman. Of the two blind men.

THE STORIES TO BE READ.

The Story of the Sower.
THE STORY.

Hearken! Behold a sower went out to sow his seed.

And as he sowed some fell by the wayside; and it was trodden down, and the fowls of the air came and devoured it.

And some fell on stony ground; and immediately it sprang up because it had no depth of earth. And when the sun was up, it was scorched, and because it had no root and lacked moisture, it withered away.

And some fell among thorns, and the thorns grew up with it, and choked it, and it yielded no fruit.

But other fell into good ground, and sprang up, and increased; and brought forth fruit, some thirty, and some sixty, and some an hundred-fold.

He that hath ears to hear, let him hear!

THE EXPLANATION.

The seed is the word of God. The sower soweth the word.

Those by the wayside are they that hear the word; but when they have heard, Satan cometh immediately, and taketh away the word that was sown, out of their hearts, lest they should believe and be saved.

They which are sown on stony ground are they who when they have heard the word, immediately receive it with joy. Yet these have no root in themselves, and so endure but for a time. Afterward, when affliction or persecution ariseth for the word's sake, immediately they are offended, and fall away.

And these are they which are sown among thorns; such as hear the word; and the cares of this world, and the deceitfulness of riches and pleasures of this life, entering in, choke the word.

And these are they which are sown on good ground; such as hear the word, and receive it in an honest and good heart, and bring forth fruit, some thirtyfold, some sixty, and some a hundred.

The Story of the Tares.

The kingdom of heaven is likened unto a man which sowed good seed in his field: but while men slept, his enemy came and sowed tares among the wheat, and went his way. But when the blade was sprung up, and brought forth fruit, then appeared the tares also. So the householder came and said unto him,

Sir, didst not thou sow good seed in thy field? From whence then hath it tares?

He said unto them,

An enemy hath done this.

The servants said unto him,

EIGHTH SUNDAY. 41

Wilt thou that we go and gather them up?

But he said,

Nay, lest while ye gather up the tares, ye root up also the wheat with them. Let both grow together until the harvest: and in the time of harvest I will say to the reapers,

Gather ye together first the tares, and bind them in bundles to burn them: but gather the wheat into my barn.

The Story of the One Pearl.

The kingdom of heaven is like unto a merchant man, seeking goodly pearls: who, when he had found one pearl of great price, went and sold all that he had and bought it.

The Story of the Net.

The kingdom of heaven is like unto a net that was cast into the sea, and gathered of every kind. When it was full, they drew to shore, and sat down, and gathered the good into vessels, but cast the bad away.

So shall it be at the end of the world: the angels shall come forth, and sever the wicked from the just, and shall cast them into the furnace of fire: there shall be wailing and gnashing of teeth.

SUMMARY OF EVENTS.

Jesus speaks in parables by the seaside.

The Sower, the Tares, the Mustard Seed, the Pearl, the Great Net.

Jesus crosses to the country of the Gergesenes and restores the demoniac. See *Bible Story* "Christ Stills the Storm."

He returns to Capernaum and sends forth the twelve disciples.

He goes to Matthew's feast and heals Jairus' daughter. See *Bible Story*.

He heals the woman sick with an issue of blood, and two blind men.

From what parts of the Bible is our narrative taken? Matt. 13-9, Mark 4-5, Luke 8.

What pictures did we have in "Bible Story" referring to this chapter?

What shall we call this eighth chapter? **The Saviour Teaches in Parables.**

In conclusion let the teacher again refer to the Scripture and Catechism answers that the scholar has learned.

THE SCRIPTURE TO BE LEARNED.

WHAT HE SAYS OF HIMSELF.

<small>What does Jesus say of Himself?</small>
I am the bread of life: he that cometh to me shall never hunger; and he that believeth on me shall never thirst. John 6: 35.

WHAT PETER SAYS OF HIM.

<small>What does Peter say of Him?</small>
Thou art the Christ the Son of the living God. Matt. 16:16. Lord, to whom shall we go? Thou hast the words of eternal life. And we believe and are sure that thou art that Christ, the Son of the living God. John 6: 68-69.

WHAT THE CATECHISM SAYS.

<small>What does the Catechism say?</small>
God gives indeed without our prayer even to the wicked also their daily bread; but we pray in this petition that He would make us sensible of His benefits, and enable us to receive our daily bread with thanksgiving.

CHAPTER IX.

The Saviour King on Land and Sea.

IN THE DESERT AND THE BORDERS OF SIDON.

THE twelve apostles sent forth by Jesus returned unto Him and told all they had done and taught. He said, Come apart into a desert place and rest awhile. For many were coming and going, and they had no time so much as to eat. And they went in a boat to the other side of the Sea of Galilee. And the people saw them going, and ran there on foot from all the cities. And Jesus went up into a mountain, and there He sat with His disciples. When evening was now come, He fed five thousand men besides women and children with five loaves and two fishes.

Why did Jesus take His disciples to the other side of the lake?

Five Thousand Fed.

How did the five thousand get there?

Tell the story of their being fed.

Perceiving that they were about to take Him by force, to make Him King, He sent His disciples to the other side in a boat, and having dismissed the multitudes, went up into the mountain alone to pray. While the boat of the disciples was tossing in the midst of the sea, Jesus came walking on the sea. Peter went down from the boat to meet Him and he began to sink, but Jesus stretched out His hand and saved him.

What were the multitudes about to do?

Where did Jesus send His disciples?

Walking on the Sea.

Relate the incident of the Saviour walking on the sea and Peter's sinking.*

The day following, the multitude on the other side saw that Jesus was not there, and they took shipping,

Why did the multitudes follow Him?

NINTH SUNDAY.

and came to Capernaum seeking Him. When they found Him they said, Master, when camest Thou hither? Jesus answered, Verily ye seek Me because ye did eat of the loaves. Labour for that meat which endureth unto everlasting life. When He said, Except ye eat the flesh of the Son of man and drink His blood, ye have no life in you; many of His disciples went back and walked no more with Him. Jesus therefore said unto the twelve, Will ye also go away? Simon Peter answered Him, Lord to whom shall we go? Thou hast the words of eternal life.

<small>The Meat That Perisheth.</small>

<small>What did He say they should eat?
Did this please them?
What did He say to the twelve?
Give Peter's answer.</small>

Then Jesus arose, and went into the borders of Tyre and Sidon. There He healed the daughter of the Canaanite woman. Coming back to the sea of Galilee, He healed a deaf and dumb man, and a great multitude of lame, blind, and maimed. Again the multitude that gathered had nothing to eat and He fed four thousand men besides women and children, with seven loaves and a few small fishes.

<small>Tell the story of the Canaanite woman.*
What other miracles did He perform?</small>

<small>The Canaanite Woman.
Four Thousand Fed</small>

And He cometh to Bethsaida. And they bring a blind man unto Him. Jesus healed the blind man, and went forth into the villages of Cæsarea Philippi. By the way He asked His disciples, Whom do men say that I am? And they said, Some say that thou art John the Baptist, others Elijah, and others, Jeremiah, or one of the prophets risen again. He saith to them, But whom say ye that I am? And Simon Peter answered and said, Thou art the Christ, the Son of the living God. Then charged He His disciples that they should tell no man that He was the

<small>Whom did He heal? How?*
What did He ask His disciples?
What answer did they give?
What reply did Peter make?
What did Jesus say to Peter?*</small>

<small>Who is Jesus?</small>

NINTH SUNDAY.

Christ. From that time forth He began to teach them that He must go unto Jerusalem and suffer many things, and be killed, and be raised again the third day.

THE STORIES TO BE READ.

Walking on the Sea.

The boat was now in the midst of the sea, distressed by the waves; for the wind was contrary. And it was dark.

And in the fourth watch of the night he came unto them, walking upon the sea, and when they saw him, they were troubled, saying, It is a spirit! And they cried out for fear. But straightway Jesus spake unto them, saying, Be of good cheer; it is I; be not afraid.

And Peter said, Lord, if it be thou, bid me come unto thee on the water. And he said, Come. And Peter went down from the boat, and walked on the water, to come to Jesus. But when he saw the wind, he was afraid; and beginning to sink, he cried, Lord, save me. And immediately Jesus stretched forth his hand, and caught him, and said unto him, O thou of little faith, wherefore didst thou doubt?

And when they were come into the ship, the wind ceased. And immediately the ship was at the land. Then they that were in the ship came, saying, Of a truth thou art the Son of God.

Healing the Daughter of the Canaanite Woman.

Behold, a woman of Canaan cried unto him, Have mercy on me, O Lord, thou Son of David; my daughter is grievously vexed with a devil.

But he answered her not a word.

And his disciples came and besought him, saying, Send her away; for she crieth after us.

But he answered, I am not sent but unto the lost sheep of the house of Israel.

Then came she and knelt before him and said, Lord, help me.

But he said, It is not meet to take the children's bread, and to

NINTH SUNDAY.

cast it to the dogs. And she said, Truth, Lord; yet the dogs eat of the crumbs which fall from their master's table.

Then Jesus answered and said unto her, O woman, great is thy faith; be it unto thee even as thou wilt. And her daughter was made whole from that very hour.

Restoring the Blind Man's Sight.

He took the blind man by the hand and led him out of the town, and when he had spit on his eyes, and put his hands upon him, he asked him if he saw aught. He looked up, and said, I see men as trees, walking. After that he put his hands again upon his eyes and made him look up. And he was restored and saw every man clearly.

What Jesus Said to Peter After the Latter Confessed Him.

Blessed art thou Simon Bar-jona! For flesh and blood hath not revealed it unto thee, but my Father which is in heaven. And I say also unto thee, That thou art Peter, and upon this rock I will build my church; and the gates of hell shall not prevail against it. And I will give unto thee the keys of heaven: and whatsoever thou shalt bind on earth shall be bound in heaven: and whatsoever thou shalt loose on earth shall be loosed in heaven.

SUMMARY OF EVENTS.

Jesus takes His disciples into a desert place to rest.

Over five thousand people gather there and He feeds them. See *Bible Story.*

He sends the disciples home and walks on the sea.

He tells the multitude not to labor for the meat that perisheth.

He heals the daughter of the Canaanite woman.

He feeds the four thousand, and heals a blind man.

He asks the disciples who men say that He is.

From what parts of the Bible is our narrative taken? Matt. 14, Mark 6, Luke 9 and John 6.

What pictures did we have in "Bible Story" referring to this chapter?

What shall we call this ninth chapter? **Jesus King on Land and Sea.**

In conclusion let the teacher again refer to the Scripture and Catechism answers that the scholar has learned.

THE SCRIPTURE TO BE LEARNED.

THE KING OF GLORY.

Lift up your heads, O ye gates; and be ye lift up, ye everlasting doors; and the King of glory shall come in.

Who is this King of glory? the Lord strong and mighty, the Lord mighty in battle.

Lift up your heads, O ye gates; even lift them up, ye everlasting doors; and the King of glory shall come in.

Who is this King of glory? The Lord of hosts, he is the King of glory. Ps. 24: 7-10.

What does Psalm 24 say of the King of glory?

WHAT THE CATECHISM SAYS AS TO OUR BEING CHARITABLE.

We should so fear and love God, as not deceitfully to belie, betray, slander, nor raise injurious reports against our neighbor, but apologize for him, speak well of him, and put the most charitable construction on all his actions.

What does the Catechism say as to our being charitable?

CHAPTER X.

The Saviour Transfigured and Training the Disciples.

ON THE MOUNTAIN AND IN THE PLAIN.

Relate the story of the Transfiguration. *

AND after six days He took Peter, James, and John and brought them up into a high mountain apart. And as He was praying, the fashion of His countenance was altered, and His face did shine as the sun, and His raiment was white as the light. And He was transfigured before them. As they came down from the mountain, He charged them that they should tell no man what things they had seen, till the Son of man were risen from the dead.

His Face Did Shine as the Sun.

Tell the story of Peter, the tribute money, and the fish.

And when they were come to Capernaum, they that received tribute money came to Peter, and said, Doth not your master pay tribute? He saith, Yes. And when he was entered into the house, Jesus spake first to him, saying, What thinkest thou, Simon? of whom do the kings of the earth take toll or tribute? of their own children, or of strangers? Peter saith to Him, From strangers. Jesus saith, Then are the children free. But lest we should offend them, go thou to the sea, and cast a hook, and take up the fish that first cometh up; and when thou hast opened its mouth, thou shalt find a piece of money. That take, and give unto them for Me and thee.

Tax from the Fish's Mouth.

TENTH SUNDAY.

And being in the house He asked them, What was it that ye disputed among yourselves by the way? But they held their peace, for they had disputed among themselves who should be the greatest. And He took a child, and set him in the midst of them, and said, Whosoever shall humble himself as this little child, the same is greatest in the kingdom of heaven. He warned them of the danger of going into temptation, through hand, foot, or eye, and of being cast into hell fire, and instructed them how to deal with their brother who sins against them. Then came Peter and said unto Him, Lord, how oft shall my brother sin against me, and I forgive him? Until seven times? Jesus said, Until seventy times seven. Then He spake the Parable of the Unmerciful Servant.

A Dispute.

Humility. Hell Fire.

Seven Times.

What dispute did the disciples have?

What did our Saviour tell them?

How does He warn us not to be a cause of offense to little ones?*

How against temptation?

What question does Peter ask Him?

What did He say?

Give the parable of the Unmerciful Servant?*

After these things, Jesus walked in Galilee. For He would not walk in Judea because the Jews sought to kill Him. Now the Jews' feast of tabernacles was at hand. His brethren therefore said unto Him, Depart hence, and go into Judea. Jesus said unto them, My time is not yet come. But when His brethren were gone up unto the feast, then went He also up, not publicly, but as it were in secret. And the Jews sought Him at the feast, and said, Where is He? But when it was the midst of the feast, Jesus went into the temple and taught.

The Feast at Hand.

Why did not Jesus go up to the feast?

What did His relatives say?
When did He go?

What did He do in the temple?

THE STORIES TO BE READ.

The Transfiguration.

And Jesus was transfigured before them. And His raiment be-

TENTH SUNDAY.

came shining, exceeding white as snow. And behold there appeared unto them Elias with Moses, And they were talking with Jesus. Then said Peter, Lord it is good for us to be here. Let us make three tabernacles; one for Thee, and one for Moses, and one for Elias. And there was a cloud that overshadowed them. And a voice came out of the cloud saying, This is my beloved Son, hear him. When the disciples heard it, they fell on their face, and were sore afraid. And suddenly, when they had looked round about, they saw no man any more, save Jesus only.

Offending These Little Ones.

Whoso shall receive one such little child in my name receiveth me. But whoso shall cause one of these little ones which believe on me to stumble, it were better for him that a millstone were hanged about his neck, and that he were drowned in the depth of the sea!

Parable of the Unmerciful Servant.

A certain king would make a reckoning with his servants. And one was brought unto him which owed him ten thousand talents. But as he had not to pay, his lord commanded him to be sold, and his wife, and children, and all that he had, and payment to be made. The servant therefore fell down before him and said, Lord, have patience with me, and I will pay thee all. Then the lord of that servant was moved with compassion, and released him and forgave him the debt. But the same servant went out and found one of his fellow servants, who owed him a hundred pence: and he laid hands on him, and took him by the throat, saying, Pay what thou owest! And his fellow servant fell down and besought him, saying, Have patience with me, and I will pay thee all. And he would not, but cast him into prison until he should pay the debt. So his fellow servants saw what was done and came and told their lord. Then his lord called him and said, O thou wicked servant, I forgave thee all that debt, because thou desiredst me: shouldest not thou also have had

TENTH SUNDAY.

compassion on thy fellow servant? And his lord delivered him to the tormentors till he should pay all. So shall my heavenly Father do unto you if ye forgive not every one his brother from your hearts.

SUMMARY OF EVENTS.

The Saviour takes Peter, James and John up into a mountain and is transfigured before them. See *Bible Story*.

He settles their dispute as to who shall be greatest by placing a little child in the midst of them.

He tells them to cut off the hand rather than enter into temptation.

He tells Peter that he must forgive until seventy times seven.

He narrates the parable of the Unmerciful Servant.

He goes up to the feast secretly and then preaches in the temple.

What picture did we have in "Bible Story" referring to this chapter?

From what parts of the Bible is our narrative taken? Matt. 17-18, Mark 9 and Luke 9.

What shall we call this tenth chapter? **The Saviour Transfigured.**

In conclusion let the teacher again refer to the Scripture and Catechism answers that the scholar has learned.

THE SCRIPTURE TO BE LEARNED.

THE LORD IS MY SHEPHERD.

Who is my Shepherd?
The Lord is my shepherd; I shall not want. He maketh me to lie down in green pastures: He leadeth me beside the still waters. He restoreth my soul: He leadeth me in the paths of righteousness for His name's sake. Yea, though I walk through the valley of the shadow of death, I will fear no evil: for Thou art with me: Thy rod and Thy staff they comfort me. Thou preparest a table before me in the presence of mine enemies: Thou anointest my head with oil; my cup runneth over. Surely goodness and mercy shall follow me all the days of my life: and I will dwell in the house of the Lord for ever. Psalm 23.

WHAT THE CATECHISM SAYS.

What does the Catechism say?
I believe in Jesus Christ, His only Son, our Lord; who was conceived by the Holy Ghost, born of the Virgin Mary; suffered under Pontius Pilate, was crucified, dead, and buried; He descended into hell; the third day He rose again from the dead; He ascended into heaven, and sitteth on the right hand of God the Father Almighty; from thence He shall come to judge the quick and the dead.

CHAPTER XI.

The Saviour the Good Shepherd.

TWICE AGAIN TO JERUSALEM.

He Knoweth Letters.

AS Jesus was teaching in the temple, the Jews gathered and said, How knoweth this man letters, having never learned. And they sought to take Him. But no man laid hands on Him. And many of the people believed and said, When Christ cometh, will He do more miracles than these which this man hath done? But the Pharisees and chief priests sent officers to take Him.

What was the Pharisees' exclamation on hearing Jesus speak?

What did the common people say?

What orders did the Pharisees give to their officers?

In the last day of the Feast, Jesus stood and cried, If **If any Man Thirst.** any man thirst, let him come unto Me and drink. Many said, Of a truth this is the Prophet. Others said, This is the Christ. But some said, Shall Christ come out of Galilee? So there was a division among the people. Then came the officers to the chief priests and Pharisees. They said, Why have ye not brought Him? The officers answered, Never man **The Officers Astonished.** spake like this man. Then answered the Pharisees, Are ye also deceived?

What did Jesus cry on the last day of the feast?

What did the people say of Christ?

What did the officers say when they came back?

Early the next morning Jesus came again into the temple, and all the people came unto Him, and He sat **I Am the Light of the World.** down and taught them. He said, I am the light of the world. Then said the Jews, Art Thou greater than our father Abraham? Jesus said,

What did Jesus say next morning in the temple?

What did the Jews ask Him about Abraham?

53

ELEVENTH SUNDAY.

<small>What did Jesus say as a result of the discussion?</small>
<small>What did the Jews do?</small>

Your father Abraham rejoiced to see My day. The Jews said, Thou art not yet fifty years old, and hast thou seen Abraham? Jesus said, Verily, verily, I say unto you, Before Abraham was, I am. Then took they up stones, but Jesus went out of the temple through the midst of them. **Your Father Abraham.**

<small>Whom did Jesus tell to wash in the pool of Siloam?</small>
<small>What did the Pharisees say to this blind man?</small>
<small>What reply did he make?</small>
<small>Tell the rest of the story.</small>

And He saw a man blind from his birth, and put clay on his eyes and told him to wash in the pool of Siloam. He went and washed, and came seeing. The Pharisees said, Give God the praise; we know that this man is a sinner. He answered, Whether He be a sinner or no, I know not. One thing I know, that, whereas I was blind, now I see. If this man were not of God, He could do nothing. They said, Thou wast altogether born in sins, and dost thou teach us! And they cast him out. **Born Blind.**

<small>How does Jesus contrast the Shepherd and the Thief?</small>

Some of the Pharisees said, Are we blind also? Jesus said, Verily, verily, I say unto you, He that entereth not by the door is a thief and a robber. But he that entereth in by the door is the shepherd of the sheep. To him the porter openeth; **Thieves and Robbers.**

<small>Tell the story of the Good Shepherd?*</small>

and the sheep hear his voice: and he calleth his own sheep by name and leadeth them out. And he goeth before them and the sheep follow him: for they know his voice. **The Good Shepherd.**

<small>Whither was Jesus bound?</small>
<small>With what reception did He meet?</small>
<small>How did the disciples wish to retaliate?</small>

And when the time was come that He should be delivered up, He sent messengers into a village of the Samaritans to make ready for Him. And they did not receive Him. And James and John said, Lord, wilt thou that we command fire to come down from heaven and consume them? But He **Fire from Heaven.**

ELEVENTH SUNDAY. 55

turned and said, Ye know not what manner of spirit ye are of, for the Son of man is not come to destroy men's lives, but to save them. And they went to another village. There met Him ten lepers and He healed them. After these things He appointed seventy disciples, and sent them two and two before His face into every city whither He Himself would come. He said unto them, The harvest truly is great, but the labourers are few.

What did Jesus say?

Ten Lepers. *How many lepers did He heal?*

Seventy Disciples. *Tell the story of the Seventy Disciples.*

And a certain lawyer stood up and tried Him, saying, Master, what shall I do to inherit eternal life? Jesus said, What is written in the law? He said, Thou shalt love the Lord thy God with all thy heart, and with all thy soul, and with all thy strength, and with all thy mind, and thy neighbor as thyself. Jesus said, Thou hast answered right: this do, and thou shalt live. The lawyer desiring to justify himself said, And who is my neighbor? And Jesus told him the Parable of the Good Samaritan, and said, Go thou, and do likewise.

The Lawyer. *What question did a lawyer ask?*

What was his own reply?

What did Jesus say?

The Good Samaritan. *How did the lawyer try to justify himself?*

Narrate the parable that Jesus then spake.

And it came to pass that as He was praying in a certain place, one of His disciples said unto Him, Lord teach us to pray. And He taught them the Lord's Prayer, and spake the Parable of the Friend at Midnight. He likewise warned them against covetousness, and told the Parable of the Rich Fool.

What prayer did Jesus teach the disciples?

Of what are we to beware?

Tell the parable of the Rich Fool.*

Parable of the Good Shepherd.

I am the good shepherd: the good shepherd giveth his life for the sheep. But he that is a hireling, and not the shepherd, seeth the wolf coming, and leaveth the sheep and fleeth; and the wolf catcheth them and scattereth the sheep. The hireling fleeth be-

ELEVENTH SUNDAY.

cause he is a hireling, and careth not for the sheep. I am the good shepherd, and know my sheep, and am known of mine. I lay down my life for the sheep. And other sheep I have, which are not of this fold: them also I must bring and they shall hear my voice; and there shall be one fold, and one shepherd.

The Rich Fool.

Beware of covetousness. For a man's life consisteth not in the abundance of the things which he possesseth. And he spake a parable, saying, The ground of a certain rich man brought forth plentifully. And he thought within himself, What shall I do, because I have no room where to bestow my fruits? And he said, This will I do. I will pull down my barns, and build greater; and there will I bestow all my fruits and my goods. And I will say to my soul, Soul, thou hast much goods laid up for many years: take thine ease, eat, drink, and be merry. But God said unto him, Thou fool, this night thy soul shall be required of thee: Then whose shall those things be, which thou hast provided? So is he that layeth up treasure for himself, and is not rich toward God.

SUMMARY OF EVENTS.

Jesus teaches in the Temple.
The Pharisees intend to arrest Jesus. Nicodemus defends Him.
Jesus the Light of the world. Greater than Abraham.
Jesus heals the man born blind, on the Sabbath.
Jesus the Good Shepherd.
Jesus starts again for Jerusalem. Heals Ten Lepers. Sends out the Seventy.
The lawyer. Parable of the Good Samaritan. See *Bible Story*.
Jesus teaches the Lord's Prayer.
Jesus warns against Covetousness. Parable of the Rich Fool.

From what parts of the Bible is our narrative taken? John 7-12.
What picture did we have in "Bible Story" referring to this chapter?
What shall we call this eleventh chapter? **The Saviour the Good Shepherd.**

Twelfth Sunday.

THE SCRIPTURE TO BE LEARNED.

NO REST FOR THE SAVIOUR.

The foxes have holes, and the birds of the air have nests; but the Son of man hath not where to lay his head. Matt. 8: 20. — *Where could the Saviour rest?*

TRUE EXALTATION.

For whosoever exalteth himself shall be abased; and he that humbleth himself shall be exalted. Luke 14: 11. — *Who is truly exalted?*

THE SUM AND SUBSTANCE OF LUKE XV.

For the Son of man is come to seek and to save that which was lost. Luke 19: 10. — *What do the Parables in Luke XV teach?*

WHAT THE CATECHISM SAYS.

Who has redeemed me . . . in order that I might be His, live under Him in His Kingdom, and serve Him in everlasting righteousness, innocence, and blessedness; even as He is risen from the dead, and lives and reigns to all eternity. This is most certainly true. — *What does the Catechism say?*

CHAPTER XII

The Saviour Eats Bread with a Chief Pharisee.

NEAR JERUSALEM.

Where was Jesus walking at the Feast?

What did the Jews say to Him?

What reply did He make?

AND it was at Jerusalem the Feast of the Dedication. And it was winter. And Jesus walked in the temple in Solomon's porch. *Tell Us Plainly.* Then came the Jews round about Him and said, How long dost thou make us to doubt? If thou be the Christ tell us plainly. Jesus answered, I told you, and ye believed not. My sheep hear My voice, and they follow Me. My Father which gave them Me is greater than all. I and My Father are one. Then the Jews took up stones again to stone Him.

What followed?

Whither did He go?

Tell the story of Mary and Martha.

But He escaped out of their hand and went away again beyond Jordan, visiting Mary and Martha at Bethany on the way to the place where John at first baptized. And there He abode. And many resorted unto Him and believed on Him there.

Whom did He heal on the Sabbath day?

How did He silence the Pharisees about healing on the Sabbath?

As He went into the house of one of the chief Pharisees to eat bread on the Sabbath day they watched Him. And there was a man before Him who had the dropsy. And Jesus said, Is it lawful to heal on the Sabbath day? And they held their peace. And He took the man and healed him, and said, Which of you shall have an ass or an ox fall into a pit, and will

In the Pharisee's House.

58

TWELFTH SUNDAY.

not straightway pull him out on the Sabbath? And they could not answer.

The Chief Places. When He saw how those who were bidden chose out the chief places, He said, When thou art bidden to a wedding, sit not down in the highest room; but go and sit down in the lowest room, that when he that bade thee cometh, he may say, Friend, go up higher. For whosoever exalteth himself shall be abased; and he that humbleth himself shall be exalted. Then said He, When thou makest a dinner or supper, call not thy friends, nor thy kinsmen, nor thy rich neighbors; but call the poor, the lame, the blind, and thou shalt be blessed. For thou shalt be recompensed at the resurrection of the just. **The Great Supper.** Then spake He the Parable of the Great Supper. And there drew near unto Him all the publicans and sinners for to hear Him. And the Pharisees and Scribes murmured saying, This man receiveth sinners and eateth with them.

The Lost Sheep. And Jesus spake the Parable of the Lost Sheep unto them, showing that there would be joy in heaven over one sinner that repenteth, more than over ninety and nine just persons which need no repentance. **The Lost Silverpiece.** And in the same way He spake the Parable of the Lost Silverpiece, saying unto them, There is joy in the presence of the angels over one sinner that repenteth. And He said, A certain man had two sons, and the younger took his journey into **The Prodigal Son.** a far country, and there wasted his substance. But when he was in want, he arose and went to his father, and said, Father I have sinned. And his father had compassion on him. But his elder brother

Margin notes:
What did He say to those who took the chief places at the feast?

Why?

Whom are we to invite to our feasts?

Tell what you know of the parable of the Lost Sheep.*

Of the Lost Silverpiece.*

TWELFTH SUNDAY.

<small>Tell the story of the Prodigal Son.</small>

was angry. Then the father said, Son, thou art ever with me, but this thy brother was dead and is alive again, and was lost, and is found. The Saviour also spake of the Rich Man, clothed in purple and fine linen, and the beggar named Lazarus which was laid at his gate, and told the Parable of the Pharisee and the Publican to certain which trusted in themselves that they were righteous, and despised others. I tell you, said the Saviour, that the publican went down to his house justified rather than the other. For every one that exalteth himself shall be abased; and he that humbleth himself shall be exalted.

<small>Of the Pharisee and the Publican.*</small>

THE STORIES TO BE READ.

Mary and Martha.

As they went, he entered into a certain village. And a woman named Martha received him into her house. And she had a sister called Mary, who sat at Jesus' feet and heard his word. But Martha came to him and said, Lord, dost thou not care that my sister hath left me to serve alone? Bid her therefore that she help me. And Jesus said unto her, Martha, Martha, thou art careful and troubled about many things. But one thing is needful, and Mary hath chosen that good part which shall not be taken away from her.

The Lost Sheep.

What man of you, having a hundred sheep, if he lose one of them, doth not leave the ninety and nine in the wilderness, and go after that which is lost until he find it. And when he hath found it, he layeth it on his shoulders, rejoicing. And when he cometh home, he calleth together his friends and neighbors, saying unto them, Rejoice with me; for I have found my sheep which was lost!

TWELFTH SUNDAY.

The Lost Silverpiece.

What woman having ten pieces of silver, if she lose one piece, doth not light a candle, and sweep the house, and seek diligently till she find it? And when she hath found it, she calleth her friends and neighbors together, saying, Rejoice with me; for I have found the piece which I had lost.

The Pharisee and the Publican

Two men went up into the Temple to pray; the one a Pharisee, and the other a publican. The Pharisee stood and prayed thus with himself, God, I thank thee that I am not as other men are, extortioners, unjust, adulterers, or even as this publican. I fast twice in the week, I give tithes of all I possess. And the publican, standing afar off, would not lift up so much as his eyes unto heaven, but smote upon his breast saying, God be merciful to me a sinner!

SUMMARY OF EVENTS.

Jesus at the Feast. He tells that He is Christ.

He eats bread on the Sabbath in a chief Pharisee's house.

Heals a man with dropsy. Tells the guests to take the lower seats.

Speaks Parables of the Great Supper, the Lost Sheep, the Lost Silverpiece, and the Prodigal Son. See *Bible Story*.

He speaks the Parables of the Rich Man and Lazarus (see *Bible Story*) and the Pharisee and the Publican.

From what parts of the Bible is our narrative taken? John 10, Luke 14, 15, 16, 17 and 18.

What pictures did we have in "Bible Story" referring to this chapter?

What shall we call this twelfth chapter? **The Saviour Eats Bread with a Chief Pharisee.**

In conclusion, let the teacher again refer to the Scripture and Catechism answers that the scholar has learned.

THE SCRIPTURE TO BE LEARNED.

WE LIVE IN HIM

How shall we live?
I am the resurrection, and the life: he that believeth in me, though he were dead, yet shall he live: And whosoever liveth and believeth in me shall never die. John 11 : 25, 26.

HIS MISSION TO THE OPPRESSED

To whom does He come?
The Spirit of the Lord is upon me, because he hath anointed me to preach the gospel to the poor; he hath sent me to heal the brokenhearted, to preach deliverance to the captives, and recovering of sight to the blind, to set at liberty them that are bruised, to preach the acceptable year of the Lord. Luke 4: 18, 19 (Isa. 61 : 1).

WHAT THE CATECHISM SAYS.

What does the Catechism say?
We pray in this petition, as in a summary, that our heavenly Father would deliver us from all manner of evil, whether it affect the body or soul, property or character, and, at last, when the hour of death shall arrive, grant us a happy end, and graciously take us from this world of sorrow to Himself in heaven.

CHAPTER XIII.
The Saviour Approaches the Crisis.
TO BETHANY AND TO JERUSALEM.

NOW a certain man was dead, named Lazarus, of Bethany. Jesus said, Where have ye laid him? They say, Lord, come and see. Jesus said, Take ye away the stone. He lifted up His eyes and prayed. And He cried, Lazarus come forth! And he that was dead came forth. Then the chief priests gathered a council and said, What do we? If we let this man alone, all men will believe on Him, and the Romans will come and take away our place. And Caiaphas, the high priest, said, Ye know nothing at all, nor do ye take into account that it is expedient for you that one man should die for the people. From that day they took counsel to put Him to death. Jesus therefore walked no more openly among the Jews.

And the Jews' Passover was nigh at hand, And they sought for Jesus, and spake one with another, as they stood in the temple, What think ye? That He will not come to the feast? Then Jesus departed from Galilee, and came into the borders of Judea by the farther side of Jordan. And the people resorted to Him again, and, as He was wont, He taught them again. Here He blessed little children, and when He had gone forth on the way, a ruler came running and

Lazarus Comes Forth.

Pharisees Enraged.

Will He Come to the Feast?

Tell the story of the raising of Lazarus from the dead.
What effect had this on the people?
What effect had it on the chief priests?
What did Caiaphas say?

What inquiries did the people make at the next Passover?
From where did Jesus start for the Passover?
What road did He take?
Whom did He bless?

THIRTEENTH SUNDAY.

Tell the story of the rich young man.

kneeled before Him and asked Him, Good Master, what shall I do that I may inherit eternal life? Jesus said, Thou knowest the commandments. And he said, All these things have I kept from my youth. *Sell and Give to the Poor.* And Jesus said, One thing thou lackest: go, sell whatsoever thou hast, and give to the poor, and thou shalt have treasure in heaven; and come, follow Me. But his countenance fell at the saying, and he went away sorrowful. For he was one that had great possessions.

What did Jesus say about people that put their trust in riches?

And Jesus said, It is easier for a camel to go through a needle's eye, than for a rich man to enter the kingdom of God. *Rich Men and Heaven.* And they were astonished and said, Who then can be saved? Jesus said, With God all things are possible. And every one that hath left houses, or brethren, or lands for My name's sake shall receive a hundredfold, and shall inherit eternal life. But many that are first shall be last; and the last shall be first. And to shew this, He spake the Parable of the Laborers in the Vineyard.

Who are those that shall be rich eternally?

Narrate the parable of the Laborers in the Vineyard.*

What did He foretell to the disciples while they were traveling?

And they were in the way going up to Jerusalem. And Jesus began to tell the Twelve what things should happen unto Him, saying,

Behold, we go up to Jerusalem, and the Son of man shall be delivered unto the chief priests and unto the scribes; and they shall condemn him to death, and shall deliver him to the Gentiles. And they shall mock him, and shall scourge him, and shall spit upon him, and the third day he shall rise again. *Christ's Prediction.*

And they understood none of these things.

To what city did they come?

Tell the story of blind Bartimeus.

Who was Zaccheus?

And they came to Jericho, and Jesus healed blind Bartimeus, who sat by the wayside begging. *Blind Bartimeus.* And behold a man named Zaccheus ran on before and climbed up into a sycamore tree to see Jesus. And Jesus looked up and *Zaccheus Climbs the Tree.*

THIRTEENTH SUNDAY.   65

said, Zaccheus come down. And he came down and received Him joyfully. And Zaccheus said, Behold, Lord, the half of my goods I give to the poor; and if I have wrongfully exacted anything of any man, I restore fourfold. And Jesus said, Today is salvation come to this house. And Jesus came to Bethany. It was six days before the passover. And they made Him a supper there, in the house of Simon the Leper. And Martha served, but Lazarus was one of them that sat at meat.

Tell how he met the Saviour and what followed.
What happened at Bethany?
What did Mary do?
Tell the story.*

Sups with Simon The Leper.

THE STORIES TO BE READ.

Parable of the Laborers in the Vineyard.

The kingdom of heaven is like unto a man that is a householder, which went out early in the morning to hire labourers into his vineyard. And when he had agreed with the labourers for a penny a day he sent them into his vineyard. And he went about the third hour, and saw others standing in the market place idle; and to them he said, Go ye also in the vineyard, and whatsoever is right I will give you. And they went their way. Again he went out about the sixth and ninth hour, and did likewise. And about the eleventh hour he went out and found others standing; and he saith unto them, Why stand ye here all the day idle? They say unto him, Because no man hath hired us. He said unto them, Go ye also in the vineyard. And when even was come, the lord of the vineyard saith unto the steward, Call the labourers, and pay them their hire, beginning from the last unto the first. And when they came that were hired about the eleventh hour they received every man a penny. And when the first came they likewise received every man a penny. And they murmured against the householder, saying, These last have spent but one hour and thou hast made them equal with us, which have borne the burden of the day. But he said to one of them, Friend, I do thee no wrong: didst not thou agree with me for a

THIRTEENTH SUNDAY.

penny? Take up that which is thine, and go thy way, it is my will to give unto this last even as unto thee. Is it not lawful for me to do what I will with my own? or is thine eye evil because I am good? So the last shall be first and the first last.

Mary Anointing Jesus with an Alabaster Box of Spikenard.

Mary took a pound of ointment of spikenard, very precious, and anointed the feet of Jesus, and wiped his feet with her hair. And the house was filled with the odour of the ointment. But Judas Iscariot said, Why was not this ointment sold for three hundred pence and given to the poor? This he said because he was a thief, and having the bag, took away what was put therein. Jesus said, Let her alone! Why trouble ye her? Ye have the poor with you always. She hath done what she could. She hath come beforehand to anoint my body to the burying. Verily, I say unto you, Wheresoever this gospel shall be preached throughout the whole world, this also that she hath done shall be spoken of for a memorial of her.

SUMMARY OF EVENTS.

The Saviour raises Lazarus from the dead. See *Bible Story*.
Many Jews believe, but the Pharisees think He ought to die.
Jesus retires into the wilderness.
The people inquire for Him before the Passover Feast.
He comes to the farther side of Jordan.
Here He blesses little children (see *Bible Story*), and speaks with the rich young man.
He utters the Parable of the Labourers in the Vineyard.
He tells the Twelve that He will die and rise again. He rebukes the sons of Zebedee. He heals blind Bartimeus and stays over night in Jericho with Zaccheus.
He comes to the home of Mary and Martha in Bethany.

From what parts of the Bible is our narrative taken? John 11, Matt. 19 and 20, Mark 10, Luke 18 and 19.
What pictures did we have in "Bible Story" referring to this chapter?
What shall we call this thirteenth chapter? **The Approach of the Crisis.**
In conclusion, let the teacher again refer to the Scripture and Catechism answers that the scholar has learned.

THE SCRIPTURE TO BE LEARNED.

THE HOUR WHEREIN THE SON OF MAN COMETH.

And at midnight there was a cry made, Behold, the bridegroom cometh; go ye out to meet him. <small>When will the Son of Man come?*</small>

And they that were ready went in with him to the marriage: and the door was shut.

Afterward came also the other virgins, saying, Lord, Lord, open to us.

But he answered and said, Verily I say unto you, I know you not.

Watch therefore, for ye know neither the day nor the hour wherein the Son of man cometh. St. Matt. 25:6, 10-13.

WHAT THE CATECHISM SAYS.

God indeed tempts no one to sin; but we pray in this petition that God would so guard and preserve us, that the devil, the world, and our own flesh, may not deceive us, nor lead us into error and unbelief, despair, and other great and shameful sins; and that, though we may be thus tempted, we may nevertheless finally prevail and gain the victory. <small>What does the Catechism say in explaining the Fifth Petition of the Lord's Prayer?</small>

---

*Teacher asks the questions until the whole class have recited these parts.

CHAPTER XIV.

The Saviour Enters Jerusalem in Triumph and Teaches in the Temple.

THE LAST SUNDAY. THE LAST MONDAY. THE LAST TUESDAY.

(Beginning of Passion Week.)

How were the disciples to prepare for the Triumphal Entry?
Describe the Triumphal Entry.

AND when they drew nigh unto Jerusalem, Jesus sent two of His disciples into a village that was over against them, and told them to loose a colt that they would find tied at the door without in the open street. And they put on it their garments, and He sat thereon. And much people that were in Jerusalem for the feast, when they heard that Jesus was coming, took branches of palm trees and went forth to meet Him. And the multitudes that went before, and that followed, cried,

Strewing Palm Branches.

Hosanna to the Son of David! Blessed is He that cometh in the name of the Lord: Hosanna in the highest!

What did Christ say in weeping over the city?

And when He was near, He beheld the city, and wept over it, saying, The days shall come that thine enemies shall not leave in thee one stone upon another, because thou knewest not the time of thy visitation!

What did the Multitude say of Him?

And when He was come into Jerusalem, all the city was stirred, saying, Who is this? And the multitude said, This is Jesus the prophet of Nazareth of Galilee. But the Pharisees said among themselves, Behold the world is gone after Him!

What did the Pharisees say?

FOURTEENTH SUNDAY. 69

And He entered into the temple. When the chief priests and the scribes saw the wonderful things that He did, and the children in the temple crying, Hosanna to the Son of David, they were moved with indignation and said, Hearest thou what these are saying? Jesus said, Did ye never read, Out of the mouths of babes thou hast perfected praise? And He left them, and went forth out of the city to Bethany and lodged there.

Hosanna to the Son of David.

What did the children do in the Temple? Describe the incident that followed.

MONDAY.

On the morrow, when they were come out from Bethany, He saw a fig tree having nothing but leaves only. And He said, Let no fruit grow on thee henceforward forever. When they came to Jerusalem, He entered into the Temple, and began to cast out them that sold and that bought, and overthrew the tables of the money-changers, and the seats of them that sold the doves; and He would not suffer that any man should carry a vessel through the Temple. He said, Is it not written, My house shall be called a house of prayer for all the nations? but ye have made it a den of thieves. But the chief priests and the scribes heard it, and sought how they might destroy Him. And when even was come He went out of the city.

Casting Out the Money Changers.

Describe the incident of the fig tree.

Tell how He cleansed the Temple.

What else did He do in the Temple? What day of the week was this?

TUESDAY.

And they went again to Jerusalem, and as He was walking in the Temple, there come to Him the chief priests and say, By what authority doest thou these things? Jesus said, I will also ask you a question, The baptism of John, was it from heaven or

By What Authority.

What question did the Chief Priests ask Jesus?

FOURTEENTH SUNDAY.

And with what question did He reply? of men? answer me. They said, We cannot tell. And Jesus said, Neither tell I you by what authority I do these things. Then He began to speak to them the Parables of the Sons Going and Refusing to go to Work, the Marriage of the King's Son, and of the Wedding Garment. And the Pharisees took counsel how they might catch Him, and asked, Is it lawful to give tribute unto Cæsar or not? The Sadducees also came likewise and attempted to entangle Him in the teaching of the resurrection, but He said, God is not the God of the dead, but of the living. And no one durst from that day forth ask Him any more questions. Then Jesus pronounced His Seven Woes and He went forth from the Temple and sat on the Mount of Olives. There He foretold the destruction of the Temple to His disciples, and spake unto them concerning the Last Things, uttering the Parables of the Ten Virgins and of the Talents.

Parables. The Seven Woes. The Last Things.

What parables did Jesus speak?
What catch question did the Pharisees have for Him?
What catch question did the Sadducees have?
Mention as many of the Seven Woes as you can. *
What two Parables did our Saviour utter on the Mt. of Olives?
Give the Parable of the Ten Virgins. *
What day was this?

THE STORIES TO BE READ.

The Seven Woes.

Then spake Jesus to the multitude, saying, The scribes and the Pharisees sit in Moses' seat. All therefore whatsoever they bid you observe, that do. But do not ye after their works.

But woe unto you, scribes and Pharisees, hypocrites! For ye neither go into the kingdom of heaven yourselves, nor suffer ye them that are entering to go in.

Woe unto you, scribes and Pharisees, hypocrites! For ye compass sea and land to make one proselyte; and when he is made, ye make him twofold more the child of hell than yourselves.

Woe unto you, ye blind guides!

FOURTEENTH SUNDAY.

Woe unto you, scribes and Pharisees, hypocrites! For ye pay tithe of mint, and anise, and cummin, and have omitted the weightier matters of the law, judgment, mercy, and faith. These ought ye to have done, and not to leave the other undone. Ye strain at a gnat, and swallow a camel.

Woe unto you, scribes and Pharisees, hypocrites! For ye make clean the outside of the cup and of the platter, but within they are full of extortion and excess.

Woe unto you, scribes and Pharisees, hypocrites! For ye are like unto whited sepulchres, which indeed appear beautiful outward, but are within full of dead men's bones.

Woe unto you, scribes and Pharisees, hypocrites! Because ye build the tombs of the prophets, and yourselves are the children of them that killed the prophets.

Ye serpents, ye generation of vipers, how can ye escape the damnation of hell!

The Ten Virgins.

Ten virgins took their lamps, and went forth to meet the bridegroom. Five of them were wise and five were foolish. They that were foolish took no oil with them. While the bridegroom tarried, they all slumbered.

And at midnight there was a cry made, Behold, the bridegroom cometh; go ye out to meet him. Then the virgins arose and trimmed their lamps, and the foolish said, Give us of your oil, for our lamps are gone out. But the wise answered, Go to them that sell and buy for yourselves. While they went, the bridegroom came. And they that were ready went in with him to the marriage. And the door was shut. Afterward came also the other virgins, saying, Lord, Lord, open to us. But he answered and said, Verily I say unto you, I know you not. Watch therefore, for ye know neither the day nor the hour wherein the Son of man cometh.

THE SCRIPTURE TO BE LEARNED.

THE INSTITUTION OF THE LORD'S SUPPER.

How does Paul describe the Institution? *

The Lord Jesus the same night in which he was betrayed took bread:

And when he had given thanks, he brake it, and said, Take, eat: this is my body, which is broken for you: this do in remembrance of me.

After the same manner also he took the cup, when he had supped, saying, This cup is the new testament in my blood: this do ye, as oft as ye drink it in remembrance of me. For as often as ye eat this bread, and drink this cup, ye do shew the Lord's death till he come. I. Cor. 11 : 23-26.

WHAT THE CATECHISM SAYS OF THE SACRAMENT OF THE ALTAR.

What does the Catechism say of the Sacrament of the Altar?

It is the true body and blood of our Lord Jesus Christ, under the bread and wine, given unto us Christians to eat and drink, as it was instituted by Christ himself.

*Teacher asks the questions until the whole class have recited these parts.

CHAPTER XV.

The Saviour Institutes the Lord's Supper and Comforts the Disciples.

WEDNESDAY. (Including Tuesday Night.)

NOW the Feast of Unleavened Bread was near. And when Jesus had finished all His sayings, He said to His disciples, Ye know that after two days is the Passover, and the Son of Man is delivered up to be crucified.

What day of the week was this?

What did Jesus say to His disciples?

Then assembled the chief priests and the scribes and the elders of the people at the palace of the high priest who was called Caiaphas, and consulted that they might take Jesus by subtilty and kill Him. But they said, Not during the Feast, lest there be an uproar among the people.

For what purpose did the Chief Priests consult?

Then one of the twelve disciples, called Judas Iscariot, went unto the chief priests and said to them, What will ye give me and I will deliver Him unto you? And they were glad, and agreed to give him thirty pieces of silver. He promised, and communed with the chief priests and captains how he might betray Him unto them in the absence of the multitude. (Jesus probably remained at Bethany all day Wednesday, but on Thursday) the disciples came to Him, saying, Where wilt Thou that we prepare the passover? And He sent Peter and John and said, Go ye into the city, and there shall meet you a man bearing a pitcher of water: follow him. And wheresoever he shall go in,

Judas Goes to the Chief Priests.

What did Judas do?

How were they to make ready for the Passover?

FIFTEENTH SUNDAY.

say ye to the goodman of the house, The Master saith, Where is the guest-chamber, where I shall eat the passover with my disciples? And he will show you a large upper room furnished and prepared. There make ready for us. The two disciples went forth and came into the city, and found as He had said, and they made ready the passover. Making Ready for the Passover.

When did Jesus come to the Passover?
What question arose?

In the evening He cometh with the twelve, and sat down and the twelve apostles with Him. And there was a strife among them, which of them should be accounted the greatest. And He said, Whether is greater, he that sitteth at meat, or he that serveth? But I am among you as he that serveth. Master and Servant.

What did Jesus do as an answer to the question?
How was it when He came to wash Peter's feet?*

And He riseth and laid aside His garments and took a towel and girded Himself, and poured water into a basin, and began to wash the disciples' feet, and to wipe them with the towel. So after He had washed their feet, and was set down again, He said, Know ye what I have done unto you? Ye call me Master and Lord: and ye say well: for so I am. I have given you an example. The servant is not greater than his lord. If ye know these things, happy are ye if ye do them!

Describe the scene when it comes out that one of the twelve is to betray the Master.

And as they sat, He was troubled and said, Verily, one of you which eateth with me shall betray me. And they began to be sorrowful and to say unto Him one by one, Is it I? He answered, It is one of the twelve that dippeth with me in the dish. Then the disciples looked one on another. Then Judas said, Master, is it I? He said, Thou hast said. Now there was leaning on Jesus' bosom one of His disciples, whom Jesus loved. Simon Peter there- One of You Shall Betray Me.

FIFTEENTH SUNDAY. 75

fore beckoned to him, that he should ask who it should be of whom He spake. He then saith unto Him, Lord, who is it? Jesus answered, He it is, to whom I shall give a sop when I have dipped it. And He gave the sop to Judas. And after the sop Satan entered into him. Then said Jesus, That thou doest, do quickly. Now no man at the table knew for what intent He spake this unto him. He then, having received the sop, went immediately out, and it was night. And the Lord warned Peter, and told him to strengthen his brethren.

Instituting the Lord's Supper. And as they did eat, Jesus took bread, and blessed and brake it, and gave it to the disciples, and said, Take, eat; this is my body, which is given for you: this do in remembrance of me. After the same manner also He took the cup, when He had supped, and gave thanks, and gave it to them, saying, Drink ye all of it. This cup is the New Testament in my blood, which is shed for you and for many for the remission of sins: this do ye, as oft as ye drink it, in remembrance of me; and they all drank of it.

What sacrament did the Lord institute? How did He do it?

Parting Words. And He spake of the mansions in His Father's house, and said, Let not your heart be troubled. Believe in me; I go to prepare a place for you. He promised to send them the Comforter, the Spirit of truth, who would take His place. He urged them to keep His commandments, to abide in His love, and to love one another. I am the vine, said He, and ye are the branches. Without me, ye can do nothing. He told them that after He had gone to the Father, they would suffer persecutions. And He lifted up His eyes to heaven and said, Father, the hour is come, glorify

What did the Lord say of His Father's house?

Whom did He promise to send in His place?

To what did He compare Himself and why?

How did He pray to His Father?

FIFTEENTH SUNDAY.

Thy Son, that Thy Son also may glorify Thee. I have finished the work which Thou gavest Me to do. And when they had sung a hymn they went out into the Mount of Olives.

THE STORY TO BE READ.

Jesus Washes Peter's Feet.

Then cometh he to Simon Peter. Peter said unto him, Lord, dost thou wash my feet! Jesus said, What I do thou knowest not now. Peter saith, Thou shalt never wash my feet. Jesus answered, If I wash thee not, thou hast no part with me. Simon Peter saith, Lord, not my feet only, but also my hands and my head. Jesus saith to him, He that is washed needeth not save to wash his feet, but is clean every whit.

SUMMARY OF EVENTS.

Two days before the feast the chief priests consult to take the Saviour by subtilty.

Judas offers to betray Him.

The Saviour sends Peter and John into the city to find a guest chamber and to make ready the passover.

He sits down with the twelve: and as an example of humility washes their feet.

He is troubled and says that one of them shall betray Him.

They ask who it is and he points out Judas.

He institutes the Lord's Supper.

He speaks parting words of comfort to the disciples and promises the Holy Spirit.

From what parts of the Bible is our narrative taken? Matt. 26, Mark 14, Luke 22, John 13-17.

There are no pictures in "Bible Story" referring to this chapter.

What shall we call this fifteenth chapter? **The Saviour Institutes the Lord's Supper and Comforts the Disciples.**

In conclusion, let the teacher again refer to the Scripture and Catechism answers that the scholar has learned.

THE SCRIPTURE TO BE LEARNED,

HE IS DESPISED AND REJECTED OF MEN.

He is despised and rejected of men; a man of sorrows, and acquainted with grief: and we hid as it were our faces from him; he was despised, and we esteemed him not. Give Isaiah's prophecy of Christ's sufferings.

Surely he hath borne our griefs, and carried our sorrows: yet we did esteem him stricken, smitten of God, and afflicted.

But he was wounded for our transgressions, he was bruised for our iniquities: the chastisement of our peace was upon him; and with his stripes we are healed.

All we like sheep have gone astray; we have turned every one to his own way; and the Lord hath laid on him the iniquity of us all.

He was oppressed, and he was afflicted, yet he opened not his mouth: he is brought as a lamb to the slaughter, and as a sheep before her shearers is dumb, so he openeth not his mouth. Isa. 53 : 3-7.

CHAPTER XVI.

The Saviour Suffers in Gethsemane and Under Pontius Pilate.

THE LAST THURSDAY AND GOOD FRIDAY.

Narrate the scene in Gethsemane.

THEY crossed the brook Cedron, and entered the garden of Gethsemane. Here Christ suf- fered and prayed while the eyes of the disciples were heavy with sleep. When He rose He said, Let us be going: behold, he is at hand that doth betray Me. And Judas and a great multitude came and laid hold on Him and led Him away to Caiaphas, where the scribes and the elders were assembled. Before Annas and Caiaphas Jesus was examined as to His teaching. He was struck with the palm of the hand, He was testified against by false witnesses and confessed that He was the Christ, the Son of God. Therefore He was declared guilty of death. When Judas saw this, he went and hanged himself.

Gethsemane. Judas Betrays. Jesus Arrested.

Tell of the betrayal by Judas.
Tell of the remorse of Judas.*

What happened in the High Priest's palace?
Tell the story of Peter's denial.*

Before the High Priest.

When the morning was come, the whole multitude bound Jesus and carried Him away to Pontius Pilate the governor. Pilate went out to them and said, What accusation bring ye against this man? They began to accuse Him that He forbade to give tribute to Caesar, saying that He Himself is Christ a King. Pilate entered into the judgment hall and called in Jesus. And he went out again and saith to

Narrate the scene before Pilate.

Away To Pilate.

SIXTEENTH SUNDAY.

the Jews, I find in Him no fault at all. When Pilate heard that He was a Galilean, he sent Him to Herod, who himself also was at Jerusalem at that time.

To whom did Pilate send Jesus?

And when Herod saw Jesus, he was exceeding glad. He hoped to have seen some miracle done by Him. He questioned with Him in many words, but Jesus answered him nothing. And the chief priests and scribes vehemently accused Him. Then Herod with his men of war set Him at naught, and mocked Him, and arrayed Him in a gorgeous robe, and sent Him again to Pilate.

Before Herod.

Narrate the scene before Herod.

Pilate called the chief priests and people together and said, Ye have brought this man unto me as one that perverteth the people. I have examined Him before you and have found no fault in Him; no, nor yet Herod: for I sent you to him; and nothing worthy of death is done unto Him: I will therefore chastise Him, and release Him.

Back to Pilate.

Give the interview of Pilate with Jesus.
What did Pilate say to the Multitude?

Now the multitude began crying aloud, desiring the governor to release unto them a prisoner, as he had ever done. There was then a notable prisoner named Barabbas whom they had desired and who had been cast into prison for sedition and murder. Pilate answered them, Will ye that I release unto you the King of the Jews? And they cried out all at once, Away with this man, and release unto us Barabbas! Pilate said, What will ye then that I shall do unto Him whom ye call the King of the Jews? They cried, Crucify Him! Crucify Him! And he said, Why? What evil hath He done? I have found no cause of death in Him. I will chastise Him

Give Us Barabbas!

Give the dialogue between Pilate and the Multitude.
What was the final result?

Crucify Him!

and let Him go. And they were instant with loud voices, requiring that He might be crucified. And the voices of them and of the chief priests prevailed. He released Barabbas and delivered Jesus to be crucified.

Peter in the Palace Yard.

But Peter stood at the door without. Then cometh John and brought in Peter. And as he was beneath in the courtyard, one of the maids of the high priest, seeing Peter warming himself, looked upon him, and saith, Thou also wast with the Nazarene. But he denied it. And he went out into the porch and the cock crew. Another maid saw him and began again to say to them that stood by, This is one of them. But he again denied it. And after a little while again they that stood by said to Peter, Of a truth thou art one of them; for thou art a Galilæan. But he began to curse and to swear, I know not this man of whom ye speak. And straightway the second time the cock crew. And the Lord turned and looked upon Peter. And Peter called to mind the word, how that Jesus said unto him, Thou shalt deny me thrice. And he went out and wept bitterly.

The Remorse of Judas.

Judas, when he saw that Jesus was condemned, cast down the thirty pieces of silver in the temple, and departed, and went and hanged himself.

The Interview of Pilate with Jesus.

Then Pilate entered into the judgment hall and called Jesus in, and said, Art thou the King of the Jews? Jesus answered, Sayest thou this thing of thyself, or did others tell it thee of me? Pilate answered, Am I a Jew? What hast thou done. Jesus answered, My kingdom is not of this world. If it were, then would my servants fight. Pilate said, Art thou a king then? Jesus answered, I am a king. To this end was I born, and for this cause came I into the world, that I should bear witness unto the truth. Pilate saith, What is truth? And he went out again unto the Jews.

SIXTEENTH SUNDAY.

Pilate Sets Jesus Before the Multitude.

Behold, I bring him forth to you, that ye may know that I find no fault in him. Then came Jesus forth, wearing the crown of thorns, and the purple robe. And Pilate saith unto them, Behold the man. When the chief priests saw him, they cried out, Crucify him, crucify him. Pilate saith unto them, Take ye him, and crucify him. And Pilate sought to release him: but the Jews cried out, If thou let this man go, thou art not Cæsar's friend. When Pilate heard that, he brought Jesus forth, and sat down in the judgment seat. And he said unto the Jews, Behold your King! But they cried out, Away with him, crucify him. Pilate saith, Shall I crucify your King? The chief priests answered, We have no king but Cæsar. When Pilate saw that he could prevail nothing, but that rather a tumult was made, he took water, and washed his hands before the multitude, saying, I am innocent of the blood of this just person; see ye to it. Then answered all the people, and said, his blood be on us, and on our children!

THURSDAY NIGHT AND GOOD FRIDAY.

Jesus suffers in Gethsemane. See *Bible Story.*
Jesus is betrayed and arrested. See *Bible Story.*
Jesus is taken to the palace of Caiaphas. See *Bible Story.*
Peter denies Jesus in the palace yard.
The remorse of Judas. He goes and hangs himself.
Jesus is bound and carried to Pontius Pilate. See *Bible Story.*
The interview of Pilate with Jesus.
Jesus is sent by Pilate to Herod. See *Bible Story.*
Herod returns Him to Pilate.
Pilate sets Jesus before the multitude and seeks to release Him.
The Jews cry for His crucifixion and the release of Barabbas.
Pilate delivers him to be crucified. See *Bible Story.*

From what parts of the Bible is this narrative taken? Matt. 26-27, Mark 14-15, Luke 22-23, John 18-19.
What pictures did we have in "Bible Story" referring to this chapter?
What shall we call this sixteenth chapter? **The Saviour Suffers in Gethsemane and Under Pontius Pilate.**

SEVENTEENTH SUNDAY.

THE SCRIPTURE TO BE LEARNED.

THE EXAMPLE OF CHRIST'S HUMILITY.

<small>How does Christ teach humility?*</small>

Let this mind be in you, which was also in Christ Jesus:

Who, being in the form of God, thought it not robbery to be equal with God:

But made himself of no reputation, and took upon him the form of a servant, and was made in the likeness of men:

And being found in fashion as a man, he humbled himself, and became obedient unto death, even the death of the cross. Phil. 2:5-8.

WHAT THE CATECHISM SAYS.

<small>What does the Catechism say?</small>

I believe that Jesus Christ, true God, begotten of the Father from eternity, and also true man, born of the Virgin Mary, is my Lord; who has redeemed me, a lost and condemned creature, secured and delivered me from all sins, from death, and from the power of the devil, not with silver and gold, but with his holy and precious blood, and with his innocent sufferings and death.

*Teacher asks the questions until the whole class have recited these parts.

CHAPTER XVII.
The Saviour Crucified, Dead and Buried.

GOOD FRIDAY.

THEN the soldiers of the governor took Jesus into the common hall and after they had mocked Him they led Him away to crucify Him. There were two malefactors led with Him to be put to death. And He bearing His cross, went forth. As they came out they found a man of Cyrene, Simon by name, and on him they laid the cross that he might bear it after Jesus. And there followed Him a great company of people, and of women who bewailed Him.

How did they mock Jesus?*

Tell how Jesus was led out to be crucified.

To Golgotha.

And when they were come unto a place called Golgotha, they gave Him wine mingled with myrrh to drink, but He received it not. There they crucified Him. Jesus said, Father, forgive them; for they know not what they do. It was the third hour. * Pilate wrote a title, JESUS OF NAZARETH, THE KING OF THE JEWS, in Hebrew, and Greek, and Latin, and put it on the cross. The soldiers divided His garments among themselves and sat down and watched Him. The women stood by the cross. Those that passed by and the chief priests reviled and mocked Him. The thieves also which were crucified with Him cast the same in His teeth. And it was about the sixth hour*, and there was a darkness over all the

Tell the story of His crucifixion.

What did the soldiers do?
What did Jesus say on the cross?
What did Pilate write?
Tell of the mother of Jesus.*
Of the Thieves.*

---

*The third hour was 9 o'clock in the morning. The sixth hour was noon. The ninth hour was 3 o'clock in the afternoon.

SEVENTEENTH SUNDAY.

earth until the ninth hour. About the ninth hour Jesus cried with a loud voice, My God, my God, why hast thou forsaken me? After this, He saith, I thirst. And straightway one of them ran, and took a sponge and filled it with vinegar, and put it on a reed, and gave Him to drink. Jesus said, It is finished: and cried with a loud voice, Father, into thy hands I commend my spirit. And having said this, He bowed His head and gave up the ghost. And the earth did quake. And the centurion watching Jesus said, Truly this was the Son of God. And all the people smote their breasts and returned. *It Is Finished.*

Tell why Jesus was taken from the cross.

That the bodies should not remain on the cross on the Sabbath, the Jews besought Pilate that their legs might be broken. But when the soldiers came to Jesus, and saw that He was dead already, one of the soldiers pierced His side with a spear, and forthwith issued thereout blood and water. When the even- ing was come, a rich man of Arimathea, named Joseph, went in boldly to Pilate and asked for the body of Jesus. Pilate gave it to Joseph. Joseph and Nicodemus took it and wound it in linen clothes with spices, and laid it in a new sepulchre, hewn out of the rock, in a garden in the place where He was crucified. And Joseph rolled a great stone to the door of the sepulchre and departed. *They Looked On Him Whom They Pierced.* *Laid in the Grave.*

Who laid Him in the grave? How?

Tell of the sepulchre.

THE STORIES TO BE READ.

The Soldiers Mock Jesus.

Then there gathered unto Him the whole band of soldiers. And they stripped him, and put on him a scarlet robe. And

SEVENTEENTH SUNDAY.

when they had platted a crown of thorns, they put it upon his head, and a reed in his right hand: and they bowed the knee before him, and mocked him, saying, Hail, King of the Jews? And they spit upon him, and took the reed and smote him on the head.

The Mother of Jesus by the Cross.

Now there stood by the cross of Jesus his mother. When Jesus, therefore, saw his mother, and the disciple standing by, whom he loved, he said unto his mother, Woman, behold thy son! Then said he to the disciple, Behold thy mother! And from that hour that disciple took her unto his own home.

Jesus and the Two Thieves.

The thieves also, which were crucified with him, cast the same in his teeth, and one of the malefactors railed on him, saying, If thou be Christ, save thyself and us! But the other answering, rebuked him saying, Dost not thou fear God, seeing thou art in the same condemnation? And we indeed justly; for we receive the due reward of our deeds: but this man hath done nothing amiss. And he said unto Jesus, Lord, remember me when thou comest in thy kingdom. And Jesus said unto him, Verily I say unto thee, To-day shalt thou be with me in paradise.

SUMMARY OF EVENTS.

Jesus is led away to be crucified.

He bears His Cross. They lay it on Simon of Cyrene.

He is offered myrrh to drink.

SEVENTEENTH SUNDAY.

He is crucified on Golgotha.

He prays, Father, forgive them.

Pilate writes a title for the cross.

The soldiers divide His garments.

The women stand by the cross; the chief priests and others mock him.

The thieves on each side speak to Him.

He says, Today shalt thou be with me in paradise.

He says to the disciple, Behold, thy mother!

At twelve o'clock there is a darkness over the earth.

Jesus cries, My God, My God, why hast thou forsaken me?

He says, I thirst; and, It is finished.

He cries, Father, into thy hands I commend my spirit: and gives up the ghost.

His body is taken from the cross and laid in the grave.

From what parts of the Bible is this narrative taken? Matt. 27, Mark 15, Luke 23, John 19.

What pictures did we have in "Bible Story" referring to this chapter?

What shall we call this seventeenth chapter? **The Saviour Crucified, Dead and Buried.**

In conclusion, let the teacher again refer to the Scripture and Catechism answers that the scholar has learned.

THE SCRIPTURE TO BE LEARNED.

WE SHALL BE MADE ALIVE IN HIM.

If in this life only we have hope in Christ, we are of all men most miserable.

But now is Christ risen from the dead, and become the firstfruits of them that slept.

For since by man came death, by man came also the resurrection of the dead. For as in Adam all die, even so in Christ shall all be made alive.

But every man in his own order: Christ the firstfruits; afterward they that are Christ's at his coming. I. Cor. 15 : 19-23.

I am the resurrection, and the life: he that believeth in me, though he were dead, yet shall he live: And whosoever liveth and believeth in me shall never die. John 11 : 25, 26.

What result does Christ's resurrection produce?*

WHAT THE CATECHISM SAYS.

* * * And will raise up me and all the dead at the last day, and will grant everlasting life to me and to all who believe in Christ. This is most certainly true.

What does the Catechism say?

---

*Teacher asks the questions until the whole class have recited these parts.

CHAPTER XVIII.
The Saviour "Rose Again from the Dead."

EASTER SUNDAY.

THE next day the chief priests and Pharisees came together unto Pilate, saying, Sir, we remember that that deceiver said, while He was yet alive, After three days I will rise again. Command therefore that the sepulchre be made sure until the third day, lest His disciples come by night, and steal Him away, and say unto the people, He is risen from the dead. Pilate said unto them, Ye have a watch; go your way, make it as sure as ye can. So they went, and made the sepulchre sure, sealing the stone, and setting a watch. *Setting a Watch at the Sepulchre.*

Tell of the watch at the sepulchre.

Tell of the women buying spices; of the earthquake and the Angel; of Mary Magdalene,* Peter and John; of Mary Magdalene and Jesus.

And when the Sabbath was past (on the evening of Saturday) Mary Magdalene, and Mary the Mother of James, and Salome had bought sweet spices that they might come and anoint Him. *The Women Purchase Spices.*

And, behold, there was a great earthquake; for the angel of the Lord descended from heaven, and rolled back the stone from the door, and sat upon it. His countenance was like lightning, and his raiment as white as snow. And for fear of him the keepers did shake, and became as dead men. *The Angel Rolls Away the Stone.*

Now Mary Magdalene cometh early, while it was yet dark, unto the tomb, and seeth the stone taken away. She runneth therefore unto Simon Peter and unto the disciple whom *Mary Magdalene Comes to the Tomb.*

Jesus loved, and saith, They have taken away the Lord out of the tomb, and we know not where they have laid Him! Then Peter and the other disciple arose and ran to the tomb. They ran together, and the other disciple outran Peter and came first to the tomb. But he did not go in. Then cometh Peter, and stooping down he entered the tomb, and saw the linen clothes lying alone. Then the other disciple also entered, and they went away again unto their own homes, wondering what had happened.

But Mary was standing without by the tomb weeping. Jesus appeared unto her, and told her to tell His brethren, I ascend unto My Father and your Father, and to My God and your God. Mary went and told them, as they mourned and wept, declaring, I have seen the Lord. And they, when they heard that He was alive, and had been seen by her, believed it not.

Jesus Appears to Her.

Very early in the morning, at the rising of the sun, the women came to the sepulchre. They said among themselves, Who shall roll us away the stone from the door of the sepulchre? And looking up they saw that the stone had been rolled away. And they entered in and found not the body of the Lord Jesus. While they were much perplexed about this, two men stood by them in dazzling apparel, and they saw a young man sitting on the right side in a white robe. He said to them, Be not affrighted; for I know ye seek Jesus of Nazareth, the crucified. He is not here, for He is risen, as He said. Go tell His disciples and Peter, that He is risen from the dead; and, behold,

The Women Enter the Tomb and Are Spoken To By Angels.

Tell of the women coming to the sepulchre.

What did they see within the sepulchre? What things did the young man say?

EIGHTEENTH SUNDAY.

He goeth before you into Galilee, there shall ye see Him. And they went out quickly from the sepulchre and fled with fear and great joy.

<small>Tell how Jesus met them.</small>
And behold Jesus met them saying, All hail! And they came up and took hold of His feet and worshiped Him. Then saith Jesus, Fear not! <small>Jesus Meets Them.</small> Go tell my brethren that they depart into Galilee and there they shall see me. And they returned and told all these things to the apostles. And their sayings appeared to them as idle talk.

<small>Tell how He met the two walking to Emmaus, and give the conversation.*</small>
And behold two of them went that day to a village called Emmaus, which was from Jerusalem <small>Jesus Walks With the Two to Emmaus.</small> about threescore furlongs. And it came to pass while they talked together of all these things which had happened, Jesus Himself drew near and expounded unto them in all the Scriptures the things concerning Himself. And they knew Him not until He vanished out of their sight. And they rose up the same hour and returned to Jerusalem, and found the eleven gathered together, saying, The Lord is risen indeed, and hath appeared to Simon. And it was at evening on the first day of the week. And the doors were shut for fear of the Jews.

<small>Tell how Jesus came to the Disciples on Easter evening.</small>
And as they thus spake, Jesus Himself stood in the midst of them, and saith unto them, Peace be unto you! But they were terrified and supposed <small>Peace Be Unto You!</small> that they had seen a spirit. And He said, Why do thoughts arise in your hearts? Behold my hands and my feet, that it is I myself. Handle Me and see. And while they yet believed not for joy, He took a piece of a broiled fish and of a honeycomb and did eat

EIGHTEENTH SUNDAY.

before them. And He said, This is what I spake unto you while I was yet with you, that it behooved Christ to suffer, and to rise from the dead the third day: and that repentance and remission of sins should be preached in My name among all nations, beginning at Jerusalem. And ye are witnesses of these things.

But Thomas was not with them when Jesus came. The **Thomas Doubts.** other disciples told him, We have seen the Lord. But he said, Except I shall see in His hands the print of the nails, and thrust my hand into His side, I will not believe. And after eight days again came *Tell the story of Thomas.* Jesus and stood in the midst and said, Peace be unto you! Then saith He to Thomas, Reach hither thy finger, and behold My hands; and reach hither thy hand, and thrust it into My side; and be not faithless, but believing. And Thomas said, My Lord and my God! Jesus saith, Thomas, because thou hast seen Me, thou hast believed: blessed are they that have not seen and yet have believed.

SUMMARY OF EVENTS.

The Jews set a watch at the Saviour's Tomb.
The Women buy spices on Saturday evening to anoint Him.
The Angel rolls the stone away early on Easter. See *Bible Story*
Mary Magdalene comes to the Tomb while it is yet dark and
    sees that the stone is taken away. She runs and tells Peter
    and John. Jesus appears to her in the garden.
The Women come at the rising of the sun and enter the Tomb.
    Angels tell them that He is risen. See *Bible Story.*
Jesus meets them on the way and says, All hail! See *Bible Story.*
Jesus meets and accompanies two of the disciples to Emmaus.
Jesus appears to the Twelve on Sunday evening.

From what parts of the Bible is this narrative taken? Matt. 27-28, Mark 16, Luke 24, John 20.

THE SCRIPTURE TO BE LEARNED.

OUR NEARNESS TO THE ASCENDED SAVIOUR.

What can sever us from the love of God in Christ Jesus?*

Who is he that condemneth? It is Christ that died, yea rather, that is risen again, who is even at the right hand of God, who also maketh intercession for us.

Who shall separate us from the love of Christ? shall tribulation, or distress, or persecution, or famine, or nakedness, or peril, or sword?

Nay, in all these things we are more than conquerors through him that loved us.

For I am persuaded, that neither death, nor life, nor angels, nor principalities, nor powers, nor things present, nor things to come,

Nor height, nor depth, nor any other creature shall be able to separate us from the love of God, which is in Christ Jesus our Lord. Rom. 8: 34-39.

WHAT THE CATECHISM SAYS.

What does the Catechism say?

For Thine is the kingdom, and the power, and the glory for ever and ever. Amen.

*Teacher asks the questions until the whole class have recited these parts.

CHAPTER XIX.
The Saviour Ascended into Heaven.
FORTY DAYS AFTER EASTER.

Peter Goes Fishing.

WHEN the eleven disciples went away into Galilee. And Jesus showed Himself again to Peter, Thomas, and Nathanael, and two other disciples at the sea of Galilee.

It was on this wise. Simon Peter saith, I go a fishing. They say, We also go with thee. They went forth and entered into a boat immediately; and that night they caught nothing. But when day was now breaking, Jesus stood on the beach and saith, Children, have ye anything to eat? They answered, No. And He said, Cast the net on the right side of the ship, and ye shall find. They cast therefore, and now they were not able to draw it for the multitude of fishes. John said, It is the Lord! When Simon Peter heard that it was the Lord, he girt his fisher's coat about himself, and did cast himself into the sea. But the other disciples came in the little boat, dragging the net full of fishes. When they got out upon the land, they saw a fire of coals there, and fish laid thereon, and bread. Jesus saith, Bring now of the fish which ye have caught. Simon Peter went up and drew the net to land full of great fishes, a hundred and fifty-three.

Jesus saith, Come and dine. And none durst ask

Tell how Jesus showed Himself to some of the disciples.

They See the Lord.

Tell how they dined together.

NINETEENTH SUNDAY.

Tell His conversation with Peter.

Him, Who art thou? knowing that it was the Lord. Jesus then cometh and taketh bread and giveth them, and fish likewise. When they had dined, Jesus asked Simon Peter whether he loved Him, and told him that when he was old he would glorify God by a martyr's death. This is now the third time that Jesus showed Himself to His disciples after He was risen from the dead.

Come and Dine.

What great commission did the Saviour give to His disciples?

Then went the eleven disciples into a mountain where Jesus had appointed them. And when they saw Him, they worshiped Him. And He said, Go ye into all the world, and preach the gospel to every creature. He that believeth and is baptized shall be saved; but he that believeth not shall be damned. And He said, All power is given unto Me in heaven and in earth. Go ye therefore and make disciples of all the nations, baptizing them into the name of the Father, and of the Son, and of the Holy Ghost, teaching them to observe all things whatsoever I commanded you; and, lo, I am with you alway, even unto the end of the world, Amen.

Go Ye Into All the World.

What did He charge them not to do? Why?

Having spoken these things concerning the kingdom of God, He charged them not to depart from Jerusalem, but to wait for the promise of the Father, which, said He, ye heard from Me. For John indeed baptized with water; but ye shall be baptized with the Holy Ghost not many days hence. They then asked Him, Lord, wilt thou at this time restore the kingdom to Israel? And He said, It is not for you to know times or seasons, which the Father hath set within His own authority. But ye shall receive power, when the Holy Ghost is

What did they ask Him?

What was His reply?

NINETEENTH SUNDAY. 95

come upon you; and ye shall be my witnesses both in Jerusalem, and in all Judea and Samaria, and unto the uttermost part of the earth.

So then after the Lord had spoken unto them, He led them out as far as to Bethany, and He lifted up His hands and blessed them. And it came to pass, while He blessed them, He was parted from them, and a cloud received Him out of their sight. He was received up into heaven, and sat on the right hand of God. *[Describe the Ascension of the Saviour.]* *[A Cloud Received Him.]*

And while they were looking steadfastly into heaven as He went, behold, two men stood by them in white apparel; which also said, Ye men of Galilee, why stand ye looking into heaven? This Jesus, which was received up from you shall so come in like manner as ye beheld Him going into heaven. *[Who stood by them?]* *[What did these men say?]*

And they returned to Jerusalem with great joy. And they went up into the upper room where they were abiding. And they continued steadfastly in prayer. In those days Peter stood up in their midst and said, Brethren, Judas who was guide to them that took Jesus, was numbered among us. His office let another take. Of the men that have been among us from the baptism of John unto the day that the Lord Jesus was received up, must one be ordained a witness of the resurrection. And they put forward two, Joseph and Matthias. And they prayed. And the lot fell upon Matthias; and he was numbered with the eleven apostles. *[Waiting In Jerusalem.]* *[How did they choose an Apostle in place of Judas?]*

THE STORY TO BE READ.

Lovest Thou Me?

So when they had broken their fast, Jesus saith to Simon

NINETEENTH SUNDAY.

Peter, Simon, son of Jonas, lovest thou me more than these? He saith unto him, Yea, Lord; thou knowest that I love thee. He saith, Feed my lambs. He saith again a second time, Simon, son of Jonas, lovest thou me? He saith unto him, Yea, Lord. Thou knowest that I love Thee. He saith, Feed my sheep. He saith unto him the third time, Simon, son of Jonas, lovest thou me? Peter was grieved because he said unto him the third time, Lovest thou me? And he saith, Lord, Thou knowest all things, Thou knowest that I love thee. Jesus said, Feed my sheep.

SUMMARY OF EVENTS.

The disciples depart into Galilee.

Simon Peter and several others go fishing.

Jesus appears to them on the beach and tells them where to cast the net.

They land a hundred and fifty-three fishes.

Jesus asks them to come and dine on the beach.

Jesus tells Simon Peter to feed His lambs.

On a high mountain Jesus gives the eleven disciples the great commission.

He tells them not to depart from Jerusalem until the promise is fulfilled.

A cloud receives Him out of sight. See *Bible Story*.

They return to Jerusalem and wait.

They choose Matthias in place of Judas.

From what parts of the Bible is this narrative taken? Matt. 28, Mark 16, Luke 24, John 21, Acts 1.

What pictures did we have in "Bible Story" referring to this Chapter?

What shall we call this nineteenth chapter? **The Saviour Ascended into Heaven.**

In conclusion, let the teacher again refer to the Scripture and Catechism answers that the scholar has learned.

Twentieth Sunday.

THE SCRIPTURE TO BE LEARNED.

PETER SPEAKETH BY THE POWER OF THE HOLY GHOST.

Jesus of Nazareth, a man approved of God among you by miracles and wonders and signs, which God did by him in the midst of you, as ye yourselves also know: <small>What did Peter, prompted by the Holy Ghost, say?*</small>

Him, being delivered by the determinate counsel and foreknowledge of God, ye have taken, and by wicked hands have crucified and slain:

Whom God hath raised up, having loosed the pains of death: because it was not possible that he should be holden of it.

Therefore being by the right hand of God exalted, and having received of the Father the promise of the Holy Ghost, he hath shed forth this, which ye now see and hear.

Therefore let all the house of Israel know assuredly, that God hath made that same Jesus, whom ye have crucified, both Lord and Christ. Acts 2: 22-24, 33, 36.

WHAT THE CATECHISM SAYS.

I believe that I cannot by my own reason or strength believe in Jesus Christ, my Lord, or come to Him; but the Holy Ghost has called me through the Gospel, enlightened me by His gifts, and sanctified and preserved me in the true faith. <small>What does the Catechism say?</small>

---

*Teacher asks the questions until the whole class have recited these parts.

CHAPTER XX.

The Holy Spirit Descends, and the Church is Founded.

FIFTY DAYS AFTER EASTER, AT JERUSALEM.

Describe what occurred on the day of Pentecost.

THE DAY of Pentecost was now come. They were all together in one place. Suddenly there was heard from heaven a sound as of the rushing of a mighty wind. It filled the house where they were sitting. And there appeared unto them tongues as of fire. And they were filled with the Holy Spirit, and began to speak with other tongues, as the Spirit gave them utterance.

What languages were spoken?

When the multitude came together, they were confounded because every man heard them speaking in his own language. Behold, they said, Are not these which speak Galileans? And how hear we, every man in the language wherein we were born? Parthians and Medes and Elamites, and the dwellers in Cappadocia, in Egypt and the parts of Libya, and sojourners from Rome, we do hear them speaking the mighty works of God.

Are Not These Galileans?

What did Peter say to the people?

But Peter, standing up with the eleven, lifted up his voice and spake forth: Ye men that dwell at Jerusalem, give ear. This is that which hath been spoken by the prophet Joel: In the last days I will pour forth of my Spirit upon all flesh. Ye men of Israel, Jesus of Nazareth, a man approved of God unto

Ye Men Give Ear!

TWENTIETH SUNDAY.

you by mighty works, ye did crucify and slay: Whom God raised up. Whereof we all are witnesses. Being therefore by the right hand of God exalted, and having received of the Father the promise of the Holy Spirit, He hath poured forth this. Know assuredly that God hath made Him both Lord and Christ, this Jesus whom ye crucified.

When they heard this, they said, Brethren, what shall **Repent and Be Baptized.** we do? And Peter said, Repent ye and be baptized every one of you. Then were they baptized, and there were added unto the church in that day about three thousand souls. Day by day continuing in the temple, and breaking bread at home, they took their food with gladness of heart, praising God.

Peter and John were going up into the temple at the hour of prayer. And a certain lame man, at the door of **A Lame Man at the Door of the Temple.** the temple which is called Beautiful, saw Peter and John about to go into the temple and asked to receive an alms. And Peter raised him up, and he began to walk. And all the people ran together in the porch that is called Solomon's, greatly wondering. And when Peter saw it, he said: Why fasten ye your eyes on us! The God of our fathers hath glorified his Servant Jesus. Whom ye denied, and killed the Prince of life! His name made this man strong. And as they spake, the captain of the temple and the Sadducees came upon them. And they put them in prison unto the morrow. And the number of men that believed came to be about five thousand.

On the morrow the rulers were gathered together. Annas was there, and Caiaphas, and John and Alexander.

Margin notes: What did the people say and do after Peter ceased speaking? Tell what you know of this first church. Tell the story of the lame man.* What did this healing lead to?

TWENTIETH SUNDAY.

Describe the trial.

And they inquired, By what power have ye done this? Peter said, In the name of Jesus Christ doth this man stand here before you whole. He is the stone which was set at nought of you the builders. And in none other is there salvation. *In the Name of Jesus Christ.*

When they beheld the boldness of Peter and John, they marveled. And as the man which was healed was standing with them, they could say nothing against it.

How did the trial end?

And they, when they had further threatened them, let them go.

Now the multitude of them that believed were of one heart and soul. Neither was there any among them that lacked; for as many as were possessed of lands or houses sold them, and brought the prices of the things that were sold, and laid them at the apostles' feet. Joseph, a man of Cyprus, having a field, sold it, and laid the money at the apostles' feet. But Ananias, with Sapphira his wife, sold a possession and kept back part of the price; and they fell down dead at the apostles' feet. And great fear came upon the whole church.

What did the church members do with their property?

Ananias and Sapphira.

Tell the story of Ananias and Sapphira.*

THE STORIES TO BE READ.

Healing the Lame Man at the Door of the Temple.

Peter fastening his eyes upon the lame man, with John, said, Look on us. And he looked, expecting to receive something. Peter said, Silver and gold have I none; but such as I have, that give I thee. In the name of Jesus Christ of Nazareth, rise up and walk. And he took him by the hand. And immediately his feet and his ankle bones received strength. And leaping up, he entered with them into the temple, walking and praising God.

TWENTIETH SUNDAY. 101

The Story of Ananias and Sapphira.

Ananias sold a possession and kept back part of the price.

But Peter said: Ananias, why hath Satan filled thy heart to lie to the Holy Ghost, and to keep back part of the price of the land? While it remained, did it not remain thine own? and after it was sold, was it not in thy power? Thou hast not lied unto men, but unto God. And Ananias hearing these words fell down and gave up the ghost. And the young men arose and wrapped him round, and carried him out, and buried him. And it was the space of three hours after, when his wife, not knowing what was done, came in. And Peter said unto her, Tell me whether ye sold the land for so much. And she said, Yea, for so much. But Peter said unto her, How is it that ye have agreed together to tempt the Spirit of the Lord? Behold, the feet of them which have buried thy husband are at the door, and they shall carry thee out. And she fell down immediately at his feet, and gave up the ghost, and the young men came in and found her dead, and they carried her out and buried her by her husband.

SUMMARY OF EVENTS.

On the day of Pentecost the Holy Spirit fills the disciples. See *Bible Story.*

They speak in many tongues, and the multitude is astonished. See *Bible Story.*

Peter preaches the resurrection of Jesus. See *Bible Story.*

Many repent and are baptized, so that the church numbers three thousand souls.

Peter and John heal a lame man at the door of the temple.

Peter preaches to the assembling crowd and is put in prison.

The next day Peter is tried before the Council.

The members of the church hold their possessions in common.

Ananias and Sapphira lie to the Holy Ghost.

From what part of the Bible is this narrative taken?   Acts 2-5.
What picture did we have in "Bible Story" referring to this chapter?
What shall we call this twentieth chapter?   **The Holy Spirit Descends, and the Church Is Founded.**

THE SCRIPTURE TO BE LEARNED.

THE SAVIOUR PREDICTS PERSECUTION.

<small>What was to happen to Christ's disciples?*</small>

And ye shall be betrayed both by parents and brethren, and kinsfolks and friends; and some of you shall they cause to be put to death.

And ye shall be hated of all men for my name's sake.

But there shall not an hair of your head perish. Luke 21:16-18.

WHAT THE CATECHISM PREDICTS OF BELIEVERS.

<small>What does the Catechism say?</small>

* * * in like manner as He calls, gathers, enlightens, and sanctifies the whole Christian Church on earth, and preserves it in union with Jesus Christ in the true faith; in which Christian Church He daily forgives abundantly all my sins, and the sins of all believers, and will raise up me and all the dead at the last day, and will grant everlasting life to me and to all who believe in Christ. This is most certainly true.

---

*Teacher asks the questions until the whole class have recited these parts.

CHAPTER XXI

The Church Is Persecuted and Extended.

TO SAMARIA AND GALILEE.

BY THE hands of the apostles many wonders were wrought among the people. Multitudes of believers were added unto the Lord. They brought forth sick folks out of the cities round about Jerusalem: and they were healed every one.

How did the church prosper in Jerusalem?

Then the high priest was filled with indignation. And he laid hands on the apostles and **The Apostles Escape From Prison.** put them in the common prison. But the angel of the Lord opened the prison doors by night. And they entered into the temple early in the morning and taught.

To what did this lead?

How did the apostles escape from prison?

The high priest sent to the prison to have them brought. But the officers returned saying, The prison truly found we shut, and the keepers before the doors; but when we had opened we found no man within. Then came one saying, Behold, the men whom ye put in prison are standing in the temple and teaching the people. Then the captain and officers went and brought them before the council. The high priest said, Did we not strictly command you not to teach in this name? And behold, ye have filled Jerusalem with your doctrine!

Describe the scene in the council and at the prison the next morning.

How did the high priest threaten?

Peter answered, We ought to obey God rather than men. The God of our fathers raised up Jesus, whom ye hanged on a tree. Him hath God exalted to be a

What was Peter's answer?

TWENTY-FIRST SUNDAY.

Saviour. And we are His witnesses of these things. So is also the Holy Ghost.

Who saved the apostles by his counsel, and what did he say?

When they heard that, they were cut to the heart, and took counsel to slay them. Then stood up one in the council, Gamaliel, and said, Ye men of Israel, take care as to what ye do. Let these men alone. If this work be of men, it will come to nought. But if it be of God, ye cannot overthrow it. And to him they agreed.

Gamaliel.

And the disciples multiplied, and the twelve said, Look ye out seven men whom we may appoint; but we will continue in prayer, and in the ministry of the Word. And they chose Stephen, and Philip, and five others. And Stephen was full of grace and power. But certain men of the synagogue of the Libertines disputed with Stephen. And when they could not withstand his wisdom, they hired men to say, We have heard him speak blasphemous words. This stirred up the people. They came upon him and brought him into the Council, and set up false witnesses. All that sat in the Council saw that his face was as the face of an angel. And the high priest said, Are these things so? Stephen said:

How did Stephen come to be a deacon?

Stephen Chosen a Deacon.

What led to his stoning?

Stephen Speaks.

Brethren and fathers, hearken: The God of glory appeared unto our father Abraham. As the time of the promise drew nigh Moses was born. This Moses our fathers refused. This is that Moses who said, A prophet shall God raise up among you. Ye stiff-necked! As your fathers did, so do ye. Which of the prophets did not your fathers persecute? And ye have now become murderers of the Righteous One!

Tell what you can of Stephen's speech.

TWENTY-FIRST SUNDAY. 105

They were cut to the heart and gnashed on him with their teeth. But he said, Behold, I see the heavens opened and the Son of man standing on the right hand of God. They stopped their ears and rushed upon him; and they stoned him. Stephen said, Lord Jesus receive my spirit, and fell asleep. The witnesses laid down their garments at the feet of a young man named Saul.

Stephen Stoned. — Describe the stoning.

That day a great persecution arose against the church in Jerusalem, and they were scattered abroad. Saul entered into every house, and seizing men and women, committed them to prison.

What arose after the stoning?

Therefore Philip went down to the city of Samaria and proclaimed Christ and the multitudes gave heed, and many palsied and lame were healed.

Philip Goes to Samaria. — Where did Philip go and what did he do?

There was a certain man in the city named Simon who used sorcery and who gave out that he was some great one. And he believed and was baptized. Now Peter and John came down from Jerusalem and laid their hands on the baptized and they received the Holy Ghost. When Simon saw that the Holy Ghost was given through the laying on of the apostles' hands he offered them money, saying, Give me also this power. But Peter said, Thy silver perish with thee. Thy heart is not right before God. And Peter and John returned to Jerusalem. Philip went south unto Gaza; and behold a eunuch of Ethiopia, under Candace, queen of the Ethiopians, was returning from Jerusalem and was met by Philip. Philip baptized him. And the Spirit of the Lord caught away Philip, and the eunuch went on his way rejoic-

Simon. — Tell what you know of Simon the Sorcerer.

The Eunuch. — Tell the story of Philip and the eunuch.*

TWENTY-FIRST SUNDAY.

What became of Philip? ing. But Philip was found at Azotus and he preached the gospel to all the cities till he came to Cæsarea.

Philip and the Eunuch.

Behold, a eunuch was sitting in his chariot and reading. And Philip heard him read the prophet Esaias, and said, Understandest thou what thou readest? And he said, How can I, except some man should guide me? And he desired Philip that he would come up and sit with him. The place which he read was this, He was led as a sheep to the slaughter; and like a lamb dumb before his shearers, so opened he not his mouth. The eunuch said, Of whom speaketh the prophet this? of himself, or of some other man? Then Philip began at the same Scripture and preached unto him Jesus. And they came unto a certain water: and the eunuch said, See, here is water: what doth hinder me to be baptized? And Philip said, If thou believest with all thine heart, thou mayest. And he said, I believe that Jesus Christ is the Son of God. And he commanded the chariot to stand still; and they went down into the water, both Philip and the eunuch; and he baptized him.

SUMMARY OF EVENTS.

The apostles heal many sick in Jerusalem.
The high priest puts the apostles into prison.
The officers are surprised at their escape.
Peter is brought before the Council and talks plainly.
Gamaliel calms the excitement.
Seven deacons are appointed to help the apostles.
The synagogue of the Libertines stirs up the Jews.
Stephen speaks and says they have murdered the Righteous One.
They stone Stephen and a persecution is begun.
Philip flees to Samaria and preaches there.
Simon the sorcerer tries to buy the gift of the Holy Ghost.
Philip baptizes the Ethiopian Eunuch.

From what part of the Bible is this narrative taken? Acts 5-8.
What shall we call this twenty-first chapter? **The Church is Persecuted and Extended to Samaria and Galilee.**

THE SCRIPTURE TO BE LEARNED.

THE GENTILES SHALL COME TO THY LIGHT

Arise, shine; for thy light is come, and the glory of the Lord is risen upon thee. Unto whom shall the light appear?*

For, behold, the darkness shall cover the earth, and gross darkness the people: but the Lord shall arise upon thee, and his glory shall be seen upon thee.

And the Gentiles shall come to thy light, and kings to the brightness of thy rising. Isa. 60:1-3.

WHAT THE CATECHISM SAYS.

Thy kingdom come. What does the Catechism say?

The kingdom of God comes indeed of itself, without our prayer; but we pray in this petition that it may come unto us also.

---

*Teacher asks the questions until the whole class have recited these parts.

CHAPTER XXII.
The Church Is Opened to the Gentiles.

Why did Paul go to Damascus?

What happened?

SAUL breathing threatenings and slaughter went unto the high priest and asked of him letters to Damascus that if he found any men or women that were disciples he might bring them bound to Jerusalem. As he drew near to Damascus sud- **Saul Stopped on his Way to Damascus.** denly there shone round about him a light from heaven, and he fell to the earth and heard a voice saying, Saul, Saul, why persecutest thou me? And he said, Who art thou, Lord? And He said, I am Jesus whom thou persecutest. And Saul arose from the earth, and when his eyes

How was he led into Damascus?

What occurred there?

were opened he saw nothing. And they led him by the hand and brought him into Damascus and he was three days without sight. A disciple named Ananias restored his sight and he arose and was baptized and **Saul Proclaims Jesus.** straightway he went into the synagogues and proclaimed that Jesus is the Son of God. All that heard him were amazed and said, Is not this the man that destroyed the disciples in Jerusalem? But Saul confounded the Jews proving that Jesus is the Christ.

Describe Paul's escape from Damascus.

What experience had he in Jerusalem?

The Jews tried to kill him and watched the gates day and night. But their plot became known to **Let Down in a Basket.** Saul, and the disciples took him by night and let him down through the wall in a basket.

When he reached Jerusalem, he tried to join himself to the disciples. And they were all afraid of him. But

TWENTY-SECOND SUNDAY. 109

Barnabas took him and brought him to the apostles. And he was with them at Jerusalem preaching boldly. And the Grecian Jews went about to kill him, but the brethren sent him off to Tarsus. So the church throughout all Judea and Galilee and Samaria had peace.

Now Peter went throughout all parts and he came down to the saints which dwelt at Lydda and healed a palsied man which had kept his bed eight years. As Lydda was near unto Joppa, when Dorcas died, they sent at once for Paul. When he was come, they showed him all the garments which Dorcas had made, and the widows stood by him weeping. But Peter prayed and restored Dorcas to life again. And he abode many days in Joppa with one Simon a tanner.

Tell the story of Peter and Dorcas.

Peter Raises Dorcas from the Dead.

And he went up upon the house top to pray and fell into a trance and saw a vision and heard a voice say, What God hath cleansed that call thou not common. While he doubted the meaning of the vision two servants and a soldier, sent from Caesarea by Cornelius, a centurion of the Italian band, called and asked whether Simon Peter were lodging there. Peter went down to the men and on the morrow accompanied them to Caesarea. Cornelius was waiting for them having called together his kinsmen and near friends. And Peter opened his mouth and preached the good tidings of peace by Jesus Christ. And the Holy Ghost fell on all who heard the word. And the Jews were amazed that the gift of the Holy Ghost was poured out on the Gentiles. And Peter commanded them to be baptized in the name of Jesus Christ. When Peter returned to Jer-

Peter on the Housetop.

Tell how Peter came to baptize Cornelius and his family.

TWENTY-SECOND SUNDAY.

usalem and explained the matter to the disciples there, they glorified God saying, Then to the Gentiles also hath God granted repentance unto life. *Cornelius Baptized.*

Tell what you know of the persecution. The persecution that arose after the death of Stephen scattered the disciples abroad as far as Phoenicia, and Cyprus, and Antioch. And they preached to none save only to Jews. But there were some men of Cyprus and Cyrene, who came to Antioch and preached to the Greeks also, and a great number believed. And the church in Jerusalem sent Barnabas to Antioch. When he was come and saw the grace of God, he was glad, and he went to Tarsus for Saul and brought him unto Antioch. For a whole year they taught the church at Antioch, and here first the disciples were called Christians. *Saul and Barnabas at Antioch.*

Of the church at Antioch.
Of the teachers there.

About that time King Herod put forth his hands to persecute the church. He killed James the brother of John with the sword. When he saw it pleased the Jews, he proceeded to seize Peter also. And he put him in prison. But an angel led Peter out and he escaped to another place. Now there was no small stir among the soldiers, what was become of Peter. And when Herod had examined the guards he commanded that they should be put to death. And Herod went down to Cæsarea and on a set day he arrayed himself in royal apparel and sat upon his throne and made an oration. And the people shouted saying, The voice of a god, and not of a man. And immediately an angel of the Lord smote him, because he gave not God

Tell of Herod's persecution.
Of Peter's imprisonment.
Of Peter's release.*
Peter Imprisoned.

Of Herod's death.

TWENTY-SECOND SUNDAY.

the glory: and he was eaten of worms, and gave up the ghost.

Peter Escapes from Prison.

Peter was kept in prison but prayer was made earnestly by the church for him. And the night before Herod was about to bring him forth, Peter was sleeping between two soldiers bound with two chains; and there were guards before the door. And behold, an angel of the Lord awoke him. And his chains fell off from his hands. And the angel said, Follow me. And when they were passed the first and the second ward, they came to the iron gate that leadeth into the city. It opened to them of its own accord. And they went out and passed on through one street, and the angel departed. When Peter had considered the thing, he came to the house of Mary the mother of John and knocked at the door of the gate. A maid came to answer, named Rhoda. And when she knew Peter's voice, she opened not the gate for joy, but ran in and told that Peter was standing before the gate. They said unto her, Thou art mad. But she confidently affirmed that it was even so. They said, It is his ghost. But Peter continued knocking, and when they had opened, they saw him, and were amazed.

SUMMARY OF EVENTS.

Paul goes to Damascus to persecute, but is converted.

The Jews attempt to kill him but he escapes.

Barnabas presents him to the disciples in Jerusalem.

Peter travels and at Joppa raises Dorcas from the dead.

Peter sees a vision, and starts to baptize Cornelius.

Saul and Barnabas upbuild the church at Antioch.

Herod puts Peter in prison, but the latter escapes.

From what part of the Bible is this narrative taken? Acts 9-12.

What shall we call this twenty-second chapter? **The Church is Opened to the Gentiles.**

In conclusion, let the teacher again refer to the Scripture and Catechism answers that the scholar has learned.

Twenty-Third Sunday.

THE SCRIPTURE TO BE LEARNED.

THE GROWTH OF THE CHURCH.

What was the result of Paul's labors in Ephesus?*

Now therefore ye are no more strangers and foreigners, but fellow citizens with the saints, and of the household of God;

And are built upon the foundation of the apostles and prophets, Jesus Christ himself being the chief cornerstone;

In whom all the building, fitly framed together, groweth unto an holy temple in the Lord:

In whom ye also are builded together for an habitation of God through the Spirit. Eph. 2:19-22.

WHAT THE CATECHISM SAYS CONCERNING THE GIFTS OF BAPTISM.

What does the Catechism say?*

It (baptism) worketh forgiveness of sins, delivers from death and the devil, and confers everlasting salvation on all who believe, as the Word and promise of God declare.

---

*Teacher asks the questions until the whole class have recited these parts.

CHAPTER XXIII.
The Church Grows in Asia.

ANTIOCH THE CENTRE OF PAUL'S FIRST MISSIONARY JOURNEY.

NOW THERE were in the church at Antioch, prophets and teachers, Barnabas, Simeon, Lucius, Manaen and Saul. And as they ministered, the Holy Ghost said, Separate me Barnabas and Saul for the work whereunto I have called them. So they sailed to Cyprus. And when they were at Salamis, they proclaimed the word of God in the synagogues of the Jews. When they had gone through the whole island unto Paphos, they found a certain sorcerer, a Jew, with the pro-consul Sergius Paulus. And Saul said, Thou shalt be blind, not seeing the sun for a season. And immediately there fell on him a mist and a darkness. Then the pro-consul believed, being astonished at the teaching of the Lord.

Who were sent out as missionaries from Antioch?

They Sailed to Cyprus.

To what island did they sail?

Give their experience on that island.

Paul and his company set sail from Paphos and came to Perga and thence to Antioch of Pisidia. And they **In Antioch of Pisidia.** went into the synagogue and sat down. And after the reading of the law and the prophets the rulers of the synagogue sent unto them saying, Brethren, if ye have any word of exhortation, say on. And Paul stood up, and beckoning with his hand said: Men of Israel and ye that fear God, hearken. Of David's seed hath God brought unto Israel a Saviour. To you is

To what city did they come in the interior of Asia Minor?

Was this Antioch the one from which they had started? (No).

What did the ruler of the synagogue say?

Tell what you can of Paul's speech.

TWENTY-THIRD SUNDAY.

the Word of this salvation. We declare unto you glad tidings, how that the promise made unto the fathers God hath fulfilled in that He raised up Jesus. Through this man is proclaimed remission of sins. Beware therefore lest that come upon you which is spoken in the prophets, Behold, ye despisers, and perish.

Tell what followed on the next Sabbath. The next Sabbath almost the whole city was gathered together to hear the Word of God. But when the Jews saw the multitudes, they were filled with jealousy, and contradicted the things which were spoken by Paul. And Paul and Barnabas spake out boldly and said, Seeing ye thrust the Word of God from you, lo, we turn to the Gentiles. And as the Gentiles heard this, they were glad, and glorified the Word of God. But the Jews stirred up a persecution against Paul and Barnabas, and cast them out of their borders.

How did the apostles fare at Iconium? They shook off the dust from their feet and they came to Iconium. A long time they tarried there speaking boldly in the Lord. But the multitude of the city was divided. *In Iconium.* And when there was an onset made to stone them, they fled to the cities of Lycaonia.

At Lystra Paul healed a cripple. When the multitudes saw it, they lifted up their voice saying, The *At Lystra.* *Tell their exciting experience at Lystra.* gods are come down to us. And they called Barnabas, Jupiter; and Paul, Mercury. And the priest of Jupiter brought oxen and garlands for a sacrifice. When the apostles heard it, they sprang forth and scarce restrained the multitudes from doing sacrifice unto them. But there came Jews thither from Antioch and Iconium. These persuaded the multitudes, and they stoned Paul,

TWENTY-THIRD SUNDAY.   115

and dragged him out of the city, supposing that he was dead. But he rose up and on the morrow went forth with Barnabas to Derbe. And when they had preached the gospel to that city, and had made many disciples, **The Return.** they returned to Lystra, Iconium, Antioch and Perga, and sailed to Antioch in Syria. And when they were come, and had gathered the church together, they rehearsed all things that God had done with them, and how He had opened a door of faith unto the Gentiles.

To what city did they go next?
How did they return?
What did they do on their return?

And certain men came from Judea and taught, saying, Except ye be circumcised after the custom of Moses, ye cannot be saved. And the brethren appointed Paul and **Paul and Barnabas Go Up to Jerusalem.** Barnabas to go up to Jerusalem unto the apostles and elders about this question. And the apostles and the elders were gathered together to consider of the matter. And when there had been much questioning, Peter rose up and said, Brethren, God made no distinction between us and the Gentiles. Now therefore why tempt ye God? We believe that we shall be saved through the grace of the Lord Jesus, in like manner as they.

Explain why Paul and Barnabas were sent up to Jerusalem.
What did Peter say in the council?

And James answered, My judgment is that we trouble **The Council at Jerusalem.** not them which from among the Gentiles turn to God; but that we write to them that they abstain from the pollutions of idols, and from fornication, and from things strangled, and from blood. And they wrote. And Paul and Barnabas tarried in Antioch, teaching and preaching the Word of the Lord, with many others also.

What did James say?

After some days Paul said unto Barnabas, Let us visit

Where were Paul and Barnabas laboring?

h

TWENTY-THIRD SUNDAY.

How did they start out on the second missionary journey?

Whom did Paul find at Lystra?

the brethren in every city wherein we proclaimed the Word, and see how they fare. And Barnabas took Mark with him and sailed away unto Cyprus; but Paul chose Silas and went through Syria and Cilicia, confirming the churches. And he came also to Derbe and to Lystra. And a certain disciple was there named Timothy, the son of a Jewess which believed; but his father was a Greek. Him would Paul have to go forth with him. And as they went on their way through the cities, they delivered the decrees which had been ordained of the apostles and elders that were at Jerusalem. So the churches were strengthened in the faith and increased in number daily.

Second Missionary Journey.

Timothy.

SUMMARY OF EVENTS.

Barnabas and Saul start on the first missionary journey.

They sail to Cyprus, traverse the island and then sail to Perga in Asia Minor.

They travel to the interior reaching the towns of Antioch, Iconium and Lystra.

They return to Antioch in Syria and tell the Church all that God had done with them.

The Church sends them up to Jerusalem with the question concerning the necessity of circumcision.

The Council at Jerusalem decides that circumcision is not necessary.

Paul starts on the second missionary journey.

He comes to Derbe and Lystra and attaches Timothy to himself.

From what part of the Bible is this narrative taken? Acts 13-16.

What shall we call this twenty-third chapter? **The Church Grows in Asia.**

In conclusion, let the teacher again refer to the Scripture and Catechism answers that the scholar has learned.

THE SCRIPTURE TO BE LEARNED.

PAUL'S SPEECH ON MARS HILL.

God that made the world and all things therein, seeing that he is Lord of heaven and earth, dwelleth not in temples made with hands; *How did Paul describe God to the Athenians?*

Neither is worshiped with men's hands, as though he needed anything, seeing he giveth to all life, and breath, and all things;

And hath made of one blood all nations of men for to dwell on all the face of the earth, and hath determined the times before appointed, and the bounds of their habitation;

That they should seek the Lord, if haply they might feel after him, and find him, though he be not far from every one of us:

For in him we live and move and have our being. Acts 17: 24-28.

WHAT THE CATECHISM SAYS.

I am the Lord thy God. Thou shalt have no other gods before me. *What does the Catechism say?*

*Teacher asks the questions until the whole class have recited these parts.

CHAPTER XXIV.
The Church Is Carried to Europe.
PAUL'S SECOND MISSIONARY JOURNEY.

Where did the travelers come to in their second journey?

AND THEY went through Phrygia and Galatia, and passing by Mysia, they came down to Troas. There a vision appeared to Paul in the night. He saw a man of Macedonia _{Come Over and Help Us.} who stood beseeching him, and saying, Come over into Macedonia and help us. Setting sail therefore from Troas, we* made a straight course to Samothracia, and the day following to Neapolis; and from thence to Philippi, which is a city of Macedonia, the first of the district, a Roman colony. And on the Sabbath day we went forth without the gate by a river side, where we supposed there was a place of prayer; and we sat down, and spake unto the women which were come together. And a certain woman named Lydia, a seller of purple, in the city of Thyatira, gave heed unto the things which were spoken by Paul.

Tell how they were called over into Europe.

Tell how they began their work in Philippi.

But a maid having an evil spirit, followed Paul and cried, These men are servants of the Most High God. This she did for many days. But Paul, being sore troubled, turned and said to the spirit, I charge thee in the name of Jesus Christ to come out of her. And it came out that very hour.

But when her masters saw that the hope of their gain

---
*From this point Luke, the writer of the history, seems to have accompanied Paul and Timothy. Hence he says "we."

was gone, they laid hold on Paul and Silas, and dragged them into the market place before the magistrates, and the multitude rose up together against them. And the magistrates commanded to beat them with rods. And when they had laid many stripes upon them, they cast them into prison, charging the jailor to keep them safely. But when it was day, the magistrates sent the sergeants, saying, Let those men go. And the jailor reported the words to Paul. But Paul said, They have beaten us publicly, uncondemned, men that are Romans, and have cast us into prison; and do they now cast us out privily? Nay verily! but let them come themselves and bring us out. And the magistrates feared when they heard that they were Romans, and they came and besought them. And they went out of the prison, and entered into the house of Lydia. And when they had seen the brethren, they departed.

In Jail at Philippi.

Why were Paul and Silas thrown into jail?
Tell the story of the jailor at Philippi.*
Tell of their release and their experience with the Roman magistrates.

Now they came to Thessalonica, where was a synagogue of the Jews; and Paul for three Sabbath days reasoned with them from the Scriptures, alleging that it behooved Christ to suffer and to rise again, and that this Jesus is Christ. Some were persuaded. But the Jews being moved with jealousy, took unto themselves certain vile fellows of the rabble, and set the city on an uproar and assaulted the house of Jason. And the brethren sent away Paul and Silas by night unto Berea. But the Jews of Thessalonica came thither likewise, stirring up the multitudes. Then immediately the brethren sent Paul as far as to the sea, and they brought him to Athens.

At Thessalonica.

What city did they reach next in their travels?
Tell of their experience at Thessalonica.

While Paul waited at Athens, his spirit was provoked

TWENTY-FOURTH SUNDAY.

as he beheld the city full of idols. So he reasoned in the synagogue and in the market place every day. And certain of the Epicurean and Stoic philosophers encountered him. And some said, What would this babbler say? And they brought him to the Areopagus, saying, May we know what this new teaching is? And when they heard of the resurrection of the dead, some mocked and others said, We will hear thee again of this matter. Howbeit certain believed, among whom was Dionysius the Areopagite, and a woman named Damaris, and others.

Tell of Paul's experiences at Athens.
At Athens.

After these things he departed from Athens, and came to Corinth. And he found a certain Jew named Aquila, with his wife Priscilla, and he came unto them; and because he was of the same trade, he abode with them, and they wrought; for by their trade they were tent-makers. And he reasoned in the synagogue every Sabbath. And when the Jews opposed themselves and blasphemed, he said, Your blood be upon your own heads; from henceforth I will go unto the Gentiles. And Crispus the ruler of the synagogue believed in the Lord; and many of the Corinthians believed and were baptized. And Paul dwelt there a year and six months, teaching the Word of God.

At Corinth.
Tell of his labors in Corinth.
How long was Paul in Corinth?

After this yet many days, Paul took his leave of the brethren, and sailed thence for Syria, having shorn his head in Cenchrea: for he had a vow. And they came to Ephesus and he entered into the synagogue and reasoned with the Jews. And when they asked him to abide a longer time, he con-

Paul Sails for Jerusalem.
Tell of Paul's voyage to Jerusalem.

sented not; but saying, I will return again unto you, if God will, he set sail from Ephesus. And when he had landed at Cæsarea, he went up and saluted the Church, and went down to Antioch.

The Jailor at Philippi.

The jailor cast them into the inner prison, and made their feet fast in the stocks. But about midnight Paul and Silas were praying and singing hymns unto God, and the prisoners were listening to them; and suddenly there was a great earthquake And the jailor being roused out of sleep and seeing the prison doors open, drew his sword, and was about to kill himself supposing that the prisoners had escaped. But Paul cried with a loud voice, saying, Do thyself no harm: for we are all here. And he called for lights, and sprang in, and, trembling for fear, fell down before Paul and Silas, and brought them out, and said, Sirs, what must I do to be saved? And they said, Believe on the Lord Jesus, and thou shalt be saved, thou and thy house. And they spake the word of the Lord unto him, with all that were in his house. And he took them the same hour of the night, and washed their stripes; and was baptized, he and all his, immediately. And he brought them into his house, and set meat before them, and rejoiced greatly, believing in God with all his house.

SUMMARY OF EVENTS.

Paul travels through Phrygia and Galatia on his second mission-
A night vision tells him to go over to Europe.   [ary journey.
He comes to Philippi, a Roman colony in Macedonia. Lydia.
Paul and Silas cast into jail.   The jailor.
When released, Paul goes to Thessalonica.
Because of the jealousy of the Jews he is sent to Athens.
He comes to Corinth and teaches there a year and six months.
He sails for Jerusalem to fulfil a vow, stopping at Ephesus on
    the way.

From what part of the Bible is this narrative taken? Acts 16-18.

What shall we call this twenty-fourth chapter? **The Church Is Carried to Europe.**

THE SCRIPTURE TO BE LEARNED.

PAUL'S PERILOUS ADVENTURES.

<small>Enumerate some of the perils of Paul.*</small> Are they ministers of Christ? I am more; in labours more abundant, in stripes above measure, in prisons more frequent, in deaths oft.

In journeyings often, in perils of waters, in perils of robbers, in perils by mine own countrymen, in perils by the heathen, in perils in the city, in perils in the wilderness, in perils in the sea, in perils among false brethren;

In weariness and painfulness, in watchings often, in hunger and thirst, in fastings often, in cold and nakedness.

If I must needs glory, I will glory of the things which concern mine infirmities. 2 Cor. 11:23, 26, 27, 30.

WHAT THE SEVENTH PETITION OF THE CATECHISM SAYS.

<small>What does the Catechism say?</small> We pray in this petition, as in a summary, that our Heavenly Father would deliver us from all manner of evil, whether it affect the body or soul, property or character, and, at last, when the hour of death shall arrive, grant us a happy end, and graciously take us from this world of sorrow to Himself in heaven.

---

*Teacher asks the questions until the whole class have recited these parts.

CHAPTER XXV.

The Apostle of the Gentiles Is Brought to Rome.

THIRD MISSIONARY JOURNEY, AND PAUL A PRISONER.

At Ephesus.

AND PAUL came to Ephesus, and went into the synagogue; and reasoned daily in the school of Tyrannus for the space of two years; so that all they which dwelt in Asia heard the Word of the Lord, both Jews and Greeks.

Where and how long was Paul in Ephesus?

Tell the result of his teaching.

And not a few of them that practiced magical arts brought their books together, and burned them, and they counted the price of them, and found it fifty thousand pieces of silver. So mightily grew the Word of the Lord and prevailed.

And about that time there arose no small stir. For *Demetrius the Silversmith.* Demetrius a silversmith, which made silver shrines of Diana, gathered together the craftsmen of like occupation and said, Sirs, ye know that by this business we have our wealth. And ye see that this Paul hath turned away much people, saying that they be no gods, which are made with hands. And the city was filled with the confusion. And after the uproar was ceased, Paul departed for Macedonia and Greece. And when he had spent three months there, he returned and hastened, if it were possible for him, to be at Jerusalem on the day of Pentecost.

Who was Demetrius?

How did he create a stir?

Where did Paul go?

Whither did he hasten after three months?

TWENTY-FIFTH SUNDAY.

Where did Paul go in Jerusalem?

Where was he found one day?

What exciting events followed?

Describe Paul's removal to Caesarea.

Describe Paul's trial before Felix.

When he was come unto Jerusalem, the brethren received him gladly. And the day following he went in unto James; and all the elders were present. And Paul rehearsed the things which God had wrought among the Gentiles. And they glorified God. **Paul Received Gladly in Jerusalem.** But the Jews from Asia saw him in the temple and laid hands on him, crying out, Men of Israel, help! This is the man that teacheth all men everywhere against the people and the law, and this place. And all the city was moved and the people dragged him out of the temple. But the chief captain took soldiers and ran down and bound him with two chains and brought him into the castle. **Arrested in the Temple.** On the morrow the captain brought Paul down before the Council. And Paul said, Brethren, I am a Pharisee. Touching the resurrection of the dead I am called in question. And there arose a great dissension. And the chief captain fearing lest Paul should be torn in pieces took him by force and brought him into the castle. Soon thereafter called unto him two of the centurions and said, Make ready two hundred soldiers, and horsemen three score and ten, and at night bring Paul safe unto Felix the governor. **The Soldiers Bring Paul to Caesarea.** And he wrote a letter. So the soldiers took Paul and brought him to the governor and delivered the letter.

After five days the high priest Ananias came down with certain elders, and with an orator, one Tertullus, and they informed the governor against Paul. But Felix deferred them. **Before Felix.** And after certain days he came with Drusilla his wife, which was a Jewess, and sent for Paul and heard him concerning the faith in

TWENTY-FIFTH SUNDAY.

Christ Jesus. And as he reasoned of the judgment to come, Felix was terrified, and answered, Go thy way for this time, and when I have a convenient season, I will call thee unto me. He hoped withal that money would be given him by Paul. But when two years were fulfilled, Felix was succeeded by Porcius Festus. And Festus commanded Paul to be brought. And the Jews stood round about him, bringing many and grievous charges. Festus, desiring to gain favor with the Jews, said, Wilt thou go up to Jerusalem, and there be judged before me? Paul said, I am standing before Cæsar's judgment seat, where I ought to be judged. To the Jews have I done no wrong, as thou very well knowest. I appeal unto Cæsar. Then Festus answered, Thou hast appealed unto Cæsar: Unto Cæsar shalt thou go.

Before Festus.
I Appeal Unto Cæsar.

Describe the trial before Festus.

How did Paul reply to Festus?

And when it was determined to sail for Italy, they delivered Paul to a centurion named Julius. At Myra, the centurion found a ship of Alexandria sailing for Italy; and he put us therein. And when we had sailed slowly many days we came with difficulty to a place called Fair Havens. And because the haven was not commodious to winter in, they weighed anchor when the south wind blew softly. But a tempestuous wind beat down from Crete and caught the ship. And when they labored exceedingly with the storm and neither sun nor stars shone upon them for many days, Paul exhorted them to be of good cheer. When the fourteenth night was come, the sailors surmised that they were drawing near to some country, and hoisting up the foresail to the wind, they made for

They Sail for Italy.

How and under whom did Paul start out for Italy?

The Great Storm.

Describe the great storm.

TWENTY-FIFTH SUNDAY.

Describe the shipwreck. the beach. Lighting upon a place where two seas met, they ran the vessel aground. The soldiers' counsel was to kill the prisoners. But the centurion commanded that they which could swim should cast themselves overboard, and the rest on planks and other things. And they all escaped safe to the land. *The Shipwreck.*

Describe their reception on the island of Malta. The island was called Melita, and the barbarians kindled a fire and received them all, because of the rain and the cold. And after three months they set sail in a ship of Alexandria, and came to Puteoli, and thence to Rome. *Safe on the Island of Malta.*

There the chief of the Jews came to him in his lodging in great number. And he expounded the matter concerning the kingdom of God and of Jesus, from morning till evening. And some believed the things that were spoken, and some disbelieved. And he said, Be it known unto you that this salvation of God is sent unto the Gentiles. *Paul Teaches and Preaches in Rome.*

What did Paul say to the Jews in Rome?

What was the result?

Paul starts on his third missionary journey.

He comes to Ephesus and for two years reasons daily in the school of Tyrannus.

The magicians bring their books together and burn them.

Demetrius the silversmith creates a great stir.

Paul hastens to Jerusalem for Pentecost and is received gladly by the brethren.

The Jews seize him in the temple and the Roman guard with difficulty gets him safely to Felix the governor in Caesarea.

Paul appears before Felix several times.

Before Festus he appeals unto Caesar.

Festus sends him to Rome, but he is shipwrecked on the way.

After being cast on the Island of Malta, he finally reaches Rome and teaches there for two years.

Twenty-Sixth Sunday.

THE SCRIPTURE TO BE LEARNED.

THE SIGNS BEFORE THE LAST DAY.

And there shall be signs in the sun, and in the moon, and in the stars; and upon the earth distress of nations, with perplexity; the sea and the waves roaring; *(What signs shall there be before the last day?*)*

Men's hearts failing them for fear, and for looking after those things which are coming on the earth: for the powers of heaven shall be shaken.

And then shall they see the Son of man coming in a cloud with power and great glory.

And when these things begin to come to pass, then look up, and lift up your heads; for your redemption draweth nigh. Luke 21 : 25-28.

WHAT THE CATECHISM SAYS CONCERNING THE TIME OF THE COMING OF THE KINGDOM OF GOD TO US.

When our heavenly Father gives us His holy Spirit, so that by His grace we believe His holy Word, and live a godly life here on earth, and in heaven forever. *(When is this coming of the Kingdom effected?)*

*Teacher asks the questions until the whole class have recited these parts.

CHAPTER XXVI.

The Final Coming of the Saviour to His Church; and the City of the Living God.

THE END OF THE WORLD. HEAVEN.

In what parts of the world was the gospel preached by the various apostles?

THUS even in Rome also was the Gospel preached by Paul the servant of Jesus Christ. At Jerusalem, Peter, James and John were the apostles of the circumcision and pillars of the church. And James also exhorted the twelve tribes of the Dispersion. Peter likewise taught the sojourners of the Dispersion in Pontus, Galatia, Cappadocia, Asia and Bithynia, and the Church that was at Babylon. John abode and wrought in Ephesus and other of the seven churches which were in Asia.

What prediction of the Lord as to Jerusalem was then fulfilled?

The Church Established.

So then the apostles went forth into all the world and were witnesses of the Lord both in Jerusalem, and in all Judea and Samaria, and to the uttermost part of the earth. Then was fulfilled the saying of the Lord to Jerusalem. Jerusalem was compassed with armies and trodden down of the Gentiles, and her house was left unto her desolate.

Jerusalem Destroyed.

For what is the church now waiting?

How will Christ come, and how shall the resurrection of the dead take place?

The Church waited and she waiteth for the coming of the Lord. Of that day and hour knoweth no man; no, not the angels which are in heaven. The Gospel shall be preached in all the world for a witness, and then shall the end come. Nation shall

The Second Coming of Christ.

TWENTY-SIXTH SUNDAY.

rise up against nation, and kingdom against kingdom. And there shall be signs in the sun, and in the moon, and in the stars. For the powers of heaven shall be shaken. And when these things begin to come to pass, lift up your heads; for your redemption draweth nigh. For the Lord himself shall descend from heaven with a shout, and with the trump of God; and the dead in Christ shall rise first: then we that are alive shall be caught up to meet the Lord. And there shall be a new heaven and a new earth, for the former things shall pass away.

<small>John's Vision.</small> And unto John who was in the isle that was called Patmos and was in the Spirit on the Lord's day, saith the Lord God, Write the things which are and the things which shall come to pass hereafter. <small>To whom and how did God reveal things which shall come to pass?</small>

And he saw one like unto the Son of man, his head white as snow, his eyes as a flame of fire, his voice as the sound of many waters, and his countenance as the sun which shineth in his strength. And He said, Fear not; I am the first and the last. I am He that liveth and was dead; and behold I am alive for evermore; and have the keys of hell and of death. <small>Describe John's vision of the Son of man.</small>

<small>Worthy Is the Lamb That Was Slain.</small> And there was a throne, and one sitting upon the throne. And there was a rainbow about the throne, like an emerald to look upon. And round about the throne were four and twenty elders in white garments and on their heads crowns of gold; and angels ten thousand times ten thousand, and thousands of thousands, saying, Worthy is the Lamb that hath been slain, to receive the power, and riches and wisdom, and might, and honor, and glory, and blessing. <small>Of the throne, and the song of the Lamb.</small>

TWENTY-SIXTH SUNDAY.

Of the blessedness of those that are come out of great tribulation.

And behold a great multitude which no man could number, standing before the throne and before the Lamb, arrayed in white robes, and palms in their hands. And they cry, Salvation unto our God and unto the Lamb. And one of the elders answered, These which are arrayed in white robes are they which came out of the great tribulation and they washed their robes and made them white in the blood of the Lamb. They shall hunger no more, neither thirst any more; neither shall the sun strike upon them, nor any heat: for the Lamb shall be their shepherd, and shall guide them unto fountains of waters of life: and God shall wipe away every tear from their eyes.

Describe the great white throne and the judgment according to the books.

And I saw a great white throne, and him that sat upon it, from whose face the earth and the heaven fled away. And I saw the dead, the great and the small, standing before the throne, and books were opened: and another book was opened, which is the book of life: and the dead were judged out of the things which were written in the books, according to their works. And the sea gave up the dead which were in it; and death and hell gave up the dead which were in them. And they were judged every man according to their works. And if any was not found written in the book of life, he was cast into the lake of fire.

The Great White Throne and the Book of Life.

Describe John's vision of heaven.

And I saw a new heaven and a new earth. And I saw the holy city, new Jerusalem, coming down out of heaven from God, made ready as a bride adorned for her husband. And I heard a great voice out of the throne saying, Behold the tabernacle of God is with men, and He shall dwell with them, and they shall

Heaven.

TWENTY-SIXTH SUNDAY. 131

be His people, and God Himself shall be with them and be their God. And death shall be no more.

And he shewed me the holy city having the glory of God. Her light was like unto a jasper stone, clear as crystal. And the building of the wall was jasper, and the city was pure gold, like unto pure glass, and the twelve gates were twelve pearls. And the street of the city was pure gold. And I saw no temple therein: for the Lord God the Almighty, and the Lamb, are the temple thereof.

And He hath put all enemies under His feet. And when all things shall be subdued unto Him, then shall the Son also Himself be subject unto Him that put all things under Him, that God may be all in all.

Of what did the various parts of the city seem to be built?

How will everything be in the end?

SUMMARY OF EVENTS.

The Church is now established in Judea, and Samaria, and in far off Rome, according to the Saviour's command.
Jerusalem is destroyed.
The Church waits for the second coming of the Lord.
John has a vision of the Son of man and of the Lamb that was slain, and of the multitude washed in His blood.
He sees the Judgment.
He sees the Holy City coming down out of heaven, and describes it and the life in heaven.
All things are subdued unto Christ, and God is all in all.

From what parts of the Bible is this narrative taken? Acts 1, Galatians 2, James 1, I. Peter 1, Luke 21, and the Revelation of St. John The Divine.

What shall we call this twenty-sixth chapter? **The Final Coming of the Saviour to His Church; and the City of the Living God.**

TWENTY-SEVENTH SUNDAY.

THE SCRIPTURE TO BE LEARNED.

GOD, THE CREATOR AND PRESERVER OF THE UNIVERSE.

How does the Psalmist contrast God and man?* Lord, thou hast been our dwelling place in all generations. Before the mountains were brought forth, or ever thou hadst formed the earth and the world, even from everlasting to everlasting, thou art God.

Thou turnest man to destruction; and sayest, Return, ye children of men.

For a thousand years in thy sight are but as yesterday when it is past, and as a watch in the night.

Thou carriest them away as with a flood; they are as a sleep: in the morning they are like grass which groweth up.

In the morning it flourisheth, and groweth up; in the evening it is cut down, and withereth. Ps. 90:1-6.

WHAT THE CATECHISM SAYS.

What does the Catechism say? I believe that God has created me and all that exists; that He has given and still preserves to me my body and soul, with all my limbs and senses, my reason and all the faculties of my mind, together with my raiment, food, home, and family, and all my property; that He daily provides me abundantly with all the necessaries of life, protects me from all danger, and preserves me and guards me against all evil.

*Teacher asks the questions until the whole class have recited these parts.

CHAPTER XXVII.
The History of the World from the First Man to the Flood.

THE GARDEN OF EDEN. THE HIGHLANDS OF ARMENIA. THE PLAIN OF SHINAR. UR OF THE CHALDEES.

IN THE beginning God created the heaven and the earth. And God said, Let the earth bring forth the living creature after his kind: and it was so. And God said, Let Us make man in Our image: and let them have dominion over all the earth. So God created man in His own image, and said, Be fruitful and multiply, and have dominion over every living thing that moveth upon the earth. And on the seventh day God ended His work. And God blessed the seventh day and sanctified it. Thus the heavens and the earth were finished.

Tell the Story of Creation.

God Creates Man.

And the Lord God planted a garden eastward in Eden. And He took the man and put him into the garden to keep it, and commanded, Of every tree thou mayest freely eat: but of the tree of the knowledge of good and evil thou shalt not eat: for in the day that thou eatest thereof thou shalt surely die.

Plants a Garden.

Tell the Story of Man in the Garden of Eden.

Now the serpent said, Ye shall not surely die! And the woman took of the fruit, and gave also unto her husband. And they heard the voice of the Lord God walking in the garden. Unto the serpent He said, I will put enmity between thy seed and the woman's seed; it shall bruise thy head, and

Man is Tempted and Falls.

i   133

TWENTY-SEVENTH SUNDAY.

How was man cursed?

thou shalt bruise his heel. Unto Adam He said, Cursed is the ground for thy sake; in the sweat of thy face shalt thou eat bread; dust thou art, and unto dust shalt thou return. So He drove out the man.

Name three of Adam's sons.

Adam and Eve had two sons, Cain and Abel. Cain rose up against Abel and slew him. And the Lord said, What hast thou done? A fugitive and a vagabond shalt thou be in the earth. And Cain went out from the presence of the Lord and dwelt in the land of Nod.

Cain and Abel.

Tell the Story of Cain.

Who was Seth?

When Adam was a hundred and thirty years old, Eve had a son and called his name Seth. For God, said she, hath appointed me another instead of Abel. And all the days that Adam lived were nine hundred and thirty years: and he died.

Seth.

How long did Adam live?

Seth had sons and daughters. The sixth in descent from Seth was Enoch. Enoch walked with God: and he was not; for God took him. All the days of Enoch were three hundred and sixty-five years. Enoch's son Methuselah reached the greatest age ever attained by man. All his days were nine hundred and sixty-nine years. Methuselah's grandson was Noah. Noah found grace in the eyes of the Lord, for he was a just man.

Who was Enoch?

Methuselah.

Who was Methuselah?

How old was he?

When men began to multiply, God saw that their wickedness was great, and He said unto Noah, Behold I will destroy them. He directed Noah to make an ark three hundred cubits in length into which Noah should go with his sons, and his wife, and his sons' wives, and two of every living thing of all flesh.

Why did God send the Flood?

Noah and the Ark.

What did he tell Noah to do?

At the end of one hundred and twenty years the ark was finished, and the Lord shut Noah in. The same day, the fountains of the great deep were broken up and the windows of heaven were opened, and it rained upon the earth forty days and forty nights. All the high hills that were under the heaven were covered, and Noah only, and they that were with him in the ark, remained alive.

The Flood. — Describe the Flood.

After more than five months, the ark rested upon the mountains of Ararat. Noah opened the window and sent forth a raven and a dove, and, when the earth was dried, went forth out of the ark, and built an altar unto the Lord and offered burnt offerings. God blessed Noah and said, Be fruitful and replenish the earth. I establish my covenant with you. I do set my bow in the cloud. Not any more shall there be a flood to destroy the earth.

Noah Goes Forth. — When and where did the ark land?

Describe what took place between God and Noah.

The sons of Noah were Shem, and Ham, and Japheth. Of them was the earth overspread. As they journeyed from the east, they found a plain in the land of Shinar and dwelt there; and they builded a city, and a tower the name of which is called Babel. But the Lord scattered them abroad. Terah was the eighth in descent from Shem. He was the father of Abraham. He took Abram his son, and Lot his son's son, and went forth from Ur to go into the land of Canaan; and they came unto Haran and dwelt there. And Terah died in Haran.

The Sons of Noah. — Who were the sons of Noah?

Babel. — What was the result of the building of the Tower of Babel?

Terah and Abram. — Tell the story of Terah and his son.

How was the story of Creation probably handed down from Adam to Noah?*

How would Abraham know the Creation story?*

THE STORY TO BE READ.

Methuselah was two hundred and forty-three years old when Adam died, and doubtless often heard him tell of the Garden of Eden, of the forbidden fruit, and how he was driven out of Paradise. Noah was born six hundred years before Methuselah died and may have often heard the history which Adam had told. Noah died one year before Abraham was born. Thus the story of Creation probably passed from Adam to Methuselah, from Methuselah to Noah, and from Noah to Terah, the father of Abraham.

SUMMARY OF EVENTS.

God creates the heavens and the earth. See *Bible Story*.

God plants a garden in Eden.

Man eats the forbidden fruit and falls into sin. See *Bible Story*.

Man is driven out from the garden.

Cain kills Abel. See *Bible Story*.

Seth and his sons. Enoch. Methuselah.

God tells Noah that He will destroy the world.

God sends the Flood. See *Bible Story*.

The sons of Noah, Shem, Ham and Japheth.

The descendants of Noah journey, and build the Tower of Babel. See *Bible Story*.

Terah, the eighth from Shem, journeys from Ur with his son Abram.

The Story of Creation is handed down from Adam to Methuselah, to Noah, to Terah, to Abraham.

From what parts of the Bible is our narrative taken? **The first eleven chapters of Genesis.**

What picture did we have in "Bible Story" referring to this chapter?

What shall we call this twenty-seventh chapter? **The History of the World from the First Man to the Flood.**

In conclusion, let the teacher again refer to the Scripture and Catechism answers that the scholar has learned.

THE SCRIPTURE TO BE LEARNED.

ABRAHAM'S FAITH.

By faith Abraham, when he was called to go out into a place which he should after receive for an inheritance, obeyed; and he went out, not knowing whither he went.

By faith he sojourned in the land of promise, as in a strange country, dwelling in tabernacles with Isaac and Jacob, the heirs with him of the same promise:

For he looked for a city which hath foundations, whose builder and maker is God. Heb. 11 : 8-10.

What can you say of the faith of Abraham? *

HOW THE CATECHISM INTERPRETS THE WORD "AMEN."

That I should be assured that such petitions are acceptable to our heavenly Father, and are heard by Him; for He Himself has commanded us to pray in this manner, and has promised that He will hear us. Amen, Amen, that is, Yea, yea, it shall be so.

What Does the Catechism say of the word "Amen"?

---

*Teacher asks the questions until the whole class have recited these parts.

CHAPTER XXVIII.

The History of the Patriarchs—Abraham.

What did God say, and promise to Abram when Abram was seventy-five years old?

WHEN ABRAM was seventy-five years old God told him to get out of his country and from his kindred and from his father's house to a land that He would show him. So Abram departed. And God promised to make of him a great nation, and make his name great, and said that in him should all the families of the earth be blessed.

What took place at Sichem and at Bethel?

And Abram came into the land of Canaan, and passed through unto the place of Sichem. Here the Lord appeared and said, Unto thy children will I give this land. And Abram builded an altar unto the Lord and removed from thence unto a mountain on the east of Bethel, and pitched his tent. There he builded an altar, calling upon the name of the Lord.

Abram Comes to Canaan.

Into what country did Abram go, and what happened to his wife there?

And he journeyed, going on still toward the south. Because of a grievous famine, he went down into Egypt to sojourn there. Here his wife was taken into Pharaoh's house; but the Lord plagued Pharaoh with great plagues, and Pharaoh said, Take thy wife and go thy way. And Abram, now very rich in cattle, in silver, and in gold, went up out of Egypt to Bethel, where his tent had been at the beginning. There Abram called on the name of the Lord.

In Egypt.

Was Abram wealthy when he went out of Egypt?

And Lot also had herds and flocks and tents, and

138

TWENTY-EIGHTH SUNDAY.

Separates from Lot. there was a strife between the herdmen of Abram and the herdmen of Lot. But Abram said, Let there be no strife. Is not the whole land before thee? Separate from me. Then Lot chose all the plain of Jordan, and pitched his tent toward Sodom. And the Lord told Abram to look toward the north, south, east and west, and that all the land which he saw should be his and his children's forever. And Abram removed his tent and dwelt in the plain in Hebron, and built there an altar.

Tell the story of Abram's separating from Lot.

It came to pass that four kings made war on the kings **Fights the Four Kings** of Sodom and Gomorrah. The latter fled and fell in the slimepits of the vale of Siddim. Then the four kings took all the goods of Sodom, and they took Lot and his goods, and departed. And there came one that had escaped and told Abram. And Abram armed his trained servants, three hundred and eighteen, and pursued them unto Dan, and brought back **Rescues Lot.** his kinsman Lot. Then the word of the Lord came unto Abram, saying, Fear not, Abram; I am thy shield, and thy exceeding great reward. But Abram said, Lord God, what wilt thou give me, seeing I go childless? The Lord said, Look now **"As the Stars."** toward heaven, and tell the stars, if thou be able to number them. So shall thy children be. And Abram believed in the Lord, and He counted it to him for righteousness.

What happened to Lot in Sodom?

What did Abram do?

What did God say to Abram after this victory?

What did Abram reply?

What did God then say?

When Abram was ninety years old, the Lord appeared **Abraham Entertains Angels.** to him and said that his name should be Abraham, and that he should be a father of many nations. Again the Lord appeared to him as

Tell the story of the Lord, the angels, and Abram.

he sat in his tent door in the heat of the day. And lo, three men stood by him. And he entertained them under the tree, and they did eat. And the Lord told Abraham that he would destroy Sodom and Gomorrah because their sin was very grievous. And Abraham said, Peradventure there be fifty righteous within the city, wilt Thou not spare the place? And the Lord said, If I find in Sodom fifty righteous, then will I spare the place for their sakes. And Abraham said, Oh let not the Lord be angry: Peradventure ten shall be found there. He said, I will not destroy it for ten's sake.

How did Abraham plead for Sodom?

Pleads for Sodom.

The next day at sunrise the Lord rained upon Sodom and upon Gomorrah brimstone and fire from out of heaven, and he overthrew those cities, and all the plain. And Abraham got up early in the morning and he looked toward Sodom, and beheld, and, lo, the smoke of the country went up as the smoke of a furnace!

What happened the next day at sunrise?

Sees Sodom Burn.

When Abraham was a hundred years old, his wife Sarah bare him a son in his old age, as the Lord had spoken. And Abraham called the name of his son Isaac. But God tempted Abraham and told him to take his only son Isaac, whom he loved, and offer him for a burnt offering. And Abraham bound Isaac and laid him on the altar. But the Angel of the Lord called unto him and said, Lay not thine hand upon the lad. For now I know that thou fearest God, seeing thou hast not withheld thine only son from me.

Tell the story of Abraham's offering up Isaac.

Offers Up Isaac.

Some years later Abraham buried Sarah his wife in

TWENTY-EIGHTH SUNDAY. 141

Buries Sarah. the field of Machpelah in Hebron, and he was old and well-stricken in years. And he sent his servant Eliezer to Mesopotamia to take a wife for his son Isaac. There Rebekah, gave the servant to drink and watered his camels, and brought him home to **Sends Eliezer** her father. Rebekah's father said, Behold, the **for Rebekah.** thing proceedeth from the Lord. Rebekah is before thee. Take her, and let her be thy master's son's wife. And she became Isaac's wife. Then Abraham died in a good old age, an old man, and full of years. And his sons Isaac and Ishmael buried him in the cave of Machpelah.

Tell what you know of the death of Abraham's wife, and of the marriage of his son Isaac.

Tell what you know of the death of Abraham.

SUMMARY OF EVENTS.

God tells Abram to get out of his country.

Abram comes to Canaan, and builds an altar at Bethel.

Abram goes into Egypt, and on his return separates from Lot.

Abram rescues Lot from captivity under the Four Kings.

God tells Abram that his children shall be as the stars.

Abraham entertains angels, and pleads for Sodom. See *Bible Story.*

God destroys Sodom. See *Bible Story.*

Abraham offers up Isaac. See *Bible Story.*

He buries Sarah. He marries Isaac to Rebekah.

He dies in a good old age.

From what parts of the Bible is our narrative taken? **Gen. Ch. 12—25.**
What picture did we have in "Bible Story" referring to this chapter?
What shall we call this twenty-eighth chapter? **The History of the Patriarch Abraham.**

In conclusion, let the teacher again refer to the Scripture and Catechism answers that the scholar has learned.

Twenty-Ninth Sunday.

THE SCRIPTURE TO BE LEARNED.

PRAISE DUE OUR FATHERS' GOD.

How does the Psalmist exhort us to praise God?* Sing aloud unto God our strength: make a joyful noise unto the God of Jacob. Take a psalm, and bring hither the timbrel, the pleasant harp with the psaltery.

Blow up the trumpet in the new moon, in the time appointed, on our solemn feast day.

For this was a statute for Israel, and a law of the God of Jacob.

This he ordained in Joseph for a testimony, when he went out through the land of Egypt: where I heard a language that I understood not. Ps. 81:1-5.

WHAT THE CATECHISM SAYS.

What does the Catechism say? Honor thy father and thy mother, that thy days may be long upon the land which the Lord thy God giveth thee.

*Teacher asks the questions until the whole class have recited these parts.

CHAPTER XXIX.
The History of Jacob and Joseph.

AFTER Abraham's death, Isaac, the son of Promise, became the head of the Chosen Race. His wife Rebekah had twins. The boys grew, and Esau was a cunning hunter, but Jacob was a plain man, dwelling in tents. One day Esau came in from the field faint and hungry while Jacob was making a pottage of lentiles. Esau asked for the pottage. Jacob said, Sell me thy birthright. Esau said, I am at the point to die: and what profit shall this birthright do me. And he sold the birthright.

What do you know of Isaac's two sons?

The Twin Brothers.

Tell the story of the birthright.

When Isaac was old and would have blessed Esau, and Jacob took the blessing, Esau cried with a bitter cry, Bless me, even me also, O my father! and wept. And Esau hated Jacob because of the blessing, and said, I will slay my brother Jacob.

What happened when Jacob took the blessing?

Rebekah called Jacob, and said, Flee thou to Laban, my brother, until thy brother's fury turn away. And Jacob went out, and lay down to sleep at Bethel, and he dreamed. The Lord said, I am the Lord God of Abraham and of Isaac; the land whereon thou liest, to thee will I give it. In thee and in thy children shall all the families of the earth be blessed. And Jacob came to Laban and married Laban's daughters Leah and Rachel and served Laban twenty years. Then God said, Arise, return unto the land of thy kindred.

Jacob Flees.

Describe the flight of Jacob.

Dreams.

Marries.

Describe Jacob's life with Laban.

143

TWENTY-NINTH SUNDAY.

Tell of Jacob's return, and of his meeting with Esau.

And Jacob sent messengers to Esau, took his wives and his eleven sons, and sent them over the ford Jabbok. And there wrestled one with him until the breaking of the day, and touched the hollow of one of Jacob's thighs and lamed him for life. The stranger said, Thy name shall be Israel: for as a prince hast thou power with God and hast prevailed. And Jacob lifted up his eyes, and behold Esau came, and ran to meet him, and embraced him: and they wept.

Returns to Canaan.

Tell of Jacob's wrestling.

Prevails with God.

God said unto Jacob, Go up to Bethel, and dwell there. So Jacob came to Bethel. And the sons of Jacob were twelve, Reuben, and Simeon, and Levi, and Judah, and Issachar, and Zebulun; Joseph and Benjamin; Dan and Naphtali; Gad and Asher. These are the sons of Jacob.

Where did Jacob go after this?
Tell of Isaac's death.
Name Jacob's sons.

Jacob's Sons.

Jacob loved Joseph more than all his children: for he was the son of his old age. But the brethren hated Joseph. When Jacob sent Joseph down to see whether it was well with them, they said, Let us slay him! But Reuben said, Cast him into this pit. Then they sold him to a company of Ishmaelites for twenty pieces of silver. These brought Joseph into Egypt unto Potiphar, a captain of Pharaoh's guard. Potiphar made him overseer in his house and over all that he had; but because he hearkened not unto his master's bad wife, he was put into the prison where the king's prisoners were bound. After two years the chief of the king's butlers who had been in ward in the prison where Joseph was, remembered Joseph one morning after Pharaoh

Joseph.

Tell the story of Joseph's being sold into Egypt.

Sold.

Tell of Potiphar, and of Joseph in prison.

In Prison.

TWENTY-NINTH SUNDAY.

had dreamed a dream which the wise men of Egypt could not interpret.
How did Joseph happen to be called before Pharaoh?

Then Pharaoh sent and called Joseph. Joseph said, **Before Pharaoh.** What God is about to do He showeth unto Pharaoh. Behold there come seven years of great plenty throughout all of Egypt; and there shall arise after them seven years of famine. Then Pharaoh set Joseph to fill the storehouses of Egypt.
Tell of Joseph before Pharaoh.

So Joseph's brethren came to buy corn among those **They Bow Down Before Joseph.** that came. Joseph saw his brethren, but made himself strange unto them, and spake roughly, and he put them all into ward three days. The third day he said, Go, carry corn, but bring your youngest brother unto me; so shall ye not die. And he took from them Simeon, and bound him before their eyes.
How did Joseph treat his brethren the first time they came?
Whom did he detain?

They came unto their father, and told him all that **Benjamin Must Go.** befel them. Jacob said, Me have ye bereaved of my children: Joseph is not, and Simeon is not, and ye will take Benjamin away! But the famine was sore, and he said, Go again, buy us a little food. Judah said, If thou wilt send our brother with us, we will go. I will be surety for him. The father said, If it must be so, take your brother, and go.
What did Jacob say?

They went down to Egypt, and were brought into **Joseph Sees Benjamin.** Joseph's house; and when Joseph came they gave him the present, and bowed themselves to him to the earth. He said, Is your father well? Is he yet alive? And he saw Benjamin, and said, God be gracious unto thee my son; and he entered into his chamber, and wept there.
Where did Joseph's brethren go again?
How did Joseph treat them the second time?

He commanded the steward to put his cup into Ben-

TWENTY-NINTH SUNDAY.

Tell the story of the silver cup.

jamin's sack's mouth. As soon as the morning was light, the men were sent away. But the steward overtook them and found the cup in Benjamin's sack. Then they rent their clothes and fell before Joseph on the ground. Judah said, O my lord, when I come to my father, and the lad be not with us, he will die. I pray thee, let me abide instead of the lad a bondman to my lord; and let the lad go with his brethren.

The Silver Cup.

What did Judah say?

What did Joseph do?

Then Joseph could not refrain himself, and he said, I am Joseph, your brother, whom ye sold into Egypt. Doth my father yet live? And he fell upon his brother Benjamin's neck and wept.

Joseph Makes Himself Known.

Who heard of all this?

What did he say to Joseph?

And the report was heard in Pharaoh's house, Joseph's brethren are come. It pleased Pharaoh, and he said, Take your father and your households, and come unto me: I will give you the good of the land of Egypt. Jacob said, It is enough; Joseph my son is yet alive: I will go and see him before I die. And the sons of Israel carried Jacob their father, and their little ones, and their goods, and came into Egypt.

Tell the story of Jacob coming into Egypt.

Jacob Moves to Egypt.

Tell of the death of Joseph.

What did he say would happen to the children of Israel?

Joseph lived an hundred and ten years, and said, I die, and God will surely visit you, and bring you unto the land which he sware to Abraham, to Isaac, and to Jacob; and he died, and all his brethren, and all that generation. And the children of Israel waxed exceedingly mighty; and the land was filled with them.

Joseph Dies.

Isaac has twin sons, Jacob and Esau.
Esau sells his birthright to Jacob. Jacob secures the blessing, and flees to Laban. See *Bible Story*.

He dreams at Bethel. He meets and marries Rachel. See *Bible Story*.
After twenty years he returns to Canaan, and meets Esau.
He wrestles with God, who changes his name to Israel.
He has twelve sons. The brothers sell Joseph into Egypt. See *Bible Story*.
Joseph is put in prison and after several years is brought before King Pharaoh to interpret the latter's dream. See *Bible Story*.
Joseph is made ruler of Egypt.
During the famine, Jacob's sons came to Egypt to Joseph to buy corn.
Joseph gives them corn, but says they must bring Benjamin next time.
Again pressed by famine, they bring Benjamin. Joseph sends them back, with the silver cup in Benjamin's sack.
Joseph makes himself known to his brethren. See *Bible Story*.
Jacob accepts Pharaoh's invitation to come and live in Egypt.
Jacob blesses his sons, and dies. Joseph tells them God will bring them back to Canaan, and dies.

From what parts of the Bible is our narrative taken? **Gen. Ch. 25—50.**

THIRTIETH SUNDAY.

THE SCRIPTURE TO BE LEARNED.

THE EXODUS.

When Israel went out of Egypt, the house of Jacob from a people of strange language; Give the Psalmist's version of the Exodus.*

Judah was his sanctuary, and Israel his dominion.

The sea saw it, and fled: Jordan was driven back.

Tremble, thou earth, at the presence of the Lord, at the presence of the God of Jacob;

Which turned the rock into a standing water, the flint into a fountain of waters. From Ps. 114.

WHAT THE CATECHISM SAYS.

Deliver us from evil. What does the Catechism say?

*Teacher asks the questions until the whole class have recited these parts.

CHAPTER XXX.
The Children of Israel Go Out of Egypt.

What did the new King of Egypt say?

THERE arose up a new king over Egypt, which knew not Joseph. He said unto his people, Behold, the people of Israel are more than we. Come on, let us deal wisely with them.

What did the Egyptians do?
With what result?
What order did Pharaoh give?

Therefore the Egyptians set taskmasters over them and made their lives bitter with hard bondage. But the more they afflicted them, the more they multiplied. Then Pharaoh charged his people, saying, Every son that is born ye shall cast into the river.

In Slavery to Pharaoh.

Tell of Moses birth, training, and of his adventure with an Egyptian.

The daughter of Pharaoh walking by the river's side, found a babe in an ark among the flags. She had compassion on it and said, This is one of the Hebrews' children. He became her son, and she called his name Moses. When grown, he went out unto his brethren and looked on their burdens, and spied an Egyptian smiting a Hebrew. He slew the Egyptian, and fled from the face of Pharaoh, and dwelt in the land of Midian.

Moses.

What happened at the fiery bush?

At Horeb the Lord appeared in a flame of fire out of the midst of a bush, and said, I have seen the affliction of my people. I will send thee unto Pharaoh, that thou mayest bring forth my people out of Egypt.

At the Fiery Bush.

What did Moses and Aaron say to Pharaoh?

Moses and Aaron, his brother, went in and told Pharaoh, Thus saith the Lord God of Israel, Let my people go. Pharaoh said, I know not the Lord. Then said the Lord, Now shalt

Moses and Aaron go before Pharaoh.

THIRTIETH SUNDAY.

thou see what I will do to Pharaoh, for with a strong hand shall he let them go.

Aaron cast down his rod before Pharaoh, and it became a serpent. Then the waters of Egypt were turned to blood. Aaron stretched out his hand and the frogs came up and covered the land. And Aaron stretched out his hand and smote the dust, and it became lice. And the Lord sent swarms of flies into the house of Pharaoh and murrain upon the horses and camels and oxen; and blains upon man and upon beast; and thunder and hail and fire, such as there was none like it since Egypt became a nation, and locusts that covered the face of the earth. *(The Ten Plagues.)* *[What did Aaron do? Describe the plagues.]*

But the Lord hardened Pharaoh's heart, and he said, See my face no more. Moses said, Thou hast spoken well, I will see thy face no more. *(Pharaoh Yields.)* *[What at last did Pharaoh say?]*

And about midnight the Lord smote all the firstborn in the land. Pharaoh called for Moses, and said, Go, serve the Lord. *[What happened? What then did Pharaoh say?]*

The children of Israel ate the Lord's Passover, and went out of Egypt about six hundred thousand men. They took their dough in kneading troughs bound up in their clothes upon their shoulders. And God led them about through the way of the wilderness of the Red sea. And Moses took the bones of Joseph with him. The Lord went before them in a pillar of cloud to lead them in the way; and by night in a pillar of fire. *(The Children o Israel Eat the Passover and Go Out of Egypt.)* *[What did Israel do? Describe their departure, and tell whither they went.]*

But the Lord hardened the heart of Pharaoh and he

THIRTIETH SUNDAY.

pursued them with his horses and chariots.
Moses said, Fear not, the Lord shall fight for you, and he stretched out his hand over the sea, and the children of Israel went through the sea upon the dry ground. And the Egyptians pursued, and the sea returned to his strength and covered all the host.

Describe what happened at the Red Sea. — **The Red Sea.**

The children of Israel celebrated their deliverance by a song of triumph and Moses led them into the wilderness, where they suffered greatly from thirst. When they came to Marah, there was bitter water, which God sweetened and they drank. From Marah they came to Elim, where there were twelve wells, and three-score and ten palm trees; and they encamped there by the waters.

What happened at Marah? — **At Marah.**

What did they find at Elim?

When they began their journey again, in the wilderness of Seir, between Elim and Sinai, they murmured against Moses and Aaron, saying, Ye have brought us into this wilderness, to kill this whole assembly with hunger. Then the Lord said, Behold, I will rain bread from heaven; and the people shall gather a portion every day. At even ye shall eat flesh, and in the morning ye shall be filled with bread. And at even the quails came up and covered the camp, and in the morning there lay a small round thing, as small as the frost on the ground, and the taste of it was like wafers made with honey. And the house of Israel called it Manna.

Tell the story of the quails, and of the manna. — **Quails and Manna in the Wilderness.**

Strengthened by this food, they journeyed on until they again began to suffer from lack of water. And they murmured, and Moses cried unto the Lord, What shall I do? They be almost ready to

What was the next incident in their journey? — **Water from the Rock.**

THIRTIETH SUNDAY.

stone me. The Lord told Moses to smite the rock in Horeb with his rod; and water came out of it, and the people drank.

When this danger of death was past, then came Amalek and fought with Israel in Rephidim. And Moses stood on the top of the hill with the rod of God in his hand, and when Moses held up his hand Israel prevailed, but when he let down his hand the Amalekites prevailed. And Aaron and Hur held up his hands steady until the going down of the sun, and Joshua discomfited Amalek with the edge of the sword.

The Amalekites Defeated. — Describe the battle with the Amalekites, and the part that Aaron and Hur took.

In the third month, after they had gone out of Egypt, they came into the wilderness of Sinai, and there Israel camped before the mount.

Reach Sinai. — Where did they come to in the third month?

SUMMARY OF EVENTS.

Four centuries after Joseph, Pharaoh oppresses Israel.
God raises up Moses as a deliverer. See *Bible Story.*
God calls him at the burning bush at Horeb.
Moses and Aaron appear before Pharaoh.
God sends the ten plagues upon Egypt, and Pharaoh yields at last. See *Bible Story.*
The children of Israel eat the Passover and depart at night. See *Bible Story.*
Pharaoh pursues them to the Red Sea.
They journey from the Red Sea to Marah, thence to Elim, thence to the wilderness of Sin, where God sends quails and manna, thence to Horeb. Water gushes from the earth.
At Rephidim they defeat the Amalekites.
In the third month they come to the wilderness of Sinai.

From what part of the Bible is our narrative taken? **Exodus, Chapters 1—19.** What pictures did we have in "Bible Story" referring to this chapter? What shall we call this thirtieth chapter? **The Children of Israel Go Out of Egypt.**

In conclusion, let the teacher again refer to the Scripture and Catechism answers that the scholar has learned.

Thirty-First Sunday.

THE SCRIPTURE TO BE LEARNED,

GOD'S WORD ON SINAI.

<small>What does God say of Himself?*</small>

And God spake all these words, saying,

I am the Lord thy God, which have brought thee out of the land of Egypt, out of the house of bondage.

Thou shalt have no other gods before me.

Thou shalt not make unto thee any graven image, or any likeness of anything that is in heaven above, or that is in the earth beneath, or that is in the water under the earth:

Thou shalt not bow down thyself to them, nor serve them: for I the Lord thy God am a jealous God, visiting the iniquity of the fathers upon the children unto the third and fourth generation of them that hate me;

And shewing mercy unto thousands of them that love me, and keep my commandments. Ex. 20:1-6.

WHAT THE CATECHISM SAYS.

<small>What does the Catechism say?</small>

We should fear, love, and trust in God above all things.

*Teacher asks the questions until the whole class have recited these parts.

CHAPTER XXXI.

The Children of Israel Come to Sinai, and Wander Forty Years in the Wilderness.

THE Lord said, Ye have seen what I did unto the Egyptians, and how I bare you on eagles' wings. Now therefore if ye will obey my voice, then ye shall be a peculiar treasure to me. The people answered, All that the Lord hath spoken, we will do.

The Lord Speaks at Sinai.

What did the Lord say first of all, to Israel at Sinai?

And it came to pass on the third day that Moses brought forth the people to meet with God. And Mt. Sinai was altogether in a smoke, because the Lord descended upon it in fire. The whole mount quaked greatly, and God spake the words beginning I am the Lord thy God, which have brought thee out of the land of Egypt. Moses wrote all the words of the Lord, and read the book to the people and made a blood covenant between them and God. And the glory of the Lord abode upon Mt. Sinai. And Moses went into the midst of the mount, and was in the mount forty days. Here he received instructions concerning the building of the Tabernacle, the offering of sacrifices, and the order of worship for Israel.

The Lord descends in Fire.

Describe the scene on Sinai on the third day.

What commandments did the Lord give? What did Moses do?

Moses in the Mount.

Where did Moses go?

What instructions did he receive?

When the people saw that Moses delayed to come down, they got Aaron to make them a molten calf of gold, and said, These be thy gods, O Israel, and sat down to eat and drink and rose up to play. And Moses came down the mountain side, carry-

The Golden Calf.

What did the people do when Moses was on the Mount?

153

THIRTY-FIRST SUNDAY.

<small>Describe the scene when Moses came down from the Mount.</small> ing two stone tables, upon which God Himself had written the ten commandments; and Joshua said to Moses, There is a noise of war in the camp. As soon as Moses came near he saw the calf, and the dancing. His anger waxed hot. He cast the tables out of his hands and brake them. He took the calf and burnt it. <small>Moses breaks the Tablets.</small> He ground it to powder and made the people drink it.

<small>Tell of the second time that Moses went up into the Mount.</small> And Moses hewed two tables of stone and rose up early and went up, and he was there with the Lord forty days. When he came down the <small>Two Other Tablets.</small> skin of his face shone, and Aaron and the children of Israel were afraid to draw near unto him.

<small>Tell of the offerings for the tabernacle.</small> Then Moses told those among the people of a willing heart to bring an offering unto the Lord. <small>Offerings for a Tabernacle.</small> And they brought bracelets, and rings, and jewels, and blue and purple and scarlet, and fine linen, and goats' hair and skins. And skilled workmen made the tabernacle, the curtains and the altars, and the table of incense, and the golden mercy-seat and cherubims, and the candlestick of gold. Thus was the tabernacle finished.

<small>Tell of the pillar of cloud and of fire.</small> One year after the flight from Egypt the tabernacle was reared up. A cloud covered it, and the <small>The Pillar of Cloud and of Fire.</small> glory of the Lord filled it. When the cloud was taken up from over the tabernacle, the children of Israel went onward in all their journeys; but if the cloud were not taken up, then they journeyed not.

And Moses anointed Aaron and his sons to minister in the priests' office. And the Lord gave the law of the meat offering, and of the sin, trespass, and peace offer-

THIRTY-FIRST SUNDAY. 155

ings. But Nadab and Abihu, sons of Aaron, took their censers, and put fire therein, and offered strange fire before the Lord. And there went out fire from the Lord, and devoured them, and they died.

Nadab and Abihu.

What laws did the Lord give?

Tell of Nadab and Abihu.

And the Lord gave unto Moses laws of food, of purification, of protection from disease, of punishment, of feasts, of the Sabbath, of the Jubilee year, of vows and of tithes. And He said, If ye walk in my statutes, I will give you rain, and the land shall yield her increase, and your threshing shall reach unto the vintage, and the vintage shall reach unto the sowing time. And I will walk among you, and will be your God, and ye shall be my people. If ye shall confess your iniquity, then will I remember my covenant with Jacob, and with Isaac, and with Abraham. I am the Lord.

God Gives Laws.

God Promises and Threatens.

What other laws did God give?

What promise did God make if they would hearken?

What did God say would happen, if they did not hearken?

And He told Moses to take the sum of all the congregation of the children of Israel, by the house of their fathers, from twenty years old and upward all that are able to go forth to war. They that were numbered were six hundred and three thousand five hundred and fifty.

Moses takes a Census.

Tell of the census.

On the twentieth day of the second month, in the second year, the cloud was taken up from off the tabernacle. And the children of Israel took their journey out of the wilderness of Sin. But the people remembered the cucumbers and the melons, and the leeks, and the onions, and the garlic, and the fish, which they did eat in Egypt, and here there was nothing at all but the manna before their eyes. Then

Israel departs from Sinai.

When did Israel's journey again begin?

THIRTY-FIRST SUNDAY.

Why did the people weep?	Moses heard the people weep, every man in the door of his tent. He said unto the Lord,
What did Moses say?	It is too heavy for me. But the Lord said, Is the Lord's hand waxed short? And a wind brought quails from the sea, and the people, all that night and all the next day, gathered the quails. But the wrath of the Lord was kindled, and He smote the
What did the Lord do?	people with a very great plague. And they buried the
What followed?	people that lusted, and journeyed unto Hazeroth.

Side notes: The People Weep. Quails and a Plague.

SUMMARY OF EVENTS.

The Lord speaks to Israel at Sinai.
On the third day He descends in fire upon the quaking mount, and gives the ten commandments.
Moses goes up into the mount, and remains forty days.
As he comes down he sees Israel worshiping the golden calf, and he breaks the tables of stone. See *Bible Story*.
After Israel is punished, Moses goes into the mount again, and brings new tables back with him.
One year after the departure from Egypt, the Tabernacle is erected, and the glory of the Lord fills it.
God gives various laws of worship and life. Nadab and Abihu are destroyed for bringing strange fire.
God promises to bless Israel if they are obedient.
Israel is numbered, and on the twentieth day of the second month of the second year, Israel begins its journey.
The people lust for food. God sends both quails and a plague.

From what parts of the Bible is our narrative taken? **Exodus, Chapters 19—40; the whole of the Book of Leviticus, and Numbers, Chapters 1—11.**
What picture did we have in "Bible Story" referring to this chapter?
What shall we call this thirty-first chapter? **The Children of Israel Come to Sinai and Wander Forty Years in the Wilderness.**
In conclusion, let the teacher again refer to the Scripture and Catechism answers that the scholar has learned.

THE SCRIPTURE TO BE LEARNED.

WE MUST NOT TEMPT GOD AS ISRAEL DID.

Harden not your hearts, as in the provocation, and as in the day of temptation in the wilderness: *(What did God say the children of Israel must not do?)*

When your fathers tempted me, proved me, and saw my work. Forty years long was I grieved with this generation, and said, It is a people that do err in their heart, and they have not known my ways:

Unto whom I sware in my wrath that they should not enter into my rest. Ps. 95:8-11.

WHAT THE CATECHISM SAYS.

God threatens to punish all those who transgress these commandments. We should, therefore, dread His displeasure, and not act contrarily to these commandments. But He promises grace and every blessing to all who keep them. We should, therefore, love and trust in Him, and cheerfully do what He has commanded us. *(What does the Catechism say?)*

*Teacher asks the questions until the whole class have recited these parts.

CHAPTER XXXII.
The Children of Israel Wander Forty Years in the Wilderness.

Where did Israel go?

ISRAEL removed from Hazeroth, and pitched in the wilderness of Paran. There the Lord told Moses to send men of every tribe to spy out the land of Canaan, and see the people and the cities. And be ye of good courage, said He. So the men went up and came unto Hebron, and unto the

Tell the story of the Twelve Spies.

brook of Eshcol, and cut down from thence a branch with one cluster of grapes, and they bare it between two upon a staff; and they brought of the

The Twelve Spies.

Tell what the Spies said.

pomegranates, and of the figs, and returned after forty days. And they showed the fruit of the land, and said, Surely it floweth with milk and honey. But the people be strong, and the cities are walled. The Amalekites dwell in the land of the south; and the Hittites, and the Jebusites, and the Amorites dwell in the mountains; and the Canaanites dwell by the sea and by the banks of Jordan.

What did Caleb say?

Caleb said, Let us go up at once and possess it. But the men with him said, We be not able to go. All the people that we saw are men of a great stature. There we saw the giants, and we were as grasshoppers in their sight.

Why would not Israel go into the land?

This discouraged all the congregation, and the people wept that night. Would God, they said, that we had died in Egypt! Let us make a cap-

Afraid to go Forward.

THIRTY-SECOND SUNDAY. 159

tain and return. At this Joshua and Caleb, who were of them that searched the land, rent their clothes, and said, The land is a good land. If the Lord delight in us, He will bring us into it. Rebel not, neither fear the people of the land. Their defence is departed from them, and the Lord is with us. But the congregation bade stone them with stones.

Joshua and Caleb.

And the glory of the Lord appeared in the tabernacle before all Israel. How long, said the Lord, will this people provoke me? I will disinherit them. All that were numbered from twenty years old upward shall not see the land which I sware unto their fathers, save Caleb and Joshua. But your little ones shall know the land which ye have despised. Forty years shall ye bear your iniquities. Tomorrow turn you and get you into the wilderness by the way of the Red Sea!

Sentenced to Wander Forty Years.

What did the Lord do, because the people were so cowardly?

Now Korah and Abiram rose up before Moses with two hundred and fifty princes, men of renown. They said to Moses and Aaron, Ye take too much upon you, seeing all the congregation is holy. Moses said, Tomorrow the Lord will show who are His, and who is holy. Take your censers, put fire therein, and put incense in them before the Lord tomorrow; and the man whom the Lord doth choose, he shall be holy. Korah and his company took every man his censer, and put fire in them, and stood at the door of the tabernacle with Moses and Aaron. And it came to pass that the ground clave asunder that was under them; and the earth opened her mouth, and swallowed them up.

Korah's Rebellion.

Tell of Korah's rebellion

To show Israel once for all that only the house of

THIRTY-SECOND SUNDAY.

Tell of Aaron's rod.

Aaron was to burn incense and be priests, God bade the head of each of the twelve tribes to bring his rod, or staff, and lay it on the altar in the tabernacle. The next day when Moses entered the tabernacle, he found Aaron's rod bringing forth buds, and blooming blossoms, and yielding almonds, while the others were only dry sticks as before. Then Aaron's rod was placed in the ark, which also contained the pot of manna and the stone tables of the law.

Aaron's Rod Blossoms.

Why did it blossom?

What was in the Ark?

Rejected by God, Israel wandered in the wilderness thirty-eight years longer. And the Lord had compassion even on those whom He had rejected. He fed them with manna, and gave them water out of the rock. At last, in the first month of the fortieth year, the Israelites again came to the southern borders of Canaan and encamped a second time in Kadesh. A new generation had succeeded the one which had been rejected. Now the supply of water failed, and the people murmured. The Lord commanded Moses to take the rod (which had been deposited in the sanctuary) and to speak to the rock. But Moses spoke to the people saying, Hear now ye rebels, and smote the rock with the rod twice. Water gushed out in abundance, and the people drank, with their beasts; but Moses and Aaron were denied entrance to the land of Canaan, for their impatience. Israel was seeking to get into Canaan and Moses sent messengers to the king of Edom, saying, Let us pass through thy country: we will not pass through the fields, or through the vineyards: we will go by the king's highway, and will not turn to the right hand nor

What did the Lord do for thirty-eight years?

What happened in the fortieth year?

At the End of Forty Years.

Tell of Moses bringing water out of the rock.

Moses Struck the Rock.

What punishment was laid on Moses and Aaron?

Edom Refuses Passage.

THIRTY-SECOND SUNDAY.

to the left, until we have passed thy borders. But Edom said, Thou shalt not pass by me, lest I come out against thee with the sword. Thou shalt not go through. So Israel turned away and journeyed unto Mount Hor. Here Aaron died in the top of the mount, and Moses put the priestly garments upon Aaron's eldest son, Eleazar. And all the house of Israel mourned for Aaron thirty days.

What did the King of Edom say?

Death of Aaron. *Whither then did Israel go, and what happened here?*

SUMMARY OF EVENTS.

Caleb, Joshua and the other ten spies go to Canaan, and bring back a large cluster of grapes.

The people are afraid to go up into Canaan.

God therefore condemns them to wander in the wilderness for thirty-eight years; forty years in all.

Korah rebels, and Aaron's rod blossoms.

At the end of the forty years, the new generation of Israel come to the borders of Canaan.

The King of Edom refuses Israel passage through his country. Israel turns to Mt. Hor. Here Aaron dies.

From what parts of the Bible is our narrative taken? **Num. Ch. 13—20.** What shall we call this thirty-second chapter? **The Children of Israel Wander Forty Years in the Wilderness.**
In conclusion, let the teacher again refer to the Scripture and Catechism answers that the scholar has learned.

Thirty-Third Sunday

THE SCRIPTURE TO BE LEARNED.

THE SYMBOL AND ITS FULFILMENT.

Give The Symbol of the Serpent and its Fulfilment in Christ.*

And as Moses lifted up the serpent in the wilderness, even so must the Son of man be lifted up:

That whosoever believeth in him should not perish, but have everlasting life.

For God so loved the world, that he gave his only begotten Son, that whosoever believeth in him should not perish, but have everlasting life. John 3:14-16.

WHAT THE CATECHISM SAYS.

What does the Catechism say?

What are such words and promises of God?

Those which our Lord Jesus Christ spake, as they are recorded in the last chapter of Mark, verse 16:

He that believeth and is baptized, shall be saved; but he that believeth not shall be damned.

*Teacher asks the questions until the whole class have recited these parts.

CHAPTER XXXIII.

The Children of Israel March to the East of Jordan.

At Mt. Hor.

ARAD the Canaanite was king in the South. He heard tell that Israel came. He fought against Israel, but Israel utterly destroyed his cities.

Who was king in the South, and what happened to him?

Then Israel left Mount Hor and journeyed eastward to compass the land of Edom. The soul of the people was much discouraged because of the way, and they again spake against God and against Moses. But the Lord sent fiery serpents which bit the people, and much people died. They said, We have sinned; pray that the Lord take away the serpents. The Lord said, make thee a fiery serpent and set it upon a pole; every one that is bitten, when he looketh upon it, shall live. And Moses made a serpent of brass, and put it upon a pole, and if a serpent had bitten any man, when he beheld the serpent of brass, he lived.

Whither did Israel go?

Fiery Serpents.

Tell about the fiery serpents.

Thereupon the children of Israel set forward. They journeyed and pitched their tents in the wilderness which is before Moab, toward the east. They had compassed the mountains of Edom, and had come to the other side of Arnon, which is the border between Moab and the Amorites. Thence they went into the valley in the country of Moab. And Sihon, king of the Amorites, would not suffer Israel to pass through

On, into Moab.

Describe the coming of the children of Israel into Moab.

THIRTY-THIRD SUNDAY.

What happened to King Sihon, and to Moab?

his border. Israel smote him with the edge of the sword, and possessed his land from Arnon unto Jabbok. Moab was undone, and Israel dwelt in all her cities and in Heshbon, the city of her king.

Sihon.

Then Israel turned and went north by the way of Bashan. There Og, the King of Bashan went out against them. But they smote him, until there was none left alive.

Tell of King Og.

Og.

Where now did the children of Israel go?
What king was afraid?
For whom did he send?

Again the children of Israel set forward, and pitched on the east of Jordan, opposite Jericho. Balak, the king of Moab, was sore afraid, and sent for Balaam, a prophet in Mesopotamia, saying, There is a people come out from Egypt that covers the face of the earth. Come and curse them for me. But God said, Thou shall not go with them; thou shalt not curse the people. So Balaam refused to come. But Balak sent again, and sent more honorable princes, and said, I will promote thee: come, curse this people. Balaam answered, If Balak would give me his house full of silver, I cannot go beyond the word of the Lord. Notwithstanding, that night, God permitted him to go. He rose up in the morning and saddled his ass, and went with the princes of Moab.

On, to the Jordan.

Tell the story of the prophet Balaam.

Balaam.

When Balak heard that Balaam was come, he went out to meet him, and brought him up into the high places of Baal that he might see Israel. And the Lord put a word in Balaam's mouth, and he said, How shall I curse, whom God hath not cursed. Let me die the death of the righteous, and let my last end be like His!

THIRTY-THIRD SUNDAY.   165

Balak said, What hast thou done? And he brought him to the top of Pisgah. Then Balaam said, The Lord is with Israel. He shall rise up as a lion, and shall not lie down until he drink of the blood of the slain. Balak brought Balaam unto the top of Peor. Then Balaam said, How goodly are thy tents, O Jacob. Blessed is he that blesseth thee, and cursed is he that curseth thee.

Then Balak's anger was kindled, and he smote his hands together and said, I called thee to curse mine enemies, and, behold, thou hast altogether blessed them these three times! Balaam said, What the Lord saith that will I speak; and he said, There shall come a star out of Jacob, and a sceptre shall rise out of Israel, and shall smite the corners of Moab, and destroy all the children of Sheth. And Balaam rose up and went to his place.

And God set Joshua before the congregation. Then Israel armed unto the war against the Midianites, and Moses sent them to the war, a thousand of every tribe. And they slew the kings of Midian. *Tell of Joshua's battle with the Midianites.*

Now the children of Reuben and of Gad had a multitude of cattle, and when they saw the land of Gilead, they said, This is a land for cattle, let this land be given unto us for a possession, and bring us not over Jordan. But Moses said, Shall your brethren go to war, and shall ye sit here? They said, We will build sheep-folds here for our cattle, and cities for our little ones, but we will go armed before the children of Israel, until we have brought them unto their place. And Moses gave them the land. *Reuben and Gad ask for Gilead.* *Tell the wish of Reuben and Gad.* *Was their wish granted? On what condition?*

The work of Moses was finished. In the fortieth year,

THIRTY-THIRD SUNDAY.

Tell what you can of Moses' farewell address to Israel. in the eleventh month, he called all Israel together and spake according to all that God had given commandment. He set before them a blessing and a curse. He bade them love the Lord God, who would bring them into the land which He had promised. He wrote the law and delivered it unto the priests. And he said, I am an hundred and twenty years old this day; I can no more go out and come in; also the Lord hath said unto me, Thou shalt not go over this Jordan. The Lord thy God, He will go over before thee; and Joshua. *Moses' Farewell to Israel.*

Tell of the death of Moses. And Moses went up from the plains of Moab unto the mountain of Nebo. And the Lord showed him all the land of Gilead, and the land of Ephraim and Manasseh, and all the land of Judah unto the utmost sea, and said, This is the land which I sware unto Abraham, unto Isaac, and unto Jacob. Here, on the mountain top, Moses, the servant of God, died. And the Lord buried him. His eye was not dim, nor his natural force abated. And Israel wept for Moses thirty days. *Death of Moses.*

> Israel destroys the Canaanites, marches round the south of Edom, and for disobedient murmuring is bitten by fiery serpents. The brazen serpent.
> They come into the country of Moab on the east of Jordan, and smite Sihon king of the Amorites, and Og king of Bashan.
> They come to the Jordan opposite Jericho.
> Balak king of Moab, sends for the prophet Balaam.
> Joshua slays the kings of Midian.
> Reuben and Gad get the land of Gilead.
> Moses makes his farewell address, and dies on Mt. Pisgah.

> From what parts of the Bible is our narrative taken? **Numbers, Chapters 20-36 and the whole Book of Deuteronomy.**
> What shall we call this thirty-third chapter? **The Children of Israel March to the East of Jordan.**

Thirty-Fourth Sunday.

THE SCRIPTURE TO BE LEARNED.

THE FULFILMENT OF THE PROMISE.

For he remembered his holy promise, and Abraham, his servant. *How did God fulfil His Promise to Israel?**

And he brought forth his people with joy, and his chosen with gladness:

And gave them the lands of the heathen: and they inherited the labour of the people;

That they might observe his statutes, and keep his laws. Praise ye the Lord. Ps. 105: 42-45.

WHAT THE CATECHISM SAYS CONCERNING THE WILL OF GOD.

When God frustrates and brings to naught every evil counsel and purpose, which would hinder us from hallowing the name of God, and prevent His kingdom from coming to us, such as the will of the devil, of the world, and of our own flesh; and when He strengthens us, and keeps us steadfast in His Word and in the faith, even unto our end. This is His gracious and good will. *What does the Catechism say?*

*Teacher asks the questions until the whole class have recited these parts.

CHAPTER XXXIV.

The Children of Israel Enter the Promised Land.

What three things did the Lord tell Joshua to do?

NOW the Lord spake unto Joshua, Moses my servant is dead; arise, go over this Jordan, thou, and all this people, unto the land which I do give them. This book of the law shall not depart out of thy mouth. Be strong and of a good courage: for the Lord thy God is with thee.

Then Joshua commanded the officers of the people saying, Prepare your victuals; for within three days ye shall pass over this Jordan. And when the people removed from their tents, and the priests bearing the ark of the covenant before the people were come unto Jordan, and the feet of the priests were dipped in the brim of the water, the waters which came down from above stood and rose up upon an heap very far, and those that came down toward the salt sea, failed, and were cut off. And all the Israelites passed over on dry ground. And when the priests' feet were lifted up unto the dry land, the waters of Jordan returned to their place, and flowed as they did before. And the children of Israel kept the passover; and they did eat of the old corn of the land. And the manna ceased.

Describe the crossing of the Jordan. *Joshua to go over Jordan.*

What did the children of Israel keep on the other side of Jordan?
What ceased?

Now Jericho was straitly shut up because of the children of Israel. And the Lord said unto Joshua, See, I have given into thine hand

Describe the Fall of Jericho. *Jericho Taken*

Jericho, and ye shall compass the city, all ye men of war, and go round about the city once. Thus shalt thou do six days. And the seventh day ye shall compass the city seven times, and the priests shall blow with the trumpets. And all the people shall shout; and the wall of the city shall fall down flat.

And so they did. And on the seventh day they compassed the city seven times. And at the seventh time, when the priests blew the trumpets, Joshua said unto the people, Shout. So the people shouted; and the wall fell down flat, and they took the city, and burned it with fire.

The Lord had commanded that all the property of the inhabitants of Jericho should be destroyed or be placed in His treasury. One man, named Achan, transgressed this command by keeping back a Babylonish garment, two hundred shekels of silver, and a wedge of gold. These he coveted, and took and hid in the earth in the midst of his tent. But when Joshua sent three thousand men to take the city of Ai, the men of Ai smote and chased them. Joshua came to God. God told him that one man had kept back a portion of the spoil. Joshua drew lots first among the twelve tribes and then among the families. The lot fell on Achan, and he confessed. Joshua sent messengers and they ran unto the tent and found the spoil. He was punished by being stoned to death with all his family.

Achan's Sin. — *What was Achan's sin, and what followed it?*

Then Joshua again led an army of thirty thousand against Ai, and took it. Having gained this foothold in the valley of the Jordan, Joshua built an altar in mount Ebal, and read all the book of the

Joshua at Ai.

THIRTY-FOURTH SUNDAY.

What did Joshua do at Ai?

law of Moses, the blessings and the cursings, to the congregation of Israel. **Reads the Law at Mt. Ebal.**

What did he do at Mt. Ebal?

When all the kings which were on this side of Jordan, in the hills, and in the valleys, and on the coasts of the great sea, heard of Joshua's advance, they gathered themselves together to fight with Joshua, with one accord. But the five kings of the Amorites **Joshua Fights the Five Kings.**

Who gathered themselves to fight against Joshua?

were overwhelmed by a hailstorm, which the Lord sent and which was so violent that there were more which died with hailstones than they whom the children of Is-

Describe the battle.

rael slew with the sword. Then spake Joshua and said in the sight of Israel, Sun, stand thou still **The Sun and Moon Stand** upon Gibeon. And the sun stood still, and **Still.** hasted not to go down about a whole day, until the people had avenged themselves upon their enemies. The five kings fled and hid themselves in a cave, where they were found, and taken out and hanged on trees.

And Joshua smote all the country of the hills and of

What became of the five kings?

the south, and of the vale, and of the springs, **onquers the Promised** and all their kings, because the Lord fought **Land.** for Israel. Thus Joshua conquered the Promised Land. And he called the heads of the ten tribes and gave out

What became the possession of Israel, and why?

by lot the land unto each tribe. And Hebron was given unto Caleb. But the tribe of Levi received no part, for the priesthood of the Lord was their inheritance. And

Describe the portioning out of the land.

the Lord gave unto Israel all the land which **The Land** he sware to give unto their fathers; and they **Divided.** possessed it and dwelt therein. There failed not of any good thing which the Lord had spoken unto Israel.

Then Joshua sent the warriors of Reuben and Gad to

THIRTY-FOURTH SUNDAY. 171

Gathers Israel and Rehearses the Promises. their tents on the other side of Jordan, and he gathered all the tribes of Israel to Shechem and rehearsed unto them their history and the Lord's fulfilment of the promises from Abraham down. And the people chose to serve the God of their fathers. And Joshua made a covenant, and wrote the words in the book of the law of God, and set up a great stone under an oak that was by the sanctuary of the Lord.

And Joshua, the son of Nun, the servant of the Lord, **Joshua Dies.** died, being an hundred and ten years old. And they buried him in Mount Ephraim. And the bones of Joseph buried they in Shechem, in the land which had been promised unto Abraham and Isaac and Jacob.

Where did Reuben and Gad go?

What was done at Shechem?

Describe Joshua's death.

Where were the bones of Joseph buried?

SUMMARY OF EVENTS.

God commands Joshua to take Israel over the Jordan into the Promised Land. They pass over on dry ground. The manna ceases.

They take Jericho. See *Bible History*. Achan sins.

They capture Ai. Joshua reads the Law of Moses to Israel.

Joshua fights the five kings of the Amorites. The sun and moon stand still. See *Bible Story*.

Joshua conquers the Promised Land and divides it out.

Joshua sends the men of Reuben and Gad to their lands.

Joshua gathers all Israel to Shechem and rehearses the promises to them. Joshua dies.

From what part of the Bible is our narrative taken? **The whole of the Book of Joshua.**

What shall we call this thirty-fourth chapter? **The Children of Israel enter the Promised Land.**

Thirty-Fifth Sunday.

THE SCRIPTURE TO BE LEARNED

THE FAITH OF THE JUDGES.

<small>How should the faith of the Judges inspire us?*</small>

Gideon, Barak, Samson, and Jephthah, who through faith subdued kingdoms, wrought righteousness, obtained promises, . . . escaped the edge of the sword, out of weakness were made strong.

Wherefore seeing we also are compassed about with so great a cloud of witnesses, let us lay aside every weight, and the sin which doth so easily beset us, and let us run with patience the race that is set before us, looking unto Jesus the author and finisher of our faith.

Hebrews 11 : 32-34, 12 : 1, 2.

WHAT THE CATECHISM SAYS.

<small>What does the Catechism say?</small>

The good and gracious will of God is done indeed without our prayer; but we pray in this petition that it may be done by us also.

*Teacher asks the questions until the whole class have recited these parts.

CHAPTER XXXV.

The Children of Israel Under the Judges.

ALL the generation of Joshua were gathered unto their fathers, and there arose another generation which followed the gods of the people round about them. The anger of the Lord was hot against Israel, and He gave them into the hands of their enemies. Nevertheless, the Lord raised up judges, which delivered them out of the land of those that spoiled them. But they hearkened not unto the Lord. Therefore God left the Perizzites and the Canaanites in the land. And the Israelites fell into the hands of the king of Mesopotamia, and were in slavery for eight years. Then the Lord heard their cries, and sent Othniel, a nephew of Caleb, who ruled them wisely. He died forty years after Joshua.

Why was Israel given over to her enemies?
Whom did God raise up to deliver them?
Israel Disobedient.
Who enslaved the Israelites?
Othniel.
What do you know of Othniel?

But again Israel fell into idolatry, and became the servant of the king of Moab for eighteen years—until Ehud came, made a dagger and hid it under his garments, and went to the king's summer parlour and killed the king with his left hand, while he offered him a present of tribute with his right hand. Then he blew a trumpet in the mountain of Ephraim and gathered the Israelites and they took the fords of Jordan, and subdued the Moabites. After him the judge was Sham-

What do you know of Ehud?
Ehud.

THIRTY-FIFTH SUNDAY.

gar, who slew six hundred Philistines with an ox-goad.

But they again did evil, and God gave them into the hand of the king of Canaan, and Sisera, the captain of the king's host had nine hundred chariots of iron, and oppressed Israel for twenty years.

Tell the story of Deborah, Barak and Sisera.

Sisera.

Deborah, the prophetess, who dwelt under the palm tree, judged Israel at that time. She sent for Barak and told him to go to Mount Tabor with ten thousand of the tribes of Naphtali and Zebulun, for the Lord would deliver Sisera, with his chariots and his multitude, into Barak's hands. Barak said, If thou wilt go go with me, then I will go. She said, I will.

Deborah.

Sisera gathered his chariots and people. Deborah said unto Barak, Up! for this is the day. Is not the Lord gone out before thee? So Barak went down from Mount Tabor, and ten thousand men after him. And the stars in their courses fought against Sisera. The river of Kishon swept them away. Their horsehoofs were broken by means of their plungings. The Lord discomfited all the host with the edge of the sword before Barak.

Tell how Sisera's life was ended.

Sisera lighted down off his chariot and fled to the tent of Jael, the wife of Heber, the Kenite. And, Jael went out to meet him and said, Turn in, my lord! And she covered him with a mantle, and stood in the door of the tent. Then she took a nail of the tent, and took a hammer in her hand, and went softly unto him, and smote the nail into his temples: for he was fast asleep and weary. So he died. And the hand of Israel prevailed against the king of Canaan, and on that day sang Deborah and Barak a song of triumph.

Jael Kills Sisera.

What did Deborah and Barak do on hearing the good news?

The land had rest forty years. But Israel again did evil,

THIRTY-FIFTH SUNDAY.

Gideon. and the Midianites and children of the east came up as grasshoppers for multitude and encamped in Israel's harvest. Israel cried unto the Lord. And the angel of the Lord appeared unto Gideon as he threshed wheat by the winepress, to hide it from the Midianites, and said, Go in this thy might, and thou shalt save Israel. Gideon asked for a sign. And a fire rose up out of the rock and consumed his offering. Then Gideon built an altar unto the Lord and threw down the altar of Baal. And God gave Gideon the sign of the wet and of the dry fleece. The spirit of the Lord came upon him, and he blew a trumpet, and sent out messengers throughout Manasseh; and unto Asher, and unto Zebulun and unto Naphtali, and they came up to meet him.

Why and how did the Lord call Gideon?

What signs did the Lord give to Gideon?

How and from where did Gideon gather an army?

But the Lord said, The people that are with thee are too many for me to give the Midianites into their hands, lest Israel vaunt. And Gideon proclaimed, Whosoever is fearful, let him go home. There returned twenty and two thousand. The Lord said, The people are yet too many. Bring them down unto the water. Every one that lappeth of the water with his tongue, as a dog, him shalt thou set by himself. The number were three hundred. The Lord said, By the three hundred will I save you.

What did the Lord do with Gideon's army?

The host of Midian was beneath in the valley. They lay along the valley like grasshoppers; and their camels were without number, as the sand by the seaside for multitude. That same night Gideon divided the three hundred men into three companies, and he put a trumpet in every man's hand, with empty pitchers, and lamps within the pitchers.

Tell of the battle between Gideon and the Midianites.

So they came to the outside of the camp, and they

THIRTY-FIFTH SUNDAY.

blew the trumpets, and brake the pitchers, and held the lamps, and stood every man in his place. And all the host ran, and cried, and fled. And the Lord set every man's sword against his fellow, throughout the host.

What did Israel wish Gideon to be? Then the men of Israel said unto Gideon, Rule thou over us, for thou hast delivered us from the hand of Midian. Gideon said, I will not rule over you, neither shall my son rule over you: the Lord shall rule over you.

What do you know of Abimelech? But Abimelech one of the sons of Gideon, wickedly slew all his brothers, and reigned over Israel until a woman threw a piece of a millstone down from a tower at Thebez, and crushed his skull.   *Abimelech.*

SUMMARY OF EVENTS.

In time, Israel disobeys the Law of God, and the Lord gives them into the hands of their enemies.
The Lord delivers Israel by raising up a long line of Judges.
Othniel, Caleb's nephew, becomes Judge, and rules wisely.
Ehud slays the king of Moab with a dagger.
Deborah and Barak defeat Sisera, who is slain in a tent.
The land has rest for forty years. Then Israel again does evil.
God raises up Gideon. Gideon gets the signs of the fire, and of the fleece.
God reduces Gideon's host to three hundred.
Gideon's three hundred conquer the host of Midianites.
Gideon refuses to rule Israel as king.
Abimelech rules Israel until his skull is crushed at Thebez.

From what parts of the Bible is our narrative taken? **Judges, Ch. 1—9.**
There are no pictures in "Bible Story" referring to this chapter.
What shall we call this thirty-fifth chapter? **The Children of Israel Under the Judges.**
In conclusion, let the teacher again refer to the Scripture and Catechism answers that the scholar has learned.

Thirty-Sixth Sunday.

THE SCRIPTURE TO BE LEARNED.

THE DEVOTION OF RUTH.

And Ruth said, Intreat me not to leave thee, or to return from following after thee: for whither thou goest, I will go; and where thou lodgest, I will lodge: thy people shall be my people, and thy God my God: Where thou diest, will I die, and there will I be buried: the Lord do so to me, and more also, if aught but death part thee and me. Ruth 1:16-17.

<small>How did Ruth assert her devotion?*</small>

WHAT THE CATECHISM SAYS.

We should so fear and love God as not to despise nor displease our parents and superiors, but honor, serve, obey, love, and esteem them.

<small>What does the Catechism say?</small>

---

*Teacher asks the questions until the whole class have recited these parts.

CHAPTER XXXVI.
The Times of the Judges: Ruth, Jephthah, Eli and Samson.

Tell the story of Ruth and Naomi.

IN THE days of the judges a man of Bethlehem, named Elimelech, together with his wife Naomi and his two sons, went to the country of Moab, because there was a famine in the land. The two sons married Orpah and Ruth, two of the women of Moab. The father died; his two sons also died; and Naomi returned to her country. The two widowed daughters proposed to go with her. Naomi said, Turn again my daughters to your own country. Orpah kissed her and remained behind. But Ruth clave unto her and said, Entreat me not to leave thee: for whither thou goest, I will go; and where thou lodgest, I will lodge: thy people shall be my people, and thy God my God: where thou diest, will I die, and there will I be buried, So they two came to Bethlehem. And Ruth went into the field to glean ears of corn after the reapers, and she came into the field of Boaz and found grace in his sight. And Naomi said, The man is near of kin to us. And Boaz said, I will do the part of a kinsman, and he went to the elders in the gate and made a compact to marry Ruth, and thus Ruth the Moabitess became the great grandmother of king David.

Ruth.

After Abimelech, there arose to defend Israel Tola.

178

THIRTY-SIXTH SUNDAY. 179

**Tola.
Jair.** He dwelt in Mount Ephraim and judged Israel twenty and three years. And after him arose Jair, a Gileadite, and judged Israel twenty and two years. He had thirty sons that rode on thirty colts, and they had thirty cities.

Who followed Abimalech as judge?
Who followed Tola?

And the children of Israel served Baal, and the gods **Israel Serves** of Syria, and the gods of Sidon, and the gods **Baal.** of Moab, and the gods of the children of Ammon, and forsook the Lord. The anger of the Lord was **The Lord** hot against them, and he sold them into the **is Angry.** hands of the Philistines.

How did Israel make the Lord angry?

By doing evil again, the children of Israel fell into the hands of the Ammonites. And Israel cried unto the Lord, We have sinned against thee. The Lord said, **Jephthah.** Did I not deliver you from the Egyptians, and from the Amorites, and from the Amalekites? Yet ye have forsaken me. Go and cry unto the gods which ye have chosen: let them deliver you. But Israel said, We have sinned. Do thou unto us whatsoever seemeth good; only deliver us. The Lord had compassion upon them and sent Jephthah, the Gileadite, a mighty man of valor, to bring victory to their armies. And Jephthah made a vow, promising to sacrifice whatsoever came forth from the doors of his house to meet him, when he returned from conquering the children of Ammon. And the Lord delivered the Ammonites into his hands and he smote twenty towns with great slaughter, and subdued them. And he came to Mizpeh to his house, and, behold, his daughter came out to meet him: and she was his only child. He rent his clothes and said, Alas, my daughter! He did with her according to the vow which he had vowed. After judging

Whom did God raise up to deliver Israel from the Ammonites?

Tell the story of Jephthah's vow.

THIRTY-SIXTH SUNDAY.

How long did Jephthah judge Israel, and how many judges succeeded him?

What happened then?

Who was Samson?

Samson.

What mighty things did he do?

How did the Philistines capture him?

Tell the story of the remainder of his life.

Israel six years, Jephthah died, and was succeeded by three judges. The children of Israel again fell into the hands of the Philistines. The time of their bondage was forty years. Eli, a good but weak man, was the high priest. Samson, the son of a Danite, was called by God to deliver Israel. From birth his hair was never to be cut, according to the vow of the Nazarite, and here was the secret of his strength. He tore the jaws of a lion apart. He caught three hundred foxes and tied burning brands to their tails. He permitted the men of Judah to bind him and deliver him to Israel's enemy, the Philistines. But the Spirit of the Lord came mightily upon him and he broke the cords upon his arms as if they were flax burnt with fire, and seizing the jawbone of an ass, he slew a thousand men. He carried the doors of the gates of Gaza, with the posts and bar, on his shoulders to the top of a hill before Hebron. He walked away with a weaver's pin and web in his hair. But finally he was delivered by Delilah into the hands of the Philistines. They put out his eyes and bound him with fetters of brass and made him grind flour in their prison-house. Praying, Let me die with the Philistines, he pulled down the temple of Dagon upon their heads, and the dead which he slew at his death were more than they which he slew in his life. He judged Israel twenty years.

SUMMARY OF EVENTS.

The Story of Ruth. Naomi's husband and sons die. Ruth returns with her to Bethlehem. She gleans in the field of Boaz. Boaz marries her. Thus she becomes the great-grandmother of King David.

The Lord raises up Jephthah the Gileadite as Judge.

He smites twenty towns of the Ammonites.

His daughter, an only child, comes out to meet him, and he does with her according to his vow.

Jephthah is succeeded by three other judges.

Then Israel falls into slavery to the Philistines for forty years.

God raises up Samson. See *Bible Story*.

From what parts of the Bible is our narrative taken? **The whole of the Book of Ruth and The Judges, Chapters 10—16.**

What picture did we have in "Bible Story" referring to this chapter?

What shall we call this thirty-sixth chapter? **The Times of the Judges: Ruth, Jephthah, Eli and Samson.**

In conclusion, let the teacher again refer to the Scripture and Catechism answers that the scholar has learned.

THE SCRIPTURE TO BE LEARNED.

SAMUEL'S PRAYER AND MONUMENT AT MIZPEH.

<small>What happened at Mizpeh?*</small>
And Samuel said, Gather all Israel to Mizpeh, and I will pray for you unto the Lord.

And the children of Israel said to Samuel, Cease not to cry unto the Lord our God for us, that he will save us out of the hand of the Philistines.

And the men of Israel went out of Mizpeh, and pursued the Philistines, and smote them, until they came under Beth-car.

Then Samuel took a stone, and set it between Mizpeh and Shen, and called the name of it Eben-ezer, saying, Hitherto hath the Lord helped us. I. Sam. 7: 5, 8, 11, 12.

WHAT THE CATECHISM SAYS.

<small>What does the Catechism say?</small>
We pray in this petition, that our heavenly Father would not regard our sins, nor deny us our requests on account of them; for we are not worthy of anything for which we pray, and have not merited it; but that He would grant us all things through grace, although we daily commit much sin, and deserve chastisement alone. We will therefore, on our part, both heartily forgive, and also readily do good to those who may injure or offend us.

CHAPTER XXXVII.
The Children of Israel Under Samuel.

SAMSON was succeeded by Samuel, the last judge and the first prophet. As a child he was brought to the house of the Lord in Shiloh by his mother Hannah.

Who was Samuel?
What do you know of his childhood?

Hophni and Phinehas, the wicked sons of Eli the high priest made themselves sons of Belial. They knew not the Lord. And the sin of the young men was very great. But Eli restrained them not. Eli was old and nearly blind, and the Lord called Samuel while Samuel slept and told him to tell Eli that God would judge his house, and would do a thing at which the ears of every one that heard it would tingle. And Eli said, It is the Lord: let him do what seemeth him good.

Eli and His Sons.

Tell of Eli and his sons.

Samuel grew, and all Israel from Dan to Beer-sheba knew that Samuel was established to be a prophet of the Lord.

Now Israel went out against the Philistines to battle, but was smitten, and lost about four thousand men. The elders of Israel thought they might be more successful if only they had the Ark of the Covenant in their midst. So the people sent to Shiloh for the Ark. And when the two wicked sons of Eli, Hophni and Phinehas, brought it into camp, all Israel shouted with a great shout, so that the earth rang again. But this gladness was turned into mourning. The Philis-

Israel's Terrible Defeat.

Tell of the battle in which Hophni and Phinehas and the ark figured.

THIRTY-SEVENTH SUNDAY.

tines said to one another, Quit yourselves like men, and fight. And Israel was smitten, and there fell of her army thirty thousand men. And the ark of God was taken. And Hophni and Phinehas were slain. And there ran a man to Shiloh and when he came, lo, Eli sat upon a seat by the wayside watching: for his heart trembled for the ark of God. And the man told Eli, Israel is fled before the Philistines, there hath been a great slaughter among the people, and thy two sons, Hophni and Phinehas are dead, and the ark of God is taken.

Tell of Eli's death. And when he made mention of the ark of God, Eli fell from off the seat backward, and broke his neck, and he died. He was ninety-eight *Eli falls dead at Shiloh.* years old, and his eyes were dim. He had judged Israel forty years.

Tell of the son of Phinehas. That day a son was born unto Phinehas. And his mother named him I-cha-bod, for, she said, *The Ark in Philistia.* The glory is departed from Israel: for the ark of God is taken. The Philistines placed the ark in the temple of their god Dagon. But the next day the idol Dagon was fallen on his face before the ark. They *Tell what happened to the ark after it was captured.* set it up again. The following day, Dagon was fallen, and his head and his hands were cut off. And they said, What shall we do with the ark? Wherever it went plagues and calamities went with it. After seven months they put it on a new cart and harnessed two young cows who took the straight way to Beth-shemesh, lowing as they went. When the men of Beth-shemesh were reaping their harvest in the valley, they saw the ark coming and rejoiced. But God smote

THIRTY-SEVENTH SUNDAY.

the men of Beth-shemesh because they looked into the ark. And they were afraid and the ark was taken to Kir-jath-je-a-rim, where it remained for many years.

But Israel could not shake off the yoke of the Philis-

Samuel at Mizpeh. tines. Samuel told them that if they would return to the Lord with all their hearts, and serve Him only, and put away the strange gods, the Lord would deliver them. The people did so, and Samuel said, Gather all Israel to Mizpeh, and I will pray for you. The Philistines had heard that the children of Israel were gathered, and as Samuel was offering up the burnt offering, they drew near to battle. But the Lord

The Battle. thundered with a great thunder, and the Philistines fled. The men of Israel pursued and smote them. Then Samuel took a stone and set it between Mizpeh and Shen, and called it Ebenezer, saying, Hitherto hath the Lord helped us. So the Philistines

Samuel the Judge. were subdued and came no more all the days of Samuel. Samuel judged Israel from year to year.

Tell the story of Samuel and the battle at Mizpeh.

When Samuel was old, he made his sons judges over

Samuel's Sons. Israel, but they walked not in his way, but took bribes and perverted judgment. Then the elders of Israel came to Samuel and said, Thy sons

"Give us a King." walk not in thy ways. Give us a king to judge us.

Tell of Samuel and his sons.

Why did Israel wish a king?

Samuel said, A king will take your sons, and appoint them for himself, for his chariots and horsemen and captains. And he will take your daughters to be confectionaries and cooks. And he will take your fields and your oliveyards—the best of them—and give them

Why did not Samuel favor a king?

THIRTY-SEVENTH SUNDAY.

to his servants. And he will take the tenth of your vineyards and give them to his officers. And he will take your goodliest young men and put them to his work. And ye shall cry out because of your king, and the Lord will not hear you.

What did the people say?

Nevertheless the people said, Nay; but we will have a king over us. They said they wished to be like all the nations, and to have a king who would go out before them to fight their battles. And the Lord said to Samuel, Make them a king.

What did God say?

SUMMARY OF EVENTS.

Samuel, the last judge and first prophet, is consecrated to God in childhood.
The high priest Eli's sons become very wicked, and he does not restrain them.
God calls Samuel and tells him that Eli shall be punished.
Israel is terribly defeated by the Philistines, the ark of God is captured, and the sons of Eli are slain.
Eli falls from his seat backward and breaks his neck when he hears the bad news.
The ark brings great plagues upon the Philistines.
They return it to Israel.
Samuel gathers all Israel to Mizpeh.
There he offers a burnt offering to the Lord, and defeats the Philistines.
Samuel judges Israel, but his sons take bribes.
The people say, "Give us a king."
The Lord said to Samuel, "Make them a king."

From what parts of the Bible is our narrative taken? **I Samuel, Chapters 1-9.**
What picture did we have in "Bible Story" referring to this chapter?
What shall we call this thirty-seventh chapter? **The Children of Israel under Samuel.**

In conclusion, let the teacher again refer to the Scripture and Catechism answers that the scholar has learned.

Thirty-Eighth Sunday.

THE SCRIPTURE TO BE LEARNED.

THE JUDGMENT OF GOD UPON SAUL.

And Samuel said, Hath the Lord as great delight in burnt offerings and sacrifices, as in obeying the voice of the Lord? Behold, to obey is better than sacrifice, and to hearken than the fat of rams. What was Samuel's Message to Saul?*

For rebellion is as the sin of witchcraft, and stubbornness is as iniquity and idolatry. Because thou hast rejected the word of the Lord, he hath also rejected thee from being king. I. Sam. 15: 22-23.

WHAT THE CATECHISM SAYS.

We should so fear and love God, as not to curse, swear, conjure, lie, or deceive, by His name; but call upon Him in every time of need, and worship Him with prayer, praise, and thanksgiving. What does the Catechism say?

*Teacher asks the questions until the whole class have recited these parts.

CHAPTER XXXVIII.

The Children of Israel Under Saul.

How did Saul happen to meet Samuel?

NOT long after the people had asked for a king, a young man came to the prophet Samuel to inquire where he might find his father's asses, which had strayed from their pasture and were lost. When Sam-

What did the Lord say, and Samuel do?

uel saw him, the Lord said, This man shall rule over my people. Samuel took a vial of oil and poured it upon Saul's head and said, The Lord hath anointed thee to be captain over his inheritance.

Samuel Anoints Saul.

Describe the gathering of the people, and the presentation of Saul unto them.

And Samuel called the people together and told them to present themselves before the Lord by their tribes. And Saul the son of Kish was chosen. But when they sought him he could not be found. He had hid himself among the stuff. And they ran, and fetched him thence. And there was not among the children of Israel a goodlier person than he: from his shoulders and upward he was higher than any of the people. And when he stood among them, all the people shouted and said, God save the king.

"God Save the King."

How did Samuel organize the kingdom?

Then Samuel told the people the manner of the kingdom and wrote it in a book, and laid it up before the Lord. And he sent all the people home.

Where did Saul go?

Saul went home to Gibeah with a band of men about him and remained there until messengers came with the tidings that the Ammonites were come up and encamped against Jabesh. Then the spirit of the Lord

THIRTY-EIGHTH SUNDAY. 189

came upon Saul and he sent messengers throughout all the borders of Israel. Three hundred thousand men of Israel and thirty thousand of Judah came out with one accord, and so completely routed the Ammonites that two of them were not left together. Then Samuel took the people to Gilgal, and there they made Saul king before the Lord.

Saul Defeats the Amorites.

When Saul had reigned two years, his son Jonathan smote a garrison of the Philistines. And the Philistines gathered thirty thousand chariots and six thousand horsemen, and people as the sand which is on the sea shore in multitude, to fight with Israel. Saul blew the trumpet throughout all the land, saying, Let the Hebrews hear. The people of Israel were distressed and did hide themselves in caves, and in thickets, and in rocks. They followed Saul trembling. Saul tarried seven days at Gilgal for Samuel, but Samuel came not. The people scattered from Saul. And Saul offered the burnt offering. As soon as he had done so, behold, Samuel came. Samuel said, What hast thou done? Saul said, I saw that the people were scattered from me, and that thou camest not. Samuel said, Thou hast done foolishly: thou hast not kept the commandment of the Lord. Thy kingdom shall not continue. And Samuel went from Gilgal. Saul dared not begin the war. And the Philistines allowed no smith in all the land of Israel, to make swords or spears. On the day of battle there was neither sword nor spear in the hand of any of the people. nor spear in the hand of any of the people.

The Philistines Gather against Israel.

Saul Offers without Samuel.

The Lord Rejects Saul.

It came to pass upon a day that Jonathan the son of

[Side notes: What kind of an army did Saul gather? Who won the battle? What did Jonathan do? What effect had this upon the Philistines? What did Saul then do? Tell the story of Saul offering a burnt offering, and its consequence. Did Israel have an abundance of weapons? Why?]

THIRTY-EIGHTH SUNDAY.

Tell the story of Jonathan and his armour bearer.

Saul decided to end this trouble, and said, Come, let us go over to the Philistines' garrison. But he told not his father. Alone with his armour-bearer he entered the Philistine camp and slew many. And there was a trembling and an earthquake that moment, and the multitude of the Philistines melted away, and they beat one another down. So the Lord saved Israel that day. *Jonathan Surprises the Philistines.*

How did the Lord save Israel?

Having defeated the Philistines Saul fought against all his enemies on every side, and gained victories over the Moabites, Ammonites and Edomites, and delivered Israel. But there was sore war against the Philistines all the days of Saul.

What victories did Saul gain?

Samuel came to Saul with the word of the Lord that he should go and smite Amalek and utterly destroy all that they had. And Saul went with two hundred thousand footmen, and he took Agag the king of the Amalekites alive, and utterly destroyed all the people with the edge of the sword. But he spared Agag, and the best of the sheep, and of the oxen, and all that was good. *Saul Smites the Amalekites.*

Describe the battle with the Amalekites.

Spares Agag.

Describe the trouble about Agag, and the meeting of Samuel and Saul.

Then the Lord told Samuel, It repenteth me that I have set up Saul to be king, for he hath not performed my commandments. And it grieved Samuel and he cried unto the Lord all night. When he rose early to go to meet Saul, Saul said, I have performed the commandment of the Lord. Samuel said, What meaneth then this bleating of the sheep in mine ears? Saul said, The people spared the best to sacrifice unto the Lord. Samuel said, Hath the Lord as great delight in burnt offerings as in

THIRTY-EIGHTH SUNDAY.

Obedience is Better than Sacrifice. obeying his voice? Behold, to obey is better than sacrifice. Saul said, I have sinned. Samuel said, Thou hast rejected the word of the Lord, and the Lord hath rejected thee.

What did Samuel say about obedience?
What followed?

SUMMARY OF EVENTS.

Samuel anoints Saul. Saul hides himself among the baggage. The people bring him out. They shout, God save the king.

Samuel tells the manner of the kingdom.

Saul goes home with a body-guard, but soon gathers three hundred thousand of Israel and completely routs the Ammonites.

Jonathan smites a garrison of Philistines, but the latter gather in great numbers against Israel.

Samuel delays. Saul foolishly offers sacrifice himself.

When Samuel comes, he tells Saul that the Lord will reject him. Saul and the people are afraid to begin battle.

Jonathan and his armour-bearer alone, aided by an earthquake, cause the Philistines to flee.

Saul engages in wars on every side, and delivers Israel.

Saul smites the Amalekites, but spares Agag and some of the spoil, contrary to the Lord's orders.

The Lord, through Samuel, rejects Saul, and tells him that obedience is better than sacrifice.

From what parts of the Bible is our narrative taken? **I. Samuel, Ch. 10—15.** None of these scenes are in "Bible Story."

What shall we call this thirty-eighth chapter? **The Children of Israel under Saul.**

In conclusion, let the teacher again refer to the Scripture and Catechism answers that the scholar has learned.

Thirty-Ninth Sunday.

THE SCRIPTURE TO BE LEARNED.

DAVID'S THANKSGIVING FOR DELIVERANCE.

<small>How does David return thanks for deliverance from Saul's hand?*</small> He delivered me from my strong enemy, and from them which hated me: for they were too strong for me.

They prevented me in the day of my calamity: but the Lord was my stay.

He brought me forth also into a large place: he delivered me, because he delighted in me.

For I have kept the ways of the Lord, and have not wickedly departed from my God. Ps. 18:17, 19, 21.

WHAT THE CATECHISM SAYS.

<small>What does the Catechism say?</small> We should so fear and love God, as not to do our neighbor any bodily harm or injury, but rather assist and comfort him in danger and want.

---

*Teacher asks the questions until the whole class have recited these parts.

CHAPTER XXXIX

The Troubles of Saul and David.

SAMUEL came no more to see Saul. The Lord said, How long wilt thou mourn for Saul? Fill thine horn with oil: I will send thee to Jesse, the Bethlehemite: for I have provided me a king. Samuel went to Bethlehem. Jesse (the grandson of Ruth) made seven of his stalwart sons pass before Samuel. Samuel said, Are here all thy children? He said, There remaineth yet the youngest: he keepeth the sheep. It was David. Samuel said, Fetch him. He sent and brought him in. Now he was of a beautiful countenance. The Lord said, This is he. Then Samuel took the oil and anointed him, and rose up and went to Ramah.

How did Samuel come to anoint David?
Describe the scene.
Samuel Anoints David.

And the Spirit of the Lord came upon David from that day forward. But the Spirit of the Lord departed from Saul. His servants said, Behold an evil spirit from God troubleth thee. Seek out a cunning player on a harp, and he shall play, and thou shalt be well. Wherefore Saul sent unto Jesse and said, Send me thy son. David came to Saul, and Saul loved him greatly, and he became Saul's armour-bearer. And David took a harp and played: so Saul was refreshed, and the evil spirit departed from him.

David Plays on the Harp for Saul.
How did David come to be brought to Saul's palace?

Now the Philistines gathered together their armies to

193

THIRTY-NINTH SUNDAY.

Tell the story of David and Goliath.

battle. And Saul set his men in array against the Philistines. And Goliath of Gath, the champion, defied the armies of Israel for forty days. Saul and all Israel were greatly afraid. Early one morning David left his sheep and came to the trench as the host was going forth to fight. And he went to meet the Philistine, and slang a stone and the stone sunk into Goliath's forehead; and he fell to the earth. The Philistines fled, and the Israelites chased them even unto Gath.

Slays Goliath.

Saul said unto Abner his captain, Whose son is this youth. Abner said, I cannot tell. The king said, Inquire. As David returned, Abner brought him before Saul. Saul said, Whose son art thou, young man? David answered, I am the son of Jesse the Bethlehemite. And Jonathan loved David as his own soul, and Saul took him that day, and would let him go home no more to his father's house. He set him over the men of war. When David returned from the slaughter, the women came out singing, Saul hath slain his thousands and David his ten thousands. But Saul was very wroth at this, and he envied David. The next day David played on the harp for Saul, and Saul cast a javelin at him. But David behaved wisely and all Israel and Judah loved him, and Michal, Saul's daughter, loved him, and David married her.

What was the result of David's bravery?

"David His Ten Thousands."

What made Saul jealous?

Saul Jealous.

Saul's jealousy became so great that he made many attempts to kill David. Warned by Jonathan, David fled from Saul's palace. He secured food and a sword from Abiathar, the high priest, and made his way to the Philistines and to the land of

Where was David obliged to go?

David Flees.

THIRTY-NINTH SUNDAY.

Moab. After many adventures, David fled into the wilderness, where he met Jonathan once again. In the wilderness of Engedi, Saul, who was searching the rocks to kill him, entered a cave and lay down to sleep, where David and his men were hiding in the dark. David cut **Cuts off Saul's Robe.** off a part of Saul's robe. When Saul had gone out of the cave, David showed him the piece of his garment. Saul was moved, and wept, and said, Thou art more righteous than I. Later on Saul again went forth to seek for David, and, as he lay sleeping in a trench in the wilderness of Ziph, David came to him by night and took his spear and his cruse of water, **Takes his Spear and Cruse.** and stood on the top of a hill afar off and cried, The King of Israel is come out as when one doth hunt a partridge in the mountains. And Saul was touched in soul, and said, I have played the fool exceedingly. David and Saul saw each other no more. For David said in his heart, I shall now perish one day by the hand of Saul: there is nothing better for me than that I should speedily escape into the land of the Philis- **David Escapes to the Philistines.** tines. David lived among the Philistines for about a year, fighting the Amalekites.

The Philistines gathered in Shunem and Saul pitched **Saul at Gilboa.** his army in Gilboa. When Saul saw the host of the Philistines, his heart greatly trembled, and when the Lord answered him not, he disguised himself and went by night to the witch at Endor and heard there that on the morrow Israel would be defeated by **The Witch at Endor.** the Philistines, and that he and his sons would die. Then Saul fell straight along on the

Tell the story of David and Saul in the wilderness of Engedi.

Tell the story of David and Saul in the wilderness of Ziph.

Why did David go to the Philistines, and what did he do there?

Tell of Saul at Gilboa.

Tell of Saul's visit to the witch at Endor.

THIRTY-NINTH SUNDAY.

earth, and there was no strength in him.

The Philistines fought against Israel. The men of Israel fled, and fell down slain in mount Gilboa. The enemy followed hard upon Saul and upon his sons. They slew Jonathan and two other sons. And the battle went sore against Saul, and the archers hit him. He said to his armour-bearer, Draw thy sword and thrust me through. But his armour-bearer would not. Therefore Saul took a sword and fell upon it. And the Philistines cut off his head.

And David lamented over Saul and Jonathan, saying: How are the mighty fallen! Tell it not in Gath, publish it not in the streets of Askelon. Ye mountains of Gilboa, let there be no dew upon you. Saul and Jonathan were lovely in their lives, and in their death they were not divided. They were swifter than eagles, they were stronger than lions. How are the mighty fallen, and the weapons of war perished!

Marginal notes: What was the result of the battle. How did Saul die? Repeat the Lament of David. Saul Slain. The Mighty Fallen!

SUMMARY OF EVENTS.

Samuel goes to Bethlehem and asks to see the sons of Jesse.
He anoints David, the youngest. See *Bible Story*.
David is taken to Saul's court, and plays on the harp.
David comes from home to the field of battle, and slays Goliath. See *Bible Story*.
Saul sets David over his men of war.
Saul grows jealous of David, and casts a javelin at him.
David flees to the wilderness, Saul tries to capture him.
David escapes to the Philistines.
Saul gathers his army against the Philistines, at Gilboa.
He visits the witch of Endor.
The battle goes against him. Jonathan is slain.
Saul falls on his sword and dies. David laments him.

What pictures did we have in "Bible Story" referring to this chapter?
What shall we call this thirty-ninth chapter? **The Troubles of Saul and David.**

Fortieth Sunday.

THE SCRIPTURE TO BE LEARNED.

DAVID'S THANKSGIVING FOR THE MERCIES OF GOD.

I will extol thee, O, Lord; for thou hast lifted me up, and hast not made my foes to rejoice over me. *How does David thank God for His mercies?**

O Lord my God, I cried unto thee, and thou hast healed me.

O Lord, thou hast brought up my soul from the grave: thou hast kept me alive, that I should not go down to the pit.

Sing unto the Lord, O ye saints of his, and give thanks at the remembrance of his holiness. Ps. 30: 1-4.

WHAT THE CATECHISM SAYS.

We should so fear and love God, as to be chaste and pure in our words and deeds, each one also loving and honoring his wife or her husband. *What does the Catechism say?*

*Teacher asks the questions until the whole class have recited these parts.

CHAPTER XL.

The Children of Israel Under David.

Tell how David became King of Judah.

WHEN David had lamented for Saul, he inquired of the Lord, Shall I go up into Judah? The Lord said, Go up. David said, Whither? He said, Unto Hebron. And the men of Judah came and anointed David King of Judah. But Abner, the commander of Saul's army, took Ish-bó-sheth, the youngest son of Saul, and made him king over Israel. There was long war between the house of Saul and the house of David; but David waxed stronger and stronger, and when he had reigned over Judah seven years and six months, Ishbosheth was slain.

David Made King.

Describe the reign of David.

Then all the tribes of Israel came to David and made him king. He was thirty years old when he began to reign. He captured Jerusalem, the stronghold of Zion, from the Jebusites.

Tell the story of David's bringing up the ark.

And David went to bring up the ark of God to Jerusalem. He gathered all the chosen men of Israel, thirty thousand. They set the ark upon a new cart and brought it out from Gibeah. Uzzah and Ahio drove the cart, and when they came to Nachon's threshing floor, Uzzah put forth his hand to the ark: for the oxen shook it. And God smote him, and he died. David was displeased, and was afraid of the Lord that day, and would not remove the ark into Jerusalem. After three months David heard that the Lord had blessed the

David Brings Up the Ark.

house where the ark was left, and he went and brought up the ark with gladness.

When the king sat in his palace, and the Lord had given him rest from his enemies, he said to Nathan the prophet, See now, I dwell in a palace of cedar, but the ark of God dwelleth within a tent. *He Wishes to Build a Temple.* *What did David wish to build? Why?* He wished to build a great temple for the ark. Nathan said, Go, do all that is in thine heart. But that night God warned Nathan not to let David build, and said that David's son should build, and that his house and his kingdom should be established forever.

After this David went to war, and enlarged his kingdom until it reached to the Red Sea. He was kind to the descendants of Saul and welcomed them to his own palace. *He Enlarges His Kingdom.* *How did David enlarge his kingdom?* In a series of battles he smote the Philistines and the Moabites and the children of Ammon. Before these wars with the enemies of Israel were entirely ended, he came back to his city, Jerusalem, and sent out his men under his general, Joab.

One eveningtide, while walking upon the roof of his palace, he saw Bathsheba, the wife of Uriah, and he sent messengers and took her. *David's Sin.* *Tell of David's dreadful sin.* And he wrote a letter to Joab, Set ye Uriah in the forefront of the hottest battle, and retire ye from him, that he may be smitten, and die. When the men of the city went out and fought with Joab, there fell some of the servants of David, and Uriah died also.

When the wife of Uriah heard that her husband was dead, she mourned for him. And when the mourning was past, David sent for her, and she became his wife, and bare him a son.

But the thing displeased the Lord, and the Lord sent

FORTIETH SUNDAY.

What parable did Nathan utter to David?

Nathan unto David. He said, There were two men in one city; the one rich, and the other poor. The rich man had exceeding many flocks and herds; but the poor man had nothing, save one little ewe lamb. It did eat of his own meat, and drank of his own cup, and lay in his bosom, and was unto him as a daughter. And there came a traveler unto the rich man, and he spared to take of his own flock and of his own herd, but took the poor man's lamb, and dressed it for the man that was come to him.

Nathan's Parable.

What did David say?

David's anger was greatly kindled, and he said, As the Lord liveth, the man that has done this thing shall surely die. Nathan said to David, Thou art the man. Thou hast slain Uriah with the sword of the children of Ammon, and hast taken his wife to be thy wife. Now therefore the sword shall never depart from thine house. And David said unto Nathan, I have sinned against the Lord.

David Excited.

What did Nathan say?

Thou Art the Man.

What did David reply?

What other punishment did David have in his children?

God gave David a son whom he called Solomon, which means "peace." But there was no more peace for David. His reign was filled with troubles which God sent as a punishment for his sins. His own children, Amnon and beautiful Absalom, gave him great pain. Absalom plotted against him and stirred up a rebellion and forced David to flee from Jerusalem. But while Absalom was living in his father's palace in Jerusalem, David gathered an army on the other side of the Jordan, and placed it under the command of Joab and two other generals. He ordered them to deal gently with Absalom, for David loved him. Absalom was defeated and killed, and David mourned for him so deeply that Joab could scarcely rouse him to

David's Children.

Tell more fully the story of Absalom.

Absalom Rebels.

FORTIETH SUNDAY.

return to Jerusalem in triumph. Soon more trouble came. The tribes of Benjamin and Judah quarreled. David's two generals became jealous of each other and Joab killed Amasa. *(David's Generals.)* *(What other punishments did David have?)*

When David was old and full of days, there was a plot against his son Solomon. And David assembled all the princes and warriors and made Solomon king over Israel. Then he stood up and said, Hear me, my people: I had in my heart to build a house of rest for the ark. But God said, Thou shalt not build because thou hast been a man of war and hast shed blood. Solomon thy son shall build. And thou, Solomon, know thou the God of thy father, and serve him with a perfect heart and with a willing mind. Be strong, and of good courage, and build. *(David Installs Solomon.)* *(What did David do for Solomon?)* *(What did David say to Solomon?)* *(What followed?)*

The people rejoiced, and offered willingly. So David slept with his fathers, and was buried in the city of David.

Abner sets up Ishbosheth, the son of Saul, as king; but he is slain, and David becomes king.
David captures Jerusalem, builds a palace, and grows great.
David brings up the Ark of God to Jerusalem.
David proposes to build a great Temple.
David wages many wars and enlarges his kingdom.
David falls into sin and marries Bathsheba.
Nathan rebukes David, and tells the parable of the ewe lamb.
David is punished for his sin by the death of his child, the wickedness of Amnon and the rebellion of Absalom.
David is obliged to flee from Jerusalem, but in a battle Absalom is slain. See *Bible Story*.
Davids generals Joab and Amasa quarrel.
David places Solomon on his throne and tells him to be strong and build the temple.

From what parts of the Bible is our narrative taken? II Samuel, Chap. 2—24; I Kings, Chap. 1—2; I Chron., Chap. 11—29.
What picture did we have in "Bible Story" referring to this chapter?
What shall we call this fortieth chapter? The Children of Israel under David.

Forty-First Sunday.

THE SCRIPTURE TO BE LEARNED.

GOD'S PROMISE CONCERNING SOLOMON.

When thou shalt sleep with thy fathers, I will set up thy seed after thee. He shall build an house for my name, and I will establish the throne of his kingdom forever. I will be his father, and he shall be my son. If he commit iniquity I will chasten him with the rod of men. . . . But my mercy shall not depart away from him. II. Sam. 7: 12-15.

THE SAVIOUR'S COMMENT ON SOLOMON.

Take no thought for your life, . . . nor yet for your body. . . . Consider the lilies of the field how they grow; they toil not, neither do they spin: and yet I say unto you, That even Solomon in all his glory was not arrayed like one of these. Matt. 6: 25, 28-29.

WHAT THE CATECHISM SAYS.

What does the Catechism say? God gives indeed without our prayer even to the wicked also their daily bread; but we pray in this petition that He would make us sensible of His benefits, and enable us to receive our daily bread with thanksgiving.

*Teacher asks the questions until the whole class have recited these parts.

CHAPTER XLI.

The Children of Israel Under Solomon.

DAVID had died in a good old age, full of days, riches and honour, Solomon his son reigning in his stead. The tribes which had united about the standard of Saul, became organized, in the continuous and successful wars of David, into a powerful empire, with might and dominion over the Canaanite world.

Describe the Empire of Israel.

At ten years of age Solomon fled from Jerusalem with his father, and at fifteen he was anointed to sit on his father's throne. Adonijah his brother sought to wrest the kingdom from him. Solomon forgave Adonijah, but when he sought again to sit upon the throne, Solomon had him put to death that day. In this conspiracy perished Shimei, Saul's last descendant, as well as Joab, David's great captain; and the high priest Abiathar was banished forever. Solomon made an alliance with Pharaoh, king of Egypt, and married his daughter.

Tell the early events in Solomon's reign.

Solomon's Empire and Troubles.

And the Lord God was with him and magnified him. God appeared unto Solomon, and said, Ask what I shall give thee. Solomon said, O Lord God, let thy promise unto David my father be established. Give me now wisdom and knowledge, that I may go out

"What shall I give thee?"

Tell of Solomon's Vision.

and come in before this people. God said, Because this was in thine heart, and thou hast not asked riches, wealth or honour, nor the life of them that hate thee, neither yet hast asked long life, I have done according to thy word. And if thou wilt keep my statutes, I will lengthen thy days.

As he reigned over Jerusalem, two women, with a child, appeared in his Judgment Hall, each claiming it as her own. Solomon said, Divide the child, and give half to the one, and half to the other. Then the woman whose the child was, said, O my lord give the other woman the child. In no wise slay it. The king said, Give it to this one. She is the mother. All Israel heard of the judgment, and they feared the king.

Tell of Solomon as Judge. "Divide The Child."

The king gathered a thousand and four hundred chariots and twelve thousand horsemen. He made silver and gold to be in Jerusalem as stones, and cedars made he to be as sycamore trees. And he reigned over all the kingdoms from the river Euphrates unto the border of Egypt; and Judah and Israel dwelt safely, every man under his vine and under his fig tree, from Dan even unto Beer-sheba, all the days of Solomon.

Tell of the prosperity in Solomon's reign. Silver and Gold as Stones.

In King Solomon's reign there came to him large caravans of merchantmen, and merchants trafficing in spices from Arabia. And the king had at sea a navy of Tarshish, with the navy of King Hiram of Tyre. It sailed out of Joppa, and once in three years came bringing gold and silver, ivory and apes and peacocks. And the navy of Hiram brought gold from Ophir, and precious stones and almug trees of which the king made pillars for the temple and the palace, and harps and

Tell of the trade and commerce of Solomon. Caravans and Navy.

FORTY-FIRST SUNDAY.

psalteries for singers. And Solomon had horses brought out of Egypt, and linen yarn. And the kings of the earth brought tribute to Solomon.

David had left his son Solomon many precious materials for the building of a Temple unto the name of the Lord, and Solomon made a league with Hiram, king of Tyre, who was to cut cedar and fir trees down on the mountains of Lebanon and make them ready and convey them by sea in floats to Joppa, that they might be brought thence to Jerusalem. Behold, the house which I build is great, said Solomon to Hiram, for great is our God above all gods. Send me therefore a master-worker in gold, in silver, in brass, in iron, in purple and crimson and blue, and a skilful engraver. Hiram sent him, and Solomon began to build in the fourth year of his reign. His builders brought great and costly stones for the foundation. It took seven and one-half years to finish building, and one hundred and eighty thousand men were employed on the work. So well was all the material prepared that no sound of axe or hammer was heard from the beginning to the end of the building.

What league did Solomon make with King Hiram of Tyre?

Hiram To Furnish Cedars from Lebanon

Materials for The Temple.

Describe the building of the Temple.

The Temple had a porch held up by two brazen pillars, and a Holy Place, where were the altars for incense, the table for shewbread and the golden candlestick of seven branches. It had the Holy of Holies, wherein stood the ark of the covenant. Around the Temple were the courts in which were the altar of burnt offering and a great brass water basin called sea. The whole building within was overlaid with pure gold.

The Temple.

Describe the Temple.

Thus the Temple was finished, and Solomon brought in the vessels and treasures that David his father had dedi-

FORTY-FIRST SUNDAY.

Tell what you can of the Dedication of the Temple.

cated, and he assembled all Israel, and the Levites brought up the tabernacle to the Temple and put the ark in the most Holy place. And when the priests were come out of the Holy place, the choirs of the Levites, arrayed in fine linen, with cymbals and psalteries and harps, and one hundred and twenty priests sounding with trumpets, lifted up their voice with the instruments, and praised the Lord, saying, For He is good; for His mercy endureth for ever. Then the glory of the Lord filled the house of God. Solomon appointed the courses of the priests to their service, and the Levites to their charges.

Solomon Dedicates it.

Glory of The Lord fills it.

But when Solomon was old, he did evil in God's sight.

How did God punish Solomon?

Wherefore the Lord said unto Solomon, I will rend the kingdom out of the hand of thy son. A prophet came to Jeroboam, and snatched the new mantle off his shoulders, and tore it into twelve pieces. He said to Jeroboam, Take thee ten pieces, for the Lord will rend the kingdom and give ten tribes to thee. Solomon sought to kill Jeroboam, but he fled into Egypt.

Tell of the prophet and Joroboam.

Solomon's Wickedness.

Solomon the ruler of a great empire.
He crushes the conspiracy of Adonijah, Shimei, Joab.
He marries Pharaoh's daughter.
God asks him, "What shall I give thee?"
He judges between the two women each claiming a little child.
He brings safety to all Israel and his fame goes out widely.
He has caravans by land and a navy of gold ships at sea.
With the aid of Hiram king of Tyre, he builds the Temple.
He dedicates the Temple.
The Queen of Sheba visits him. See *Bible Story*.
He does evil and worships idols, to please his wives.
The Lord declares that he will rend Solomon's kingdom.

From what parts of the Bible is our narrative taken? **I Kings, Chapters 2—11, II Chronicles, Chapters 1—9.**

What picture did we have in "Bible Story" referring to this chapter? What shall we call this forty-first chapter? **The Children of Israel Under Solomon.**

Forty-Second Sunday.

THE SCRIPTURE TO BE LEARNED.

JUDAH AND ISRAEL FORSOOK GOD AND WERE FORSAKEN BY HIM.

How hath the Lord covered the daughter of Zion with a cloud in his anger, and cast down from heaven unto the earth the beauty of Israel, and remembered not his footstool in the day of his anger! <small>How did God punish Israel and Judah?*</small>

The Lord hath swallowed up all the habitations of Jacob, and hath not pitied: he hath thrown down in his wrath the strongholds of the daughter of Judah; he hath brought them down to the ground.

He burned against Jacob like a flaming fire, which devoureth round about. . . . Lam. 2: 1-3.

WHAT THE CATECHISM SAYS.

And lead us not into temptation. But deliver us from evil. <small>What does the Catechism say?</small>

---

*Teacher asks the questions until the whole class have recited these parts.

CHAPTER XLII.

The Kingdom of Solomon Divided.

Who was Solomon's son?

What happened at Shechem?

REHOBOAM, son of Solomon, reigned in his father's stead. He went to Shechem, where all Israel was come to make him king. But Israel had called Jeroboam out of Egypt, and with Jeroboam as spokesman, they said to King Rehoboam, Make the heavy yoke of thy father lighter, and we will serve thee. Rehoboam said, Depart for three days, then come again. Rehoboam consulted with the old men, and they advised him, Speak good words to this people, then they will be thy servants forever.

Make the Yoke Lighter, Rehoboam!

What did the old men, and the young men advise?

But Rehoboam consulted with the young men that were grown up with him, and they gave counsel, Thus shalt thou say, My little finger shall be thicker than my father's loins. I will add to your yoke.

What did King Rehoboam say?

So Jeroboam and all the people came to the king the third day, as the king had appointed. And the king answered roughly, and said, My father chastised you with whips, but I will chastise you with scorpions.

Not with Whips but with Scorpions.

Describe the scenes that followed.

Then the people answered, What portion have we in David? To your tents, O Israel! Now see to thine own house! King Rehoboam sent his collector of taxes, and all Israel stoned him with stones, that he died. Then the

FORTY-SECOND SUNDAY.

To Your Tents O Israel! king made speed to get up to his chariot, to flee to Jerusalem. So Israel rebelled against the house of David. And they sent for Jeroboam, and made him king over all Israel: there was none that followed the house of David, but the tribe of Judah only.

[Who still called Rehoboam king?]

Thus the children of Israel were divided thereafter into two kingdoms. The two tribes of Judah and Benjamin remained faithful to David's grandson Rehoboam, and formed the kingdom of Judah. But the other ten tribes chose Jeroboam as their king and formed the kingdom of Israel. The kingdom of Israel was in the north, and was composed of the countries afterward called Samaria and Galilee. King Rehoboam and Judah possessed the capital city Jerusalem.

The Children of Israel Divided into Two.

[Tell of the Division, and describe each of the two kingdoms.]

King Jeroboam (Is.)* built Shechem in Mount Ephraim as his capital. He said to his people, It is too much for you to go up to Jerusalem; and he made two calves of gold, and he set the one in Bethel and the other in Dan, and said, Behold thy gods, O Israel, which brought thee up out of the land of Egypt. And this thing became a sin: for the people went to worship.

Jeroboam Makes Golden Calves.

[What did Jeroboam do to keep his people from Jerusalem?]

[Was this right?]

In Jerusalem King Rehoboam (Ju.) preserved the true worship of the Lord in the Temple, and the priests and the Levites through all Israel left their possessions and their cities and came to him.

[What did King Rehoboam do in Jerusalem?]

Nevertheless he had not been reigning five years before he forsook the law of God, and allowed his people to fall into idolatry. Then the Lord punished him and

[What was Rehoboam's sin?]

---

*From this point on the kings of Judah will be marked Ju.; and the kings of Israel will be marked Is.

FORTY-SECOND SUNDAY.

<small>Who invaded his territory as a punishment?</small>
took away the superiority which Judah had enjoyed over Israel. His territory was invaded by Shishak, the Lybian king of Egypt. <small>Rehoboam Defeated by Egypt.</small>

<small>What followed?</small>
Jerusalem was captured, and the treasures which David and Solomon had collected were taken away to Egypt.

In his stead his son Abijah (Ju.) reigned over Judah.

<small>Who succeeded Abijah in Judah?</small>
But Abijah (Ju.) walked in all the sins of his fathers, and his reign was cut short, and his son Asa (Ju.) reigned in his stead.

<small>What did Asa do?</small>
In his days the land was quiet ten years, and he did that which was right in the eyes of the Lord. <small>Asa King of Judah.</small>

<small>Tell of Asa's army.</small>
And Asa (Ju.) had an army out of Judah of three hundred thousand that bare targets and spears; and two hundred and eighty thousand out of Benjamin that bare shields and drew bows.

<small>Tell of Asa and the Ethiopians.</small>
There came out against them Zerah the Ethiopian, with a host of a thousand thousand. Then Asa (Ju.) went out against them, and he cried, Lord, it is nothing with Thee to help, whether with many, or with them that have no power. Help us, O Lord our God; for we rest on Thee, and in Thy name we go out against this multitude. <small>In Thy Name We Go Against the Multitude.</small>

So the Lord smote the Ethiopians, and they fled and were overthrown and destroyed before the Lord. And there was no more war unto the thirty-fifth year of his reign.

<small>How did Asa get rid of King Baasha?</small>
The next year Baasha, king of Israel came up against Asa. Then Asa (Ju.) took silver and gold out of the treasures of the Temple and his palace and sent them to Ben-hadad, king of Syria, and bribed him to break his league with Baasha (Is.). <small>Asa Bribes Ben-hadad.</small>

<small>What did a prophet tell Asa?</small>
Ben-hadad hearkened unto Asa (Ju.) and smote the cities of Baasha (Is.).

But a seer came to Asa (Ju.) and said, Because thou hast relied on the king of Syria, and not on the Lord, thou hast done foolishly: therefore from henceforth thou shalt have wars. Then Asa (Ju.) was in a rage, and put the seer in a prison-house and oppressed some of the people. In the thirty-ninth year of this reign, he was diseased in his feet; yet in his disease he sought not to the Lord, but to the physicians. He died in the forty-first year of his reign and was buried in his own sepulchre in the city of David.

He is in a Rage.

Asa Dies.

How did Asa deal with the prophet?

Describe Asa's death.

SUMMARY OF EVENTS.

Rehoboam, son of Solomon, is king.
At Shechem he rejects the counsel of the old men and declares roughly that he will be heavier on Israel than was his father.
Israel rebels and makes Jeroboam king. The kingdom is divided forever.
Jeroboam builds a capital and sets up two calves of gold for the people to worship.
Rehoboam at first preserves the true worship at Jerusalem, but then falls into idolatry.
As a punishment Jerusalem is captured by Shishak king of Egypt.
Rehoboam is succeeded by his son Abijah.
Abijah is succeeded by Asa, who took away the strange gods, and defeated the Ethiopian king, but took the treasure of the Temple to make alliance with the king of Persia, and died a miserable death in the forty-first year of his reign.

From what parts of the Bible is our narrative taken? I Kings, Chap. 12—15, II Chron., Chap. 10—16.

There are no pictures in "Bible Story" referring to this chapter.

What shall we call this forty-second chapter? **The Kingdom of Solomon Divided.**

In conclusion let the teacher again refer to the Scripture and Catechism answers that the scholar has learned.

THE SCRIPTURE TO BE LEARNED.

REVENGE IS FORBIDDEN.

<small>What does the apostle say of revenge?*</small> Dearly beloved, avenge not yourselves, but rather give place unto wrath: for it is written, Vengeance is mine; I will repay, saith the Lord.

Therefore if thine enemy hunger, feed him; if he thirst, give him drink: for in so doing thou shalt heap coals of fire on his head.

Be not overcome of evil, but overcome evil with good. Rom. 12: 19-21.

WHAT THE CATECHISM SAYS.

<small>What does the Catechism say?</small> We should so fear and love God as not to desire by craftiness to gain possession of our neighbor's inheritance or home, or to obtain it under the pretext of a legal right, but be ready to assist and serve him in the preservation of his own.

*Teacher asks the questions until the whole class have recited these parts.

CHAPTER XLIII.

The Early and Wicked Kings of Israel.

IN Judah the three successors of Solomon, Rehoboam (Ju.) and his son Abijah (Ju.) and his grandson Asa (Ju.) were dead. But Jeroboam (Is.) the first king of Israel was still ruling in his capital at Shechem. After he had set up the golden calves, a prophet came to reprove him for offering sacrifice to the calf at Bethel. The king tried to seize and lay hold on the prophet, but his hand, which he put forth against the prophet, withered, and he could not pull it in again. He had therefore to beg the prophet to entreat God to restore the hand, and the Lord restored it. But he kept on in his evil way. He made priests of the lowest of the people. Such sin did this thing become, that the Lord determined to cut off his house. His son, the only good member of his family, the one Israel hoped would succeed him, fell sick and died, and Jeroboam (Is.) himself died, after a reign of twenty-two years.

Jeroboam at Bethel.

His Hand Withers.

Who were kings of Judah at the time of our lesson?

Who was king of Israel?

What did Jeroboam set up?

Narrate the scene between the king and the prophet.

How did God punish Jeroboam?

Nadab (Is.), a son of his, reigned over Israel for two years, but he walked in the evil way of his father, and the next year, during a war with the Philistines, Baasha (Is.) a captain of the house of Issachar, conspired against Nadab, and slew him while he was laying siege to the town of Gibbethon, and reigned in his stead. To make sure of holding the throne, he smote the whole family of Jehoram (Is.), and left not anyone to the family that breathed, but

Nadab.

Baasha Murders Him.

Tell of King Baasha.

destroyed them all. He made fresh war on Judah, and fortified Ramah so near the border of Judah that Judah was threatened, and Asa (Ju.) its king sent a bribe to Benhadad, king at Damascus, to get the latter to break his treaty with Baasha and go to war against Baasha (Is.). Benhadad did so and captured Baasha's cities of Dan, Abel and Ijou in the north, and overran the land around the Sea of Galilee. Baasha (Is.) was compelled to withdraw his forces from the south near the borders of Judah and to go north to meet the king of Syria. He left off building Ramah, and lived in Tirzah. He reigned twenty-four years. But the word of the Lord came against Baasha (Is.), saying, As I exalted thee out of the dust, and thou hast made my people to sin, behold I will take away the posterity of Baasha, and will make thy family like the family of Jeroboam.

So Baasha (Is.) slept with his fathers, and was buried in Tirzah; and his son Elah (Is.) reigned in his stead for two years. But while Elah (Is.) was drinking himself drunk in the house of his steward in his capital Tirzah, Zimri, one of his military officers, went in, and smote him and killed him. As soon as Zimri (Is.) sat on the throne, he slew all the family of Baasha: he left not one neither of his kinsfolks, nor of his friends. Thus did Zimri destroy all the house of Baasha according to the word of the Lord, for the sins of Baasha.

Zimri (Is.) reigned for seven days in Tirzah. Then the news came to the army of Israel, which was encamped against Gibbethon, that Zimri had conspired and slain the king. Then all the army made Omri, the commander of the host, king over Israel, that

FORTY-THIRD SUNDAY. 215

day in camp. Omri and the army marched against the conspirator, and besieged him at the capital Tirzah. When Zimri saw that the city was captured, he went into the palace of the king's house and burnt the king's house over him with fire, and died. Then the people were divided into two parts. Half of them followed a certain Tibni and wished to make him king; and half followed Omri. In the civil war which followed, the party of Omri prevailed, and he became the founder of the strongest family that sat on the throne of Israel. Omri (Is.) warred against Benhadad, king of Damascus. Omri (Is.) also oppressed Moab for many days. After reigning in Tirzah for six years, he bought a hill a few miles northeast of the ancient capital Shechem, rising on every side from deep valleys, for two talents of silver, and built a city there, which he named "Samaria" after the owner of the hill, and which became the capital of his kingdom. He reigned six years in Samaria, and did evil, and slept with his fathers.

Tell of the wars of Omri.

Omri's Deeds.

Tell of Omri's building a capital.

Builds a Capital.

The son of Omri was Ahab, the greatest, strongest and most wicked of all the kings of Israel. He reigned over Israel in Samaria twenty-two years, and he did evil in the sight of the Lord above all that were before him. At Samaria he began much building, while at Jezreel he erected another palace.

Who was Ahab?

How long did he reign; were his deeds good or evil?

Ahab King.

King Ahab (Is.) mingled and made alliance with neighboring heathen nations, who worshiped idols. Among these were the wealthy trading cities of Tyre and Sidon. Ahab (Is.) took to wife Jezebel, the daughter of King of the Sidonians, and went and served her god Baal and wor-

Marries Jezebel.

Tell of Ahab and Jezebel.

o

shiped him. From the time of his marriage, he was under the influence of this wicked woman. For her he reared up a temple and an altar of Baal in his capital Samaria. And he made a grove for wicked worship, and did more to provoke the Lord God of Israel to anger than all the kings of Israel that were before him. For her temple, Jezebel brought no less than eight hundred and fifty heathen priests into the kingdom, and they did eat at her own table. She persecuted the prophets of the Lord God and cut them off with such fury that they fled, and one hundred of them hid in caves, and were fed in secret by Obadiah, the governor of the king's house, for he feared the Lord greatly. Thus the Israelites were forsaking the Lord's covenant and had thrown down his altars, and worshiped idols, and there were only seven thousand men in all Israel which had not bowed the knee to Jezebel's god Baal.

What did Jezebel do?

She Brings in Baal.

SUMMARY OF EVENTS.

Jeroboam king of Israel sacrifices to the golden calf.
He is cut off by the Lord. His son Nadab king for two years.
Baasha slays Nadab and is king for twenty-four years.
His son Elah reigns for two years, and while drinking is killed
   by one of his captains, Zimri.
Zimri reigns for seven days, when the army makes Omri king.
Omri removes the capital to Samaria. He reigns twelve years.
Wicked Ahab, the son of Omri, reigns twenty-two years. He
   marries Jezebel. He rears a temple of Baal for her.
Jezebel brings in 850 heathen priests, and Israel bows to idols.

From what parts of the Bible is this narrative taken? **I Kings, Ch. 13—16.**
What shall we call this forty-third chapter? **The Early and Wicked Kings of Israel.**
In conclusion let the teacher again refer to the Scripture and Catechism answers that the scholar has learned.

THE SCRIPTURE TO BE LEARNED.

AN ILLUSTRATION OF THE POWER OF PRAYER.

Elias was a man subject to like passions as we are, and he prayed earnestly that it might not rain: and it rained not on the earth by the space of three years and six months. Illustrate the Power of Prayer.*

And he prayed again, and the heaven gave rain, and the earth brought forth her fruit. James 5: 17-18.

WHAT THE CATECHISM SAYS ABOUT THINGS FOR WHICH WE SHALL PRAY.

All things that pertain to the wants and the support of this present life; such as food, raiment, money, goods, house and land, and other property; a believing spouse and good children; trustworthy servants and faithful magistrates, favorable seasons, peace and health; education and honor; true friends, good neighbors, and the like. What does the Catechism say?

---

*Teacher asks the questions until the whole class have recited these parts.

CHAPTER XLIV.
Ahab and Elijah.

Describe the prophet Elijah.

A SOLITARY man, with long, thick hair hanging down his back, a mantle of sheepskin, and a girdle around his loins, stood suddenly before Ahab (Is.). It was Elijah the Tishbite, of the inhabitants of Gilead, the greatest prophet since the time of Samuel. He said unto Ahab, As the Lord God of Israel liveth, before whom I stand, there shall not be dew nor rain these years, but according to my word. And he fled and got himself hence and turned eastward and hid himself by the brook Cherith, and the ravens brought him bread and flesh. When the brook dried up, he went to Sarepta, near the seaside, and was fed by a poor widow whose barrel of meal wasted not, and whose cruse of oil did not fail, during the years of the famine. Meanwhile the famine was sore in Samaria, and Ahab had said unto his governor, Go into the land, unto all fountains of water, and unto all brooks, and see if we may find grass to save the horses and mules alive, that we lose not all the beasts, and they had divided the land between them to pass through it all, Ahab going one way by himself, and the governor another way by himself.

What did Elijah say to Ahab?

Tell his subsequent wanderings.

No Rain for Three Years.

What did Ahab do when the famine was great?

Ahab Searching for Grass.

When God told Elijah to show himself to Ahab, what happened?

After many days the word of the Lord came to Elijah saying, Go, show thyself unto Ahab; and I will send rain upon the earth. And Elijah went, and, as the governor was in the way, behold, Elijah met him: and he knew him, and fell on his face, and said, Art thou my lord Elijah? He answered, I am: go, tell thy lord, Behold, Elijah is here. So the governor went and told Ahab; and Ahab went to meet Elijah.

Elijah Comes.

When Ahab saw Elijah, he said, Art thou he that troubleth Israel? He answered, I have not troubled Israel; but thou and thy father's house, in that ye have forsaken the commandments of the Lord, and thou hast followed Baal. Now therefore gather all Israel unto Mount Carmel, and gather the four hundred and fifty prophets of Baal, and the four hundred prophets of the groves.

All Israel on Mt. Carmel.

Ahab sent unto all Israel, and gathered the prophets together unto Mount Carmel. And Elijah came and said to the people, How long halt ye between two opinions? if the Lord be God, follow Him: but if Baal, then follow him. The people answered him not a word.

Then Elijah proposed that he on the one hand and Baal's prophets on the other, make an offering, each unto their God; and the God that answereth by fire, let him be God. And all the people said, It is well spoken. When the people saw that there was no answer to the Baal offering, and that on Elijah's prayer the fire of the Lord fell and consumed the burnt sacrifice, they fell on their faces and said, The Lord, He is God; the Lord, He is God. And at Elijah's command the prophets of Baal were slain.

The God that Answereth by Fire.

Then said Elijah unto Ahab, Get thee up, for there is a sound of abundance of rain. And Elijah went up to the top of Carmel; and he cast himself down upon the

Tell of Elijah on top of the Mount.

What did Ahab say to Elijah?

What did Elijah propose in reply?

Describe the scene on Mt. Carmel.

earth and said to his servant, Go up now, look toward the sea. He went up, and looked, and said, There is nothing. He said, Go again, seven times. At the seventh time he said, Behold there ariseth a little cloud out of the sea, like a man's hand. Elijah said, Go up, say unto Ahab, Prepare thy chariot, and get thee down, that the rain stop thee not. In the meanwhile the heaven was black with clouds and wind, And Ahab rode, and went to Jezreel. Elijah ran before Ahab to the entrance of Jezreel.

A Little Cloud.

Tell of the storm.

Rain!

Arriving at the palace, Ahab told Jezebel all that Elijah had done, and how he had slain all her prophets. Then Jezebel flew into a rage and sent a messenger unto Elijah, saying, So let the gods do unto me, and more also, if I make not thy life as theirs by to-morrow. But Elijah arose and ran for his life and came to Beer-sheba in the southernmost part of Palestine, and went a day's journey into the wilderness, and came and sat down under a juniper tree, fainting, and asking the Lord to let him die. But an angel of the Lord came and touched him on the shoulder. The prophet looked up and saw a fire of coals, and a cake baken on it, and a cruse of water at his head. He ate and drank, and went in the strength of this food unto Mount Horeb, and he lodged in a cave.

What message did Jezebel send to Elijah?

Jezebel's Threat.

Describe Elijah's flight.

How was Elijah encouraged?

Fed by Ravens.

And behold the word of the Lord came unto him and said, What doest thou here, Elijah? He said, I have been very jealous for the Lord God of hosts: the children of Israel have forsaken Thy covenant, thrown down thine altars, and slain thy prophets with the sword; and I, even I only am left; and they

Tell of Elijah's interview with the Lord.

What Doest Thou Here, Elijah?

FORTY-FOURTH SUNDAY.

seek my life to take it away. Then, behold, the Lord passed by, and a great and strong wind rent the mountains, and brake in pieces the rock; but the Lord was not **The Still Small Voice.** in the wind, and after the wind an earthquake; but the Lord was not in the earthquake: and after the earthquake a fire, but the Lord was not in the fire: and after the fire a still small voice.

When Elijah heard it, he wrapped his face in his mantle. The Lord told him to anoint Hazael to be king over **Elijah's Commission.** Syria, Jehu to be king over Israel, and Elisha to be prophet in his own place. He told Elijah that there were still seven thousand faithful followers left in the land.

So Elijah departed, and he found Elisha ploughing with twelve yoke of oxen before him. Elijah passed by **Elijah's Mantle.** and cast his mantle upon him. Elisha left the oxen, and ran after Elijah.

Marginal notes: What did Elijah do, at these great sights? What did the Lord tell Elijah to do? How did he encourage Elijah? Tell of the call of Elisha.

Elijah appears suddenly before Ahab, and announces a three years' drought.

Elijah flees to the brook Cherith, and thence to the widow of Sarepta. After three years, he goes to Ahab to announce rain.

Elijah calls down fire upon his offering on Mt. Carmel, and slays the prophets of Baal. See *Bible Story*.

Elijah awaits the approach of the storm which comes, and Ahab rides before it.

Elijah, threatened by Jezebel, runs for his life and comes to the wilderness. The Lord feeds him.

The strong wind, the earthquake, the fire, and the still voice.

Elijah is commissioned to anoint kings. He casts his mantle upon Elisha.

From what part of the Bible is this narrative taken? **I Kings, Chap. 17—19.**
What picture did we have in "Bible Story" referring to this chapter?
What shall we call this forty-fourth chapter? **Ahab and Elijah.**

THE SCRIPTURE TO BE LEARNED.

THE RIGHTEOUS LORD HATETH INIQUITY.

<small>How doth the righteous Lord look upon iniquity?*</small>
The Lord trieth the righteous: but the wicked and him that loveth violence his soul hateth.

Upon the wicked he shall rain snares, fire and brimstone, and an horrible tempest: this shall be the portion of their cup.

For the righteous Lord loveth righteousness; his countenance doth behold the upright. Psalm 11: 5-7.

WHAT THE CATECHISM SAYS ABOUT HALLOWING AND PROFANING THE NAME OF GOD.

<small>What does the Catechism say?</small>
When the Word of God is taught in its truth and purity, and we, as the children of God, lead holy lives in accordance with it; to this may our blessed Father in heaven help us! But whoever teaches and lives otherwise than as God's word prescribes, profanes the Name of God among us; from this preserve us, Heavenly Father!

---

*Teacher asks the questions until the whole class have recited these parts.

CHAPTER XLV.

The Destruction of Ahab.

BENHADAD, king of Syria, had wrested a great part of Israel from Ahab's father. Ahab did according to Benhadad's demands, until at length Benhadad gathered all his host together and invaded Israel for the purpose of subjugating it completely. He went up with thirty-two kings and shut up Ahab within his capital Samaria, and besieged Samaria and warred against it.

Who invaded Israel?

Benhadad Besieges Samaria.

How did he go up?

Sending messengers into the city, he said unto Ahab, Thy silver and thy gold is mine; thy wives also and thy children are mine. The king of Israel answered, My lord, O king, according to thy saying, I am thine, and all that I have. The messengers came again and said, I will send my servants tomorrow, and they shall search thine houses, and whatsoever is pleasant in thine eyes, they shall put it in their hand, and take it away.

What message did he send to Ahab?

His First Demand.

What was his second message?

His Second Demand.

Then the king called all the elders and said, Mark, how this man seeketh mischief. The elders and the people said, Hearken not unto him. Wherefore he told the messengers, This thing I may not do. Benhadad vowed vengeance. Ahab replied that it was better to be boastful after battle than before. When Benhadad heard this message, as he was drinking with

What did the king do about it?

Ahab's Refusal.

What was king Ahab's reply?

223

the kings in the pavilions, he said to his soldiers, Set yourselves in array.

But a prophet told Ahab that the Lord would deliver him. Though he had only seven thousand men, he went out at noon. Now Benhadad was drinking himself drunk in the pavilions, he and the thirty-two kings that helped him, and the Syrians fled, and Benhadad escaped on a horse with the horsemen, and the king of Israel went out and smote the horses and chariots, and slew the Syrians with a great slaughter.

At the return of the year, Benhadad again came up to fight against Israel. And the children of Israel were like two little flocks of kids; but the Syrians filled the country. In the seventh day the battle was joined: and the children of Israel slew a hundred thousand of the Syrian footmen in one day. But the rest fled to Aphek, into the city, and Benhadad into an inner chamber. Then Ahab spared him and made a treaty with him, and sent him away.

As Ahab passed by on his homeward road, a prophet cried to him, Thus saith the Lord, Because thou hast let go a man whom I appointed to utter destruction, therefore thy life shall go for his life. And the king came to Samaria heavy and displeased.

Now Naboth the Jezreelite had a vineyard hard by the summer palace of Ahab, and Ahab said unto Naboth, Give me thy vineyard that I may have it for a garden, because it is near my house: and I will give thee a better vineyard; or, if it seem good to thee, I will give thee the worth of it in money. Naboth said, The Lord forbid that I should give the in-

FORTY-FIFTH SUNDAY.

heritance of my fathers. Ahab came into his house and he would not eat. Jezebel his wife said, Dost thou now govern the kingdom of Israel? Arise, and eat bread, and let thine heart be merry; I will give thee the vineyard. She had two men to bear false witness against Naboth, and had him stoned. Then she said to Ahab, Arise, take the vineyard: for Naboth is dead. And Ahab went down to the vineyard to take possession. There Elijah met him. Ahab said, Hast thou found me, O mine enemy. He answered, I have found thee. In the place where dogs licked the blood of Naboth shall dogs lick thy blood, even thine. And Ahab rent his clothes, and fasted and humbled himself.

Jezebel Gets It for Ahab.

The Dogs Shall Lick Thy Blood.

How did it affect Ahab?
What did Jezebel say?
What did Jezebel do?

Describe the meeting of Elijah and Ahab.

At this time Jehoshaphat, the son of Asa, was on the throne in Judah. He was energetic and strengthened himself against Israel and every foe, and walked in the commandments of the Lord. He had riches and honour in abundance, and the Lord was with him. He took away the idols and sent teachers and priests throughout all the cities of Judah to teach the people out of the book of the law. He built castles and strong cities and had mighty men of valour in Jerusalem. The fear of the Lord fell on surrounding kingdoms and they made no war on him, but the Philistines brought him presents and the Arabians gave him flocks. He organized his army and put garrisons in all the walled cities of Judah, and carried his conquests to the Red Sea. After the manner of Solomon he prepared to send a navy to Ophir for gold, but the ships were wrecked before they had left their port.

Jehoshaphat's Greatness.

Who was Jehoshaphat?

Tell what he did for Judah.

Like what king was he in some respects?

Jehoshaphat (Ju.) made peace with Ahab (Is.) and

came down to him. Ahab said, Wilt thou go with me to battle against Syria? They went, Jehoshaphat in his kingly robes and Ahab in disguise. The king of Syria had commanded his chariots to fight neither with small nor great, but only with the king of Israel. And when the chariot captains saw Jehoshaphat they said, Surely it is the king of Israel! And they turned to fight against him: and Jehoshaphat cried out. And when the chariots perceived it was not the king of Israel, they turned back. But a certain man drew a bow at a venture, and smote the king of Israel. The latter said to his chariot-man, Turn; for I am wounded. But he led the battle until the even: and about the time of the sun going down he died. And the blood ran out of the wound into the midst of the chariot. And one washed the chariot in the pool of Samaria; and the dogs licked up his blood, according to the word of the Lord.

Sidenotes: What did Ahab and Jehoshaphat do together? How did Ahab go into battle? How did Jehoshaphat go in? Describe the battle. Tell how Ahab died. What happened at Naboth's vineyard? Wilt Thou Go with Me to Battle? Ahab in Disguise. Fight Only Ahab. An Arrow Smote Him. The Dogs Licked His Blood.

SUMMARY OF EVENTS.

The king of Syria wars against Ahab, is defeated but spared.
While Ahab is on the way home a prophet declares that because Ahab spared the Syrian king's life, he will lose his own.
Jezebel secures Naboth's vineyard for Ahab by killing its owner.
Elijah says that the dogs shall lick Ahab's blood in the spot where they licked Naboth's.
Jehoshaphat king of Judah flourishes, and is righteous.
Ahab and Jehoshaphat go out to battle against the king of Syria.
Ahab is mortally wounded and dies. The dogs licked his blood.

From what parts of the Bible is this narrative taken? **I Kings, Chapters 20—22, II Chronicles 17, 18.**
There are no pictures in "Bible Story" referring to this chapter.
What shall we call this forty-fifth chapter? **The Destruction of Ahab.**

Forty-Sixth Sunday.

THE SCRIPTURE TO BE LEARNED.

THE GIFTS OF PROPHECY AND CHARITY.

Though I have the gift of prophecy, and understand all mysteries, and all knowledge; and though I have all faith, so that I could remove mountains, and have not charity, I am nothing. *(What did Paul say of Prophecy and of Charity?*)*

And though I bestow all my goods to feed the poor, and though I give my body to be burned, and have not charity, it profiteth me nothing. Charity never faileth: but whether there be prophecies, they shall fail: whether there be tongues they shall cease; whether there be knowledge, it shall vanish away. . . . And now abideth faith, hope, charity, these three. I Cor. 13: 2-3, 8, 13.

WHAT THE CATECHISM SAYS.

Confession consists of two parts: the one is, that we confess our sins; the other, that we receive absolution or forgiveness through the pastor as of God himself, in no wise doubting, but firmly believing that our sins are thus forgiven before God in heaven. *(What does the Catechism say?)*

*Teacher asks the questions until the whole class have recited these parts.

CHAPTER XLVI.
The Prophet Elisha.

What happened to Ahab's son?

What happened to Elijah?

What did Elisha do for Jehoshaphat?

What did the Moabites suppose?

What did they cry?

What was the result?

What did Elisha do for the poor widow?

AHAB had two sons and a daughter. One son reigned two years and then fell down through a lattice in his upper chamber in the palace at Samaria and was sick, and died. During the reign of the other son over Israel, Elijah left a double portion of his spirit and his mantle to Elisha, and went up by a whirlwind into heaven, being parted from Elisha by a chariot of fire and horses of fire. Ahab's second son Jehoram, wicked though he was, did not altogether resist the prophet Elisha. When he as king of Israel made an alliance with Jehoshaphat (Ju.) against the rebellious Moabites, Elisha, for Jehoshaphat's sake filled the barren valley with water, that the army might have to drink. On the next morning, when the Moabites saw the reflected light of the rising sun as it shone upon the standing water, they supposed that the water was blood, and that the armies of the three kings had quarreled and smitten one another, and they cried, Now therefore Moab, to the spoil! but the Israelites smote them, and went forward pursuing them even into their own country.

To Heaven in a Whirlwind.

Water, not Blood.

To the Spoil!

The spirit of Elijah rested on Elisha. He multiplied the oil of a poor widow and relieved her from the fear of her creditors. He promised the

Elisha Helps.

kindly woman in Shunem a son, and brought back again the life of the child when he died in the hot harvest field. During a famine he preserved the lives of the sons of the prophets at Gilgal when they were eating of pottage into which one had cast a lap full of poisonous gourds while it was seething in the pot. With twenty loaves of barley he fed a large number of people.

<small>Death in the Pot.</small>

<small>What for the woman in Shunem?
What for the sons of the prophets?
With what did he feed the people?</small>

And Naaman, captain of the army of the king of Syria, a great man with his master and a mighty man of valour, but a leper, was sent by his king to the king of Israel, with a letter saying, Behold I have sent Naaman my servant to thee, that thou mayest recover him of his leprosy. The king of Israel read the letter and said, Am I God, to kill and to make alive, that this man doth send unto me to recover a man of his leprosy? When Elisha had heard that the king had rent his clothes, he said, Let the man come unto me. So Naaman came with his horses and with his chariot, and stood at the door of the house of Elisha. Elisha sent a messenger to him saying, Go and wash in Jordan seven times, and thou shalt be clean.

<small>Naaman.
Wash in Jordan.</small>

<small>Tell the story of Naaman the leper.</small>

But Naaman was wroth and went away, and said, I thought he would surely come out to me. Are not the rivers of Damascus better than all the waters of Israel? So he turned away in a rage.

<small>Are Not the Rivers of Damascus Better?</small>

His servants came near and said, If the prophet had bid thee do some great thing, wouldest thou not have done it? How much rather, then, when he saith to thee, Wash, and be clean. Then he went down and dipped himself in Jordan seven times, and his flesh came again, and he was clean. And he returned to Elisha and said, Now I know that there is no God in all the earth, but in Israel.

<small>No God But in Israel.</small>

But the king of Syria made war against Israel. And Elisha told the king of Israel the whereabouts of his enemy. The latter was sore troubled and called his servants and said, Which one of us is for the King of Israel? And one said, Elisha telleth the king of Israel the words that thou speakest in thy bedchamber. He said, Go, spy where he is. It was told, Behold, he is in Dothan. Therefore sent he by night, and surrounded the city. When Elisha's servant rose early, he said, Alas, my master! how shall we do? Elisha answered, Fear not: for they that be with us are more than they that be with them. And the Lord opened the eyes of the young man: and behold the mountain was full of horses and chariots of fire round about Elisha.

<small>What did Elisha tell the king of Israel?</small>

<small>Elisha Tells Syrian Secrets.</small>

<small>What did the king of Syria think?</small>

<small>What did the king of Syria do?</small>

<small>Tell of Elisha's servant.</small>

<small>Those With Us More Than Those Against Us.</small>

<small>What did the servant see?</small>

After this, Benhadad gathered all his host and went up and besieged Samaria. It brought on a great famine. Elisha tells the angered king that tomorrow at this time flour and barley would be sold lower than ever before in the city. That night the Lord caused the Syrians to hear a noise which they supposed to be the noise of the horses and chariots of a great host arriving from Egypt, and they fled and left their tents and garments and vessels. And the people went out and spoiled the tents of the Syrians. So a measure of fine flour was sold for a shekel.

<small>What place did Benhadad besiege?</small>

<small>What did the king of Israel do?</small>

<small>Tomorrow Wheat at a Shekel a Bushel.</small>

<small>What did Elisha promise?</small>

<small>How did this actually come to pass?</small>

Elisha came to Damascus, and Benhadad the king of Syria was sick. The king sent Hazael to ask, Shall I recover? Elisha said, He shall surely

<small>Thou Shalt Be King.</small>

die, and the man of God wept. Hazael said, Why weepeth my lord? Elisha answered, Because I know the evil that thou wilt do unto the children of Israel. Hazael replied, But what! Is thy servant a dog, that he should do this great thing? Elisha answered, The Lord hath showed me that thou shalt be king over Syria. Hazael came to his master, and murdered him, and reigned in his stead.

Tell the story of Elisha and Hazael.

Now the son of Jehoshaphat (Ju.) had married the daughter of Ahab (Is.) and Jezebel. This daughter, Athaliah, was as wicked as her mother Jezebel, and her husband began his reign by murdering his brothers and by introducing the worship of Baal. The Philistines and Arabians plundered Jerusalem and carried away all the king's treasures, and the Lord smote him with disease, and he died in agony, according to a prophecy of Elisha.

Athaliah Brings Disaster to Judah.

Who was Athaliah?

What wicked things did her husband do, and how did he die?

SUMMARY OF EVENTS.

Elijah leaving his mantle to Elisha goes by a whirlwind to heaven.
Elisha fills a barren valley with water, that the Israelites may defeat the Moabites.
Elisha multiplies the oil of a widow and raises to life her son.
Removes death from the pot of the prophet. Feeds a multitude.
He heals Naaman the Syrian. He is fearless at Dothan, being protected by the Lord's horses and chariots of fire.
Amid siege and famine he predicts plenty.
He tells Hazael he will be king of Syria and will oppress Israel.
He prophecies that the husband of Athaliah will be smitten with disease.

From what parts of the Bible is this narrative taken?   II Kings, Chap. 2—8, II Chron., 22.
There are no pictures in "Bible Story" referring to this chapter.
What shall we call this forty-sixth chapter?   **The Prophet Elisha.**

P

FORTY-SEVENTH SUNDAY.

THE SCRIPTURE TO BE LEARNED.

A KINGDOM DIVIDED AGAINST ITSELF MUST FALL.

Is it possible to serve two Masters?* No man can serve two masters: for either he will hate the one, and love the other; or else he will hold to the one, and despise the other. Ye cannot serve God and mammon.

Therefore I say unto you, Take no thought for your life, what ye shall eat, or what ye shall drink; nor yet for your body, what ye shall put on. Is not the life more than meat, and the body than raiment? Matt. 6: 24-25.

WHAT THE CATECHISM SAYS.

What does the Catechism say? We should so fear and love God, as not to alienate our neighbor's wife from him, entice away his servants, nor let loose his cattle, but use our endeavors that they may remain and discharge their duty to him.

*Teacher asks the questions until the whole class have recited these parts.

CHAPTER XLVII.
Jehu, Jezebel and Joash, Amaziah and Uzziah.

Joram Wounded.

JORAM, the second son of Ahab, was king in Israel. And the yoke of his mother Jezebel was oppressing the land. He went to war against Hazael king of Syria; and the Syrians wounded Joram. And he left the army and went back to his summer palace in Jezreel to be healed.

Who was Joram?

Did his mother Jezebel have any authority?

What happened to Joram?

Elisha called one of the children of the prophets and said, Go to the army: look out Jehu, and carry him to an inner chamber, and say, Thus saith the Lord, I have anointed thee king over Israel. Then open the door, and flee, and tarry not.

Go To Jehu.

What did Elisha tell a son of a prophet to do?

So the young man went and said, I have an errand to thee, O captain. And he went into the house and said, Thus saith the Lord God of Israel, I have anointed thee to be king, and thou shalt smite the house of Ahab.

Tell how the young man did what he was told.

Then Jehu came forth. And the captains hasted and took every man his garment, and put it under him on the top of the stairs, and blew with trumpets, saying, Jehu is king.

Jehu King.

What did the captains do?

So Jehu rode in a chariot and went to Jezreel. A watchman on the tower spied the company of Jehu, and told the sick king.

What did Jehu do?

Tell the story of the watchman, Jehu, and the king.

He Rideth Furiously.

The watchman said, The driving is like the driving of Jehu; for he driveth furiously. Joram said, Make ready. His chariot was made ready. And Joram, king of Israel, went out in his chariot and met Jehu in the portion of Naboth the Jezreel-

What did King Joram finally do?

FORTY-SEVENTH SUNDAY.

ite. When he saw Jehu, he said, Is it peace, Jehu? He answered, What peace, so long as the witchcrafts of thy mother Jezebel are so many?

Describe the meeting between Joram and Jehu.

Joram turned his hands, and fled, and said, There is treachery. And Jehu drew a bow with his full strength, and smote Joram between his arms, and the arrow went out at his heart, and he sunk down in his chariot. Jehu said, Take and cast him in the field of Naboth. **There is Treachery!**

Where was the body of Joram cast?

Where did Jehu go then?

When Jehu was come to Jezreel, Jezebel heard of it; and she painted her face, and tired her head, and looked out of the palace window and taunted him. Jehu said, Throw her down. So they threw her down: and some of her blood was sprinkled on the wall, and on the horses, and he trod her under foot. And the dogs ate her flesh as Elijah had said. Then Jehu slew all that remained of the house of Ahab and all his great men. He burnt the images of Baal, and brake down the temple of Baal, and slew the priests of Baal, and destroyed Baal out of Israel, and restored the worship of the Lord. But he took no heed to walk in the law of the Lord with all his heart, and the Lord began to cut Israel short; and Hazael smote them. And Jehu slept with his fathers, and the time that he reigned over Israel was twenty-eight years. **Throw Jezebel down.**

Tell the story of the death of Jezebel.

What prophecy was fulfilled?

Whither did Jehu go next?

How did he root out the worship of Baal?

Did Jehu do right all his life?

Jehu Roots Out Baal.

Now wicked Athaliah was the daughter of Ahab and Jezebel. She married the king of Judah, and destroyed her children and grandchildren, that she might reign over the land of Judah herself. But Joash, an infant son of the dead king, had been stolen away from the king's sons which were slain, and had been hid with his nurse in a **Athaliah Murders Her Families.**

What did wicked Athaliah do when she heard that her son was dead?

Tell the story of little Joash.

Little Joash Hid.

FORTY-SEVENTH SUNDAY.

bedchamber in the Temple, by his aunt, the wife of the high priest.

The seventh year the high priest brought the captains and the guard into the Temple and showed them the king's son. Then the high priest proclaimed Joash king in the Temple, and put the crown upon him; and they clapped their hands and said, God save the king!

Joash Crowned.

How was he proclaimed king?

When Athaliah heard the noise of the guard and the people, she came into the Temple, and behold the king stood by a pillar, and the trumpeters by the king, and all the people rejoiced. Athaliah cried, Treason! Treason! But the priest commanded her to be taken out and slain.

Treason.

What became of Athaliah?

Then all the people went into the Temple of Baal and brake it down. Joash (Ju.) was seven years old when he began to reign and he reigned forty years in Jerusalem. And he did that which was right in the sight of the Lord. He destroyed idols and repaired the Temple. The people brought offerings and they were put into a chest with a hole in the lid of it, on the right side of the altar, and when there was much money, it was laid out to the overseers and carpenters, and masons and hewers of stone, and for vessels of gold and vessels of silver.

Joash Repairs the Temple.

Tell how Joash repaired the Temple.

But Joash (Ju.) was persuaded by some of the princes to worship idols. Then Hazael and the host of Syria came up to Jerusalem. And Joash took of the hallowed things in the Temple and all the gold and gave it to Hazael, and Hazael went away from Jerusalem. But Joash (Ju.) was slain by his servants.

Takes of the Temple Gold.

What was Joash persuaded to do?

What happened?

How did Joash get rid of Hazael?

What happened to Joash?

FORTY-SEVENTH SUNDAY.

Who was Amaziah? Did he do right?

His son Amaziah (Ju.) reigned twenty-nine years and did that which was right, but not with a perfect heart.

Tell of the reign of Uzziah.

Amaziah's son was Uzziah (Ju.). He was sixteen years old when he began to reign, and he reigned fifty-two years in Jerusalem. He fought the Philistines and the Ammonites, and built towers, *Uzziah King.* and digged wells for the flocks. He had a host of fighting men and prepared for them shields and spears and helmets and bows and slings, and he made engines to be upon the towers and bulwarks of Jerusalem to shoot arrows and great stones. And his name was marvellously spread abroad, but pride was his destruction. For he went into the Temple to burn incense, and the priests withstood him, and said, It appertaineth not unto thee, go out! And he was wroth, and had a censer in his hand and the leprosy rose up in his forehead. The Lord had smitten him.

What military equipment did he prepare?

What caused his downfall? Describe it.

The Fall of Pride.

SUMMARY OF EVENTS.

Jehu is anointed and proclaimed king.
He rides furiously in a chariot to Jezreel.
He kills Joram and Jezebel.
He breaks down the temple of Baal and slays the priests of Baal.
Athaliah, daughter of Ahab and mother of the king of Judah, destroys her children and grandchildren.
The high priest proclaims Joash king and slays Athaliah.
Joash reigns forty years and repairs the temple.
Amaziah reigns twenty-nine years.
Uzziah reigns fifty-two years and makes Jerusalem a great military centre. Uzziah is stricken with leprosy by the Lord.

From what parts of the Bible is our narrative taken? **II Kings, Chapters 9—15, II Chronicles, Chapters 22—26.**

There are no pictures in "Bible Story" referring to this chapter.

What shall we call this forty-seventh chapter? **Jehu, Jezebel and Joash, Amaziah and Uzziah.**

In conclusion let the teacher again refer to the Scripture and Catechism answers that the scholar has learned.

Forty-Eighth Sunday.

THE SCRIPTURE TO BE LEARNED.

GOD'S MESSAGE TO CAPTIVE ISRAEL.

But if the wicked will turn from all his sins that he hath committed, and keep all my statutes, and do that which is lawful and right, he shall surely live, he shall not die. *(How will God deal with him who repents?*)*

All his transgressions that he hath committed, they shall not be mentioned unto him: in his righteousness that he hath done he shall live.

Have I any pleasure at all that the wicked should die? said the Lord God: and not that he should return from his ways, and live? Ezek. 18: 21-23.

WHAT THE CATECHISM SAYS.

The good and gracious will of God is done indeed without our prayer; but we pray in this petition that it may be done by us also. *(What does the Catechism say?)*

---

*Teacher asks the questions until the whole class have recited these parts.

CHAPTER XLVIII.

Israel in Prosperity, Confusion and Captivity. The Empires of The East.

Who was Jeroboam II?

How long did he reign?

What did he do for Israel?

IN the fifteenth year of Amaziah (Ju.) Jeroboam II. (Is.) began to reign in Samaria and reigned forty-one years. He enlarged the boundaries of Israel to their farthest limits. He reconquered the territory of Moab and captured Damascus. Except in the northeast, the ancient empire of Israel was free from foreign power. There was wealth unheard of since the days of Solomon. Great estates, **Jeroboam II Enlarges Israel.**

How did the rich live?

with palaces of hewn stone and beds of ivory and silken couches were in the land. Their masters ate and drank, as they stretched themselves upon their couches, and sang to the sound of the **The Palaces of the Rich.** viol. The needy and helpless were wronged by the violence and robbery of the rich. The courts and judges took bribes. The prophets Amos and Hosea **Amos and Hosea.** foretold the coming doom. In less than

What prophets predicted doom?

What happened in less than twenty years?

twenty years after Jeroboam II. (Is.) died, the proud kingdom of Israel ceased to exist. Four of the six kings who succeeded him were struck down by assassins, and one died in captivity.

What warriors were now coming to trouble Israel?

The kingdom of Assyria for a half century had been in trouble, and had given Israel rest. But now it had broken the kingdom of Damascus and **The Assyrians Come Three Times.** was again coming toward Israel and the Great

How did the king of Israel get rid of the Assyrians the first time?

Sea. The first time the Assyrians came, the king of Israel bought him off for one thousand talents of silver.

FORTY-EIGHTH SUNDAY.

The next time the king of Assyria came, it was because the king of Israel had made alliance with the Syrians to fight against Assyria. In the battle Israel was defeated, and a part of the people were led into captivity, as had been foretold by the prophets.

Then the king of Israel with the king of Syria came **Ahaz of Judah.** up to war against Ahaz, the king of Judah, in Jerusalem. Ahaz was one of the most wicked and idolatrous of the kings of Judah. To punish Ahaz, the Lord allowed Israel and Syria to defeat him and to kill one hundred and twenty thousand of his men. Jerusalem would have fallen into the hands of the king of Israel, if Isaiah the prophet had not told the people to repent and to defend themselves against the attack. Ahaz took the silver and gold of the Temple and sent it for a present to the king of Assyria, so that the king of Assyria would come up against the armies that were besieging Jerusalem. The king of Assyria, Tiglath-Pileser, did so, and captured Damascus and slew the king of Syria, and carried the tribes **Into Captivity.** of Reuben, Gad and Manasseh into captivity. Five years afterward Tiglath-Pileser died. Then the king of Israel refused to pay tribute to Shalmaneser, his successor, and sent messengers to the king of Egypt to deliver him from Assyria.

Then Shalmaneser, king of Assyria, came up throughout all the land, and went up to Samaria, and captured the king and besieged Samaria three years. Shalmaneser died before the city yielded to the pressure of starvation, but Sargon, his successor, took the city. It was given up **Samaria Captured.** to plunder. More than twenty-seven thousand of its inhabitants were carried away into

FORTY-EIGHTH SUNDAY.

<small>Tell all that followed the capture.</small>
captivity, and over those left behind there was placed an Assyrian governor to collect the tribute.

<small>To what place was Israel carried?</small>
Thus was Israel carried away into Assyria, and placed in the cities of the Medes. For they had sinned against
<small>Of what was this the punishment?</small>
the Lord their God, which had brought them up out of the land of Egypt, and had feared <small>Israel in Captivity.</small> other gods. And they followed vanity, and went after the heathen that were round about them. Therefore the Lord
<small>Who only was left in the Holy Land?</small>
was very angry with them, and removed them out of his sight: there was none left but the tribe of Judah only.

<small>How was the deserted land colonized?</small>
And the king of Assyria brought men from Babylon, and from Cuthnah, and other cities, and <small>Heathen Brought to Settle In</small> placed them in the cities of Samaria instead of
<small>How were these new settlers taught?</small>
the children of Israel; and he sent one of the <small>Israel.</small> priests to teach them how they should fear the Lord.

Of the great kingdoms and empires of this world which God employed as a rod to chastise the children of Israel,
<small>Tell what you can of the kingdom of Syria.</small>
the first was Syria. It lay north of Israel and <small>The Three Empires.</small> its capital was Damascus. Its kings were the three Benhadads, with Hazael, who murdered Benhadad II., coming in between. Israel and Syria united against Judah; but Judah called in Tiglath-Pileser, king of Assyria, and he carried the people of Syria away to Assyria.

<small>Tell what you can of the empire of Assyria.</small>
The second empire was the far-more powerful Assyrian monarchy. Assyria was a colony of Babel. It lay east of Israel and included the region watered by the Euphrates and the Tigris. Its capital <small>Assyria.</small> was Nineveh. Tiglath-Pileser carried the inhabitants of Syria and the northern part of Israel into captivity, and his successor Shalmaneser completed the destruction of Israel and carried away the remainder of the people. Sennacherib, on his march to Egypt, besieged Jerusalem dur-

FORTY-EIGHTH SUNDAY. 241

ing the reign of Hezekiah, king of Judah. Esarhaddon, his son and successor, carried Manasseh, king of Judah, captive to Babylon.

Babylon. The third empire was the Babylonian, which succeeded the Assyrian, and was succeeded by the empire of the Medes and Persians. Nebuchadnezzar, who was the destroyer of the kingdom of Judah, made this empire exceedingly great. Nebuchadnezzar's son, perhaps Belshazzar, was murdered probably by Darius the Mede, and Darius was conquered by Cyrus the Persian.

Tell what you can of the Babylonian Monarchy.

SUMMARY OF EVENTS.

The reign of Jeroboam in Israel. The glory and the wickedness of Israel at this time. Amos. Hosea.

The Assyrians come to Israel, and the king of Israel buys them off.

The Assyrians again come to Israel and take part of the people into captivity.

Israel and Syria go up to war against wicked Ahaz of Judah.

Ahaz presents the treasures of the Temple to the king of Assyria.

The king, Tiglath-Pileser, of Assyria, comes up against Israel and carries the tribes of Reuben, Gad and Manasseh into captivity.

Shalmaneser besieges Samaria, and Sargon takes it and carries the rest of Israel into captivity.

Sargon places heathen from abroad as colonists in Israel.

The first kingdom to chastise Israel was Syria. The second was the Assyrian monarchy. The third was the Babylonian monarchy.

From what parts of the Bible is this narrative taken? **II Kings, Chap. 13—17, II Chron., Chap. 28.**

There are no pictures in "Bible Story" referring to this chapter.

What shall we call this forty-eighth chapter? **Israel In Prosperity, Confusion and Captivity.**

Forty-Ninth Sunday.

THE SCRIPTURE TO BE LEARNED.

LOVE FOR THE HOUSE OF GOD.

<small>How does the psalmist praise God's House?</small>

How amiable are thy tabernacles, O Lord of hosts! My soul longeth, yea, even fainteth for the courts of the Lord: my heart and my flesh crieth out for the living God.

Yea, the sparrow hath found an house, and the swallow a nest for herself, where she may lay her young, even thine altars, O Lord of hosts, my king, and my God.

Blessed are they that dwell in thy house: they will be still praising thee. Selah. Ps. 84: 1-4.

WHAT THE CATECHISM SAYS.

<small>What does the Catechism say?</small>

Remember the Sabbath day to keep it holy.

*Teacher asks the questions until the whole class have recited these parts.

CHAPTER .XLIX.
Judah under King Hezekiah.

THE kingdom of Israel had been destroyed, and its people been led into captivity. Six years before this occurred, the kingdom of Judah had received one of her three most perfect kings. His name was Hezekiah. In his day Isaiah was the great prophet of Israel. He was the central figure in the politics of his age. Isaiah spake for the Holy One of Israel, the Lord of hosts with whose glory the whole earth is filled. In the midst of these bloody wars, he pointed to a Prince of Peace, who would yet be born. This Prince would be a Wonderful Counsellor, a Mighty God, an Everlasting Father. At the coming of this Prince, Isaiah saw that the everlasting hills do bow, the valleys are raised, the moon puts on the brightness of the sun. The deserts and dry places gush with waters. The serpent forgets his fangs, the lion and the lamb sleep side by side, and the hand of the child is on the mane of the tiger. Nations gaze till they forget the murderous work of war, and the garments rolled in blood. Sorrow and sighing pass away, and the ransomed of the Lord come with garlands upon their foreheads and songs of joy on their lips.

Who came to the throne of Judah six years before Israel was led into captivity?

What kind of king was he?

Who was the great prophet in his day?

Hezekiah on the Throne.

Isaiah The Prophet.

What did Isaiah prophesy? Picture the scene.

Isaiah was the great adviser of King Hezekiah. Hezekiah did that which was right in the sight of the Lord, according to all that his father David did. He trusted in

Did Hezekiah do right or wrong?

FORTY-NINTH SUNDAY.

the Lord God of Israel, and he prospered whithersoever he went forth. He pulled down the idols, and brake in pieces the brazen serpent. In the first month of the first year of his reign he opened the closed doors of the House of the Lord which had long lain in neglect. He brought in the priests and the Levites and told them to sanctify themselves and to carry forth the filthiness out of the holy place. For this, said he, have our fathers fallen by the sword, and our sons and daughters and wives are taken into captivity. And the priests cleansed it, and offered burnt offerings, and Hezekiah set the Levites in the house of the Lord with cymbals, with psalteries, and with harps, according to the commandment of David. And when the burnt offerings began, the song of the Lord began also with the trumpets, and all the congregation worshiped, and the singers sang, and the trumpeters sounded. And the people consecrated themselves unto the Lord. So the service of the Temple was set in order.

And the king sent letters throughout all Israel, from Dan even to Beersheba, saying, Ye children of Israel, turn again unto the Lord God of Abraham, Isaac, and Israel, and he will return to those who are left of you, who are escaped out of the hand of the kings of Assyria. And be not like your fathers and like your brethren, who trespassed against the Lord God of their fathers. Who therefore gave them up to desolation. So the posts passed from city to city, through the country of Ephraim and Manasseh, even unto Zebulun: but they laughed them to scorn and mocked them. Nevertheless some of Asher and Manasseh and of Zebulun humbled themselves, and

Margin notes:
- Describe what Hezekiah did to the Temple.
- Describe the services in the Temple.
- What letters did Hezekiah send, and to whom?
- Where did the letter carriers go? How were they received?

Side headings:
- Hezekiah Opens the Temple.
- Institutes Services.
- Invites All Israel to the Passover.

FORTY-NINTH SUNDAY. 245

came to Jerusalem. And there assembled at Jerusalem much people to keep the Passover, and they kept it four- teen days. All that came, the strangers out of Israel, and those that dwelt in Jerusalem, rejoiced. So there was great joy in Jerusalem: for since the time of Solomon the son of David there was not the like in Jerusalem.

The great Assembly at Jerusalem.

Describe the Great Passover Feast at Jerusalem. What did they do at the end of the Passover?

King Hezekiah filled the public treasury, smote the Philistines even unto Gaza, and built the pool and conduit that brought water within the city in time of siege.

Deeds of Hezekiah.

Mention some of the great deeds of King Hezekiah.

In spite of the protest of Isaiah, Hezekiah rebelled against the king of Assyria. Then Sennacherib king of Assyria came up and took all the walled cities of Judah. Captives and spoil were dragged away. Hezekiah was shut up like a caged bird within his city. But Hezekiah sent word to Sennacherib saying, I have offended; return from me, that which thou puttest upon me will I bear. Then Hezekiah took all the silver in the Temple, and in the treasuries of the palace, and stripped off the gold from the doors and pillars of the Temple, and gave it to the king of Assyria. The daughters of the king and the young men and women of the palace were among the captives who were sent to Nineveh.

Sennacherib Comes.

Against whom did Hezekiah rebel? Was Isaiah in favor of it? Describe the result.

The people rejoiced at the deliverance of Jerusalem, but soon the Assyrian king again sent his generals and a great host against Jerusalem, who besieged it and uttered blasphemies against the Lord. Hezekiah rent his clothes and went into the house of the Lord and prayed, O Lord our God, save us out of his

Jerusalem Besieged.

Tell of the second siege.

Tell of Hezekiah's Prayer.

FORTY-NINTH SUNDAY.

hand, that all the kingdoms of the earth may know that Thou art the Lord God, even Thou only. **Hezekiah Prays.** Then Isaiah the prophet sent unto Hezekiah saying, Thus saith the Lord concerning the king of Assyria, He shall not come into this city, nor shoot an arrow there. By the way that he came, by the same shall he return.

What did Isaiah say to Hezekiah?

And it came to pass that night that the angel of the Lord went out, and smote in the camp of the Assyrians one hundred and eighty thousand; and when Israel arose early in the morning, behold the enemy were all dead corpses. **Host Smitten With Pestilence.**

How was the siege brought to an end?

SUMMARY OF EVENTS.

Hezekiah ascends the throne of Judah.
Isaiah is his leading prophet.
The Prophecies of Isaiah.
Hezekiah opens the Temple and reorganizes the services there.
He sends letters of invitation throughout Israel, asking them to repent and to celebrate the Passover.
The Passover is celebrated for fourteen days with great joy.
The idols and altars are broken down throughout Judah.
The deeds of Hezekiah.
Sennacherib shuts up Hezekiah in Jerusalem.
Hezekiah gives him gold and silver to go away.
The army of Sennacherib returns, and Hezekiah prays unto God.
Isaiah declares that Jerusalem will be delivered.
That night the angel of the Lord smites the Assyrian army with a pestilence.

From what parts of the Bible is this narrative taken? **II Kings, Chapters 18—20, II Chronicles, Chapters 29—32.**

There are no pictures in "Bible Story" referring to this chapter.

What shall we call this forty-ninth chapter? **Judah Under King Hezekiah.**

In conclusion let the teacher again refer to the Scripture and Catechism answers that the scholar has learned.

THE SCRIPTURE TO BE LEARNED.

THE LAMENTATION OF THE JEWS IN CAPTIVITY.

By the rivers of Babylon, there we sat down, yea, we wept, when we remembered Zion.

What was the lamentation of the Jews in captivity?*

We hanged our harps upon the willows in the midst thereof. For there they that carried us away captive required of us a song; and they that wasted us required of us mirth, saying, Sing us one of the songs of Zion.

How shall we sing the Lord's song in a strange land? If I forget thee, O Jerusalem, let my right hand forget her cunning. Ps. 137: 1-5.

WHAT THE CATECHISM SAYS.

We should so fear and love God, as not to rob our neighbor of his money or property, nor bring it into our possession by unfair dealing or fraudulent means, but rather assist him to improve and protect it.

What does the Catechism say?

---

*Teacher asks the questions until the whole class have recited these parts.

CHAPTER L.
Josiah, Jeremiah, and the Fall of Judah. The Babylonian Captivity.

Who was Josiah?

When and how long did he reign?

How did he cleanse his realm from Baal worship?

JOSIAH was the great grandson of Hezekiah. He was eight years old when he began to reign. He reigned thirty-one years in Jerusalem, and he did that which was right in the sight of the Lord. While he was still young, he began to purge Judah and Jerusalem from the carved and the molten images and to break down the altars of Baal. *Young Josiah Casts Out Baal.* The vessels used in the service of Baal and the host of heaven were brought forth and burned in the Kidron valley; the altars reared by Manasseh were demolished, the chariots of the sun were burned.

In the eighteenth year of his reign, he sent Shaphan the scribe, and the governor of the city, and the son of the recorder, to repair the Temple of the Lord his God. And when they brought out the money that was in the house of the Lord, Hilkiah found a book of the law of the Lord given by Moses. And Hilkiah gave the book to Shaphan. Then Shaphan told the king, and he read it before the king. When the king heard the words of the law, he rent his clothes.

What did Hilkiah find? Where?

What did he do with it?

What did Shaphan do?

What did the king do?

Finds the Book of the Law.

Then the king gathered together all the elders of Judah and Jerusalem. And he with the priests and Levites and all the inhabitants of Jerusalem, great and small, went up into the Temple. And he read

Reads it to the People.

in their ears all the words of the book that was found.

Then the king stood by a pillar and made a covenant before the Lord to keep his commandments with all their heart and all their soul, to perform the words that were written in this book. And all the people stood to the covenant.

What covenant did the king make with the Lord?

And the king commanded all the people to keep the Passover as it was written in the book. Surely such a Passover was not held from the days of the judges that judged Israel, nor in all the days of the kings of Israel. And like unto him there was no king that turned to the Lord with all his heart, and with all his soul, and with all his might, according to the law of Moses. But when the king of Egypt went up against the king of Assyria, king Josiah went out against the king of Egypt, and the king of Egypt slew him at Megiddo. And his servants carried him in a chariot dead from Megiddo, and brought him to Jerusalem and buried him in his own sepulchre. And all Judah and Jerusalem mourned for Josiah. And Jeremiah the prophet lamented.

What did they keep?

Keep a Great Passover.

What praise is given to King Josiah?

How and where did he meet his death?

Killed at Megiddo.

Who lamented him?

Eleven years later Nebuchadnezzar king of Babylon came up against Jerusalem, and the city was besieged. And he carried away from Jerusalem all the princes and the mighty men of valour, even ten thousand captives, and all the craftsmen, and the king, and the officers and the mighty, even them the king of Babylon brought captive to Babylon.

Nebuchadnezzar Carries Captives Away.

Who came up to besiege Jerusalem?

Whom did he take into captivity?

Nevertheless at Jerusalem the chief of the priests and the people still transgressed after the abominations of the heathen and polluted the house of the Lord. And

Did the people that were left heed this punishment

the Lord God of their fathers sent to them by his messengers but they mocked the messengers, and misused his prophets. *The Wrath of God.*

Through the anger of the Lord, the last king, Zedekiah, rebelled against the king of Babylon. And Nebuchadnezzar came, he, and all his host, against Jerusalem, and pitched against it; and they built forts round about it. The city was besieged over a year, and the famine prevailed and the city was broken up, and the men of war fled by night. The army of the Chaldees pursued the king and took him and brought him to the king of Babylon. They slew his sons, and put out his eyes, and bound him with fetters of brass, and carried him to Babylon. The captain of the guard burnt the Temple and the king's palace and all the houses, and they brake down the walls of Jerusalem, and carried away the rest of the people that were left in the city. There was no compassion upon young man, or maiden, old man, or him that stooped for age. Them that escaped the sword were carried away to Babylon, to fulfil the word of the Lord by the mouth of the prophet Jeremiah. So Judah was carried away out of their land. *Zedekiah. Jerusalem Destroyed. Judah Captive.*

Jeremiah, the son of the high priest Hilkiah, had exhorted the people in vain to yield to Babylon, and then had announced the destruction of the holy city and the removal to Babylon. But he comforted them also, and told them that they should return after a captivity of seventy years. Nebuchadnezzar permitted him to remain in the Holy Land and labor among those who had been left. Seated upon the ruins of Jerusalem he announced that instead of the old *Jeremiah the Prophet.*

covenant between God and the nation, which had been broken by the prophets' sins, the Lord would establish a new and everlasting covenant, inscribed in the human heart.

Ezekiel was the prophet who labored after the same manner among the captives in Babylon. He drove out the delusions and hopes awakened by false prophets, and comforted the people by telling of a deliverance approaching, and of another still far distant. He told that the Lord would set up one Shepherd among his people, and that his servant David should feed them. He foresaw a new temple and a new Jerusalem. By the rivers of Babylon these captives sat down and wept when they remembered Zion.

Who was Ezekiel?

Ezekiel in Captivity.

What prophecies did he utter?

SUMMARY OF EVENTS.

Josiah begins to reign at the age of eight years.
He does right and roots out the worship of Baal.
While repairing the Temple, Shaphan the scribe finds the Book of the Law.
The king reads the Book to all the people and makes a covenant to keep it. He celebrates a great passover.
He fights against Egypt at Megiddo, and is killed.
Nebuchadnezzar besieges Jerusalem and carries away 10,000 captives to Babylon.
Nevertheless Jerusalem does not repent.
Nebuchadnezzar comes again, captures king Zedekiah and puts out his eyes, burns the Temple, breaks down the walls of Jerusalem and carries the rest of the people into captivity.
The prophet Jeremiah. The prophet Ezekiel.

From what parts of the Bible is this narrative taken? **II Kings, Chap. 22—25; II Chron, Chap. 34—36; Jere., Chap. 39.**
There are no pictures in "Bible Story" referring to this chapter.
What shall we call this fiftieth chapter? **Josiah, Jeremiah, and the Fall of Judah; The Babylonian Captivity.**

Fifty-First Sunday.

THE SCRIPTURE TO BE LEARNED.

Give David's song for the Church, and the peace thereof.*

THE GRANDEUR OF JERUSALEM.

I was glad when they said unto me, Let us go into the house of the Lord. Our feet shall stand within thy gates, O Jerusalem.

Jerusalem is builded as a city that is compact together: Whither the tribes go up, the tribes of the Lord, unto the testimony of Israel, to give thanks unto the name of the Lord. . . .

Pray for the peace of Jerusalem: they shall prosper that love thee.

Peace be within thy walls, and prosperity within thy palaces. Psalm 122: 1-4, 6-7.

WHAT THE CATECHISM SAYS.

What does the Catechism say?

Thy kingdom come.

*Teacher asks the questions until the whole class have recited these parts.

CHAPTER LI.
The Captive Daniel at Babylon: Return of the Captives and the Rebuilding of Jerusalem.

AMONG the youths of royal and noble families, who were carried away to Babylon, and brought up in the court of king Nebuchadnezzar, and who were taught the learning and tongue of the Chaldeans, was one who would not eat the king's meat nor drink the king's wine. God gave him knowledge and skill in all learning and wisdom, and he had understanding in all visions and dreams.

Who was Daniel?
Where was he?
What kind of young man was he?

Troubled by a Dream. Nebuchadnezzar dreamed, and his spirit was troubled, and his sleep brake from him. The king forgot the dream and knew not the interpretation, and all the wise men enchanters and magicians of the realm could not disclose it unto him. Then was the youth Daniel brought in before the king, and he said, There is a God in heaven that revealeth secrets, and he hath made known to king Nebuchadnezzar what shall be in the latter days.

What happened to Nebuchadnezzar?

What did David say?

The Great Image. Thou, O king, sawest a great image, and the form thereof was terrible. Its head was of fine gold, its breast and its arms of silver, its thighs of brass, its legs of iron, its feet part of iron and part of clay.

Repeat the dream.

A stone was cut out without hands, which smote the image upon its feet, and brake them to pieces. Then were

FIFTY-FIRST SUNDAY.

the iron, the clay, the brass, the silver, and the gold broken to pieces together, and became like the chaff of the summer threshing-floors; and the wind carried them away; and the stone that smote the image became a great mountain, and filled the whole earth.

This is the dream. Thou, O king, art a king of kings. Thou art this head of gold. After thee shall rise another kingdom inferior to thee, and another third kingdom of brass, which shall bear rule over all the earth. And the fourth kingdom shall be strong as iron; and whereas thou sawest the feet and toes part of potter's clay and part of iron, the kingdom shall be divided. It shall be partly strong, and partly broken.

Repeat the interpretation.
The Interpretation of the Dream.

And in the days of these kings shall the God of heaven set up a kingdom which shall never be destroyed. It shall break in pieces and consume all these kingdoms and it shall stand forever. The stone was cut out of the mountain without hands, and it brake in pieces the iron, the brass, the clay, the silver and the gold.

What is the interpretation of the stone? (Ans. It is the Kingdom of Christ).

The king answered, Of a truth your God is a God of gods. Then he made Daniel a great man and ruler over the whole province of Babylon.

What did the king say and do to Daniel?
Daniel a Great Man.

Nebuchadnezzar dreamed again, and Daniel told him its interpretation was that he should dwell with the beasts of the field, and be made to eat grass as oxen, until he knew that the Most High ruleth among men. At the end of twelve months the king walked in the palace at Babylon, and spake, Is not this great Babylon that I have built by the might of my power. The same hour was the thing fulfilled, and Nebuchadnezzar was driven from men, and

What was the king's second dream?
The King to Eat Grass as an Ox.
What actually happened?

FIFTY-FIRST SUNDAY. 255

did eat grass as oxen. When his reason returned, he praised and honoured the King of heaven.

Belshazzar's Feast. The second king after Nebuchadnezzar was Belshazzar. He made a great feast to a thousand of his lords. While he tasted the wine, he commanded to bring the golden and silver vessels which his father Nebuchadnezzar had taken out of the Temple which had been in Jerusalem. Then they brought the vessels and the king and his princes drank in them and praised the gods of gold and of iron and of stone. *Tell of Belshazzar's feast.*

In the same hour came forth fingers of a man's hand, **Fingers Writing on the Wall.** and wrote over against the candlestick upon the plaster of the wall. Then was king Belshazzar troubled, and his countenance was changed, and his knees smote one against another. Then was Daniel brought in and he said, Thou, O Belshazzar, hast not humbled thy heart, but hast lifted up thyself against the Lord of heaven, and they have brought the vessels of His house before thee, and the God in Whose hand thy breath is, hast thou not glorified. This is the **Mene, Mene.** writing that was written, MENE, MENE, TEKEL, UPHARSIN. This is the interpretation: God hath finished thy kingdom. Thou art weighed in the balances, and art found wanting. Thy kingdom is divided and given to the Medes and Persians. *What happened to the king? Who was brought in? How did he interpret the writing?*

In that night was Belshazzar the king of the Chaldeans **Belshazzar Slain.** slain, and Darius the Mede took the kingdom. And Daniel prospered in the reign of Darius, and in the reign of Cyrus the Persian. *What happened that night? Who were Belshazzar's successors?*

In the first year of Cyrus king of Persia, he made a

FIFTY-FIRST SUNDAY.

What did Cyrus say he was charged to do?
What did he do?
Who was Cyrus?

proclamation saying, The Lord of heaven hath charged me to build Him a house at Jerusalem. Cyrus sent back over forty-two thousand of the captives and gave unto them the five thousand four hundred vessels of gold and silver which Nebuchadnezzar had taken from the Temple. *Cyrus Will Rebuild the Temple.*

What did the builders do?

In the second year of their return, the builders laid the foundation of the Temple, and all the people shouted with a great shout, when they praised the Lord, because the foundation of the Temple was laid. But many of the fathers that had seen the first Temple, wept. But they were hindered in the work by their neighbors, whose services they had rejected because they were idolaters. Under the encouragement of the prophets Haggai and Zechariah, with the high priest Jeshua, they went on with the building, and completed and consecrated it five hundred and fifteen years before Christ. *They Lay the Foundation.*

What did many of the old men do?
Who hindered the work?
What prophets encouraged the builders?
When was the new Temple consecrated?

SUMMARY OF EVENTS.

Daniel in the court of Nebuchadnezzar.
He interprets the dream of the Great Image.
He interprets a second dream for Nebuchadnezzar.
Belshazzar's feast.
Daniel interprets the handwriting on the wall for Belshazzar.
Belshazzar is slain, and succeeded by Darius and Cyrus.
Cyrus sends 42,000 captives back to Jerusalem to rebuild the Temple.
The new Temple is consecrated B. C. 515.

From what parts of the Bible is this narrative taken? **Daniel Ch. 1—6, Ezra Ch. 1—6.**
What picture did we have in "Bible Story" referring to this chapter?
What shall we call this fifty-first chapter? **The Captive Daniel at Babylon, The Return of the Captives and the Rebuilding of Jerusalem.**

Fifty-Second Sunday.

THE SCRIPTURE TO BE LEARNED.

A NEW HEAVEN AND A NEW EARTH.

And I saw a new heaven and a new earth: for the first heaven and the first earth were passed away; and there was no more sea. What can you say of the heavenly Jerusalem?*

And I John saw the holy city, new Jerusalem, coming down from God out of heaven, prepared as a bride adorned for her husband.

And I heard a great voice out of heaven saying, Behold the tabernacle of God is with men, and he will dwell with them, and they shall be his people, and God himself shall be with them, and be their God.

And God shall wipe away all tears from their eyes; and there shall be no more death, neither sorrow, nor crying, neither shall there be any more pain: for the former things are passed away.

And he that sat upon the throne said, Behold, I make all things new. Rev. 21 : 1-5.

WHAT THE CATECHISM SAYS.

For thine is the kingdom, and the power, and the glory, forever and ever. Amen. What does the Catechism say?

*Teacher asks the questions until the whole class have recited these parts.

CHAPTER LII.

The Old Testament, Looking to the Coming of the Saviour.

When did a second company return to Jerusalem from Babylon? Who led them?

What did they bring with them?

What did Ezra do in Jerusalem?

When did Nehemiah come to Jerusalem? Who was Nehemiah?

What work did he do?

How did they keep at it?

Whom did Nehemiah put away?

DURING the reign of Artaxerxes a second company of colonists, under Ezra the scribe, went up from Babylon to Jerusalem with silver and gold which the king had offered, and Ezra put away idolatry from among the people and instructed them in the Law.

Thirteen years afterward word came to Nehemiah, cupbearer of king Artaxerxes in the palace at Shushan that the returned captives were in great affliction, and that the wall of Jerusalem was broken down. The king sent him to Jerusalem and he repaired the wall. Every one of the builders had his sword girded by his side, and half of them wrought in the work, and the other half held the spears, and shields and bows against the enemies. Thus the wall was finished. Nehemiah reformed the people, and drove out of Jerusalem those who refused to put away their pagan wives.

After Ezra, Nehemiah Goes to Jerusalem.

And the prophet Haggai comforted the chosen people when the glory of their restored Temple appeared unto them as nothing. He told them to be strong and work, and that the Spirit of the Lord was remaining among them. For yet once, saith the Lord of hosts, it is

The Prophet Haggai.

FIFTY-SECOND SUNDAY.

a little while, and I will shake the heavens, and the earth, and I will shake all nations, and the Desire of all nations shall come: and the glory of this latter house shall be greater than of the former, and in this place will I give peace. *What Prophet comforted the people? What did he say?*

Likewise also Zechariah told them that many and strong nations would come to seek the Lord of hosts in Jerusalem, and to pray before the Lord. Rejoice greatly, said he, O daughter of Jerusalem: behold, thy King **The Prophet Zechariah.** cometh unto thee: He is just, and having salvation; lowly, and riding upon an ass, and upon a colt the foal of an ass. In that day there shall be a fountain opened to the house of David and to the inhabitants of Jerusalem for sin and for uncleanness. And Malachi, the last of the prophets of the Old Testament, **The Prophet Malachi.** in the days of Nehemiah, prophesied this word of the Lord: Behold, I will send my messenger, and he shall prepare the way before Me; and the Lord, whom ye seek, shall suddenly come to His Temple. Unto you that fear My name, shall the *Sun of Righteousness* arise with healing in his wings. Behold I will send Elijah the prophet before the coming of the great and dreadful day of the Lord; and he shall turn the heart of the fathers to the children, and the heart of the children to their fathers. *What prophecies did Zechariah utter? What did Malachi say of the Messenger? What of the Sun of Righteousness? What of Elijah? Who was this second Elijah? (Ans. John the Baptist.)*

Thus the God of Abraham and of Isaac and of Jacob **Trained to Look for a Heavenly Jerusalem.** had trained the chosen race to look for a Messiah, and had prepared the world to look for a kingdom and a city whose builder is God. Then, more than three centuries before the Christian Era, prophecy ceased. Alexander the Great succeeded Cyrus. *To what had God trained the chosen race?*

He entered the Temple at Jerusalem. Under Ptolemy king of Egypt one hundred thousand Jews were carried captive to that land. Heathen generals came to desecrate their Temple, the Jews rallied around a bold leader Mattathias the priest, whose five sons, called the Maccabees, defeated all the armies sent against them. Pompey the Roman general pulled down the walls of Jerusalem, but allowed the Jews to worship as before. Julius Cæsar appointed a governor for Judea: but he was soon succeeded by his son Herod the Great, who bore the title of king. Twenty or more years before our era, Herod began to rebuild the ruined temple and the chief part of it was finished the year Christ was born. *Interval Between the Old and the New Testaments.*

Thus in Bible History are seen the trace and results of the sin of Adam, coming down through Cain, the Flood and the hard-hearted Pharaoh; through the heathen peoples in the Promised Land; through the evil kings of Israel and Judah; through the prophets that spake falsely and the people that wrought iniquity. The end of it was misery, woe and desolation. *Sin in Bible History.*

Thus also in Bible History are seen the promise and the call to salvation, given to Adam before he was driven from the garden, given to Abel and Enoch and Noah; given to Abraham and Isaac and Jacob; given to Moses and Joshua and Samuel; given to David and the faithful among his descendants, given to the priests and the prophets. Thus came the law and the prophets, the expectation of a Messiah, and the root from which, according to the *The Promise of Salvation in Bible History.*

FIFTY-SECOND SUNDAY.

flesh, Christ, the son of David, the Son of man, the Son of God, did spring.

SUMMARY OF EVENTS.

Ezra goes up from Babylon to the returned captives at Jerusalem.

He puts away idolatry and instructs the people in the Law.

Thirteen years later Nehemiah goes up and rebuilds the wall of Jerusalem. He reforms the people.

Haggai comforts the people with prophecy.

Zechariah and Malachi prophesy of the coming Christ.

Thus the Lord God of Abraham prepared the world for a Saviour.

Alexander the Great, Ptolemy, and the Maccabees, Pompey, Julius Caesar and Herod the Great.

The progress of sin in Bible History.

The progress of the promise of a Messiah.

From what parts of the Bible is this narrative taken? **Ezra, Chap. 7—10; the whole of the Book of Nehemiah, the Apocryphal Books.**

There are no pictures in "Bible Story" referring to this chapter.

What shall we call this fifty-second chapter? **The Old Testament, Looking to the Coming of the Saviour.**

In conclusion let the teacher again refer to the Scripture and Catechism answers that the scholar has learned.

www.ingramcontent.com/pod-product-compliance
Lightning Source LLC
Chambersburg PA
CBHW031942230426
43672CB00010B/2023